OXFORD WORLD'S CLASSICS

THE LUSÍADS

LUÍS VAZ DE CAMÕES was born in 1524/5, probably in Lisbon, and educated probably at Portugal's national university at Coimbra. By the mid-1540s he was back in Lisbon, frequenting the fringe of the court and writing his earliest love lyrics. Banished, perhaps because of amorous intrigue, he enlisted in 1547 as a common soldier in the garrison at Ceuta in Morocco and lost his left eye in battle. In 1553, after being jailed for brawling in Lisbon during the Corpus Christi procession, he sailed for India, seeing action in the Red Sea and off the Indian and Arabian coasts, and spending seventeen years in all in Goa, Macau, and Mozambique. During these years he published a dedicatory poem to a book about medicinal plants, and wrote a vast body of lyrical poetry. Much of *The Lusíads* was evidently completed by the time of his shipwreck in 1559 off Cambodia. In 1570 he returned to Lisbon where his epic of the Portuguese nation was published in 1572. He died in poverty in 1580, oppressed by the national disaster of Alcácer-Kebir in Morocco, and aware that Portugal was fated to pass under the rule of Spain.

LANDEG WHITE worked for sixteen years in the West Indies and Africa. His books include studies of V. S. Naipaul, of Malawian and Mozambican history, and of southern African praise poetry, together with three collections of his own poetry. He teaches at the Universidade Aberta in Portugal.

OXFORD WORLD'S CLASSICS

*For over 100 years Oxford World's Classics have brought
readers closer to the world's great literature. Now with over 700
titles—from the 4,000-year-old myths of Mesopotamia to the
twentieth century's greatest novels—the series makes available
lesser-known as well as celebrated writing.*

*The pocket-sized hardbacks of the early years contained
introductions by Virginia Woolf, T. S. Eliot, Graham Greene,
and other literary figures which enriched the experience of reading.
Today the series is recognized for its fine scholarship and
reliability in texts that span world literature, drama and poetry,
religion, philosophy and politics. Each edition includes perceptive
commentary and essential background information to meet the
changing needs of readers.*

OXFORD WORLD'S CLASSICS

═══

LUÍS VAZ DE CAMÕES

The Lusíads

═══

Translated with an Introduction and Notes by
LANDEG WHITE

OXFORD
UNIVERSITY PRESS

OXFORD
UNIVERSITY PRESS

Great Clarendon Street, Oxford OX2 6DP

Oxford University Press is a department of the University of Oxford.
It furthers the University's objective of excellence in research, scholarship,
and education by publishing worldwide in

Oxford New York

Athens Auckland Bangkok Bogotá Buenos Aires Calcutta
Cape Town Chennai Dar es Salaam Delhi Florence Hong Kong Istanbul
Karachi Kuala Lumpur Madrid Melbourne Mexico City Mumbai
Nairobi Paris São Paulo Shanghai Singapore Taipei Tokyo Toronto Warsaw

with associated companies in Berlin Ibadan

Oxford is a registered trade mark of Oxford University Press
in the UK and in certain other countries

Published in the United States
by Oxford University Press Inc., New York

First published as a World's Classics paperback 1997
Reissued as an Oxford World's Classics paperback 2001
Reissued 2008

British Library Cataloguing in Publication Data

Data available

Library of Congress Cataloging in Publication Data

Camões, Luís de, 1524?–1580.
[Lusíadas. English]
The Lusiads / Luís Vas de Camões ; translated with an introduction
and notes by Landeg White
(Oxford world's classics)
Includes bibliographical references (p.).
I. White, Landeg. II. Title. III. Series.
PQ9199.A2W5 1997 869.1′2–dc21 97–19376

ISBN 978-0-19-953996-3

7

Typeset by Graphicraft Typesetters Ltd., Hong Kong
Printed in Great Britain by
Clays Ltd, St Ives plc

For Maria Alice
as before

CONTENTS

Introduction   ix

Translator's Note   xxi

Select Bibliography   xxiii

Chronology of Camões   xxv

Maps   xxvii–xxviii

THE LUSÍADS   1

  Canto One   3

  Canto Two   25

  Canto Three   48

  Canto Four   77

  Canto Five   98

  Canto Six   119

  Canto Seven   139

  Canto Eight   157

  Canto Nine   177

  Canto Ten   197

Explanatory Notes   229

INTRODUCTION

In the register of Lisbon's India House for 1550 occurs the following entry: 'Luís de Camões, son of Simão Vaz de Camões and Ana de Sá residents of Lisbon, in Mouraria, squire, aged 25 years. Accepted on the guarantee of his father, travelling by the man-of-war *S. Pedro dos Burgalese.*' Three years later in 1553, there is a further entry, describing one Fernando Casado, another squire resident in Lisbon, and continuing: 'in his place was Luís de Camões, son of Simão Vaz de Camões and Ana de Sá, squire, receiving 2$400 *reis* like the others.'

Why Luís Vaz de Camões failed to sail in 1550 on the *S. Pedro dos Burgalese*, no one knows. But we do know why he sailed for India in 1553. The previous June, during one of Lisbon's biggest religious festivals, the Corpus Christi procession, he had fought a duel with one Gonçalo Borges, keeper of the King's harness, and wounded him with a sword thrust. He was jailed in the Tronco prison, and released on payment of a fine of 4,000 *reis* and an undertaking to proceed to India as a common soldier.

Had Camões never written a line of poetry, these three obscure references would probably comprise all we knew of his existence. They tell us, far from conclusively, that he was born in 1524 or 1525, of parents living in the Mouraria district of Lisbon, that his father's name carried weight with the India House, that his status was that of *escudeiro*, literally 'shield-bearer' or squire, belonging to the lower orders of the nobility, and that he had a capacity, amply confirmed by legend, for getting himself into deep trouble. Most important of all, they confirm his departure for India, for it was in India that he became a great poet, the first European artist to cross the equator and experience Africa and India at first hand. The result is *The Lusiads*, an epic of European thought and action in the sixteenth century.

The 'India' to which Camões sailed was far more than a territory. It was the heart of a trading system of which the Portuguese had seized control with astonishing speed. In 1509 Francisco de Almeida, the first viceroy, destroyed a combined Egyptian–Gujarati fleet off Diu, the only force capable of withstanding Portuguese warships. This was followed by the capture of Goa (1510), Malacca (1511), and Ormuz (1515), together with most of the city states of the East African coast. Within just seventeen years of Vasco da Gama's epic voyage, the Portuguese held and dominated all the most important sea routes and trading networks of the Indian Ocean, the Persian Gulf, and the South China seas. It was a ruthless demonstration of naval might, and the first instance of a new concept of empire built on control of the oceans.

Yet, by the time Camões arrived in Goa, on the only one of four ships to survive that year's outward voyage, it was all beginning to unravel. Though cities continued to be added to the empire (including Macau in 1554), the great days were over. The Portuguese crown had not the resources to maintain an overseas fleet, nor Portugal the manpower for colonial administration. Trade required not just military control but the goods and bullion to keep silks and spices flowing westwards, and the hope that the empire could finance itself with the profits of the gold mines of south-east Africa proved illusory. In Camões's single letter home from Goa, which he labels 'the mother of villains and stepmother of honest men', there is already a strong whiff of what was later to be recognizable as the odour of an empire in decline. French and English warships were already marauding and the Dutch were about to join the scene. The point is important, for underlying the manifest heroics of *The Lusíads* there is a note of elegy, of absences and regret. It had all happened before Camões's time.

Six years after *The Lusíads* was published, with its closing appeal for the imperial adventure to be rekindled, came the disaster of Alcácer-Kebir when the mad King Sebastião's mammoth invasion of Morocco ended in his death and the destruction or enslavement of all but one hundred of his army of over 20,000. In despair, Camões wrote to a friend, 'All will see that so dear to me was my country I was content to die not only in it but with it'. He died on 10 June 1580, just before the throne passed to Philip II of Spain. According to one early biographer, he was buried in a borrowed shroud. Three hundred years later, what were assumed to be his remains were re-buried in the great monastery of the Jerónimos at Belém.

The European maritime empires which changed the world for ever have had their day, but 'discoveries' is not a word we need balk at. The confirmation by late-fifteenth-century Europeans that the world was much larger than the Mediterranean basin with parts of the east attached, was matched a century later by proof that the earth was not the centre of the universe but a wandering planet in a universe that was not unique. Both discoveries posed a challenge to existing beliefs from which the world, in and beyond Europe, is still recovering.

Camões completed *The Lusíads* and died without knowing of the Polish astronomer Copernicus and his theories. In canto 10, it is the Ptolemaic system of concentric spheres which Tethys explains to da Gama. But the new geographical discoveries of the previous century, and the unprecedented encounters between peoples they entailed, are at the very heart of his epic. In cantos 3 to 5, da Gama explains to the Sultan of Malindi exactly where Europe is, country by country, and how Portugal came to sponsor his present voyage. The explanation involves more than geography. From Christ's manifestation at the Battle of Ourique to da Gama sitting on the beach at St Helen's Bay, north of Cape Town, using the astrolabe to determine his position, we are swept as in no other Renaissance poem from the world of religion to the world of science.

But then it is the Sultan of Malindi who gives da Gama a pilot to navigate the last stretch across the Indian Ocean to Calicut. When the fleet arrives, it is Monsayeed, a Muslim from Morocco, who tells da Gama about the history, religion, and social and political systems of India, before proceeding in canto 7 to tell the Hindu Samorin of Malabar everything he knows about the Portuguese, information supplemented in canto 8 as Paulo da Gama gives a lesson in Portuguese history to one of the Samorin's officials. There are other mini-encounters, some friendly, some violent—what other epic contains so many different nationalities? The poem concludes in canto 10 with a guided tour of Europe, Africa, the Middle East, India, China, Japan, various Pacific and Indian Ocean islands, and finally the Americas and Antarctica (with a reference to Magellan's circumnavigation of the globe), as Tethys explains to the Portuguese the momentous consequences of their voyage to India in demonstrating to mankind the dimensions and wealth of the planet mankind inhabits. Nothing quite like this happened again until December 1968, when the Apollo 8 spacecraft showed us the first pictures of Earth taken from space.

Over three centuries of colonial rule have blunted our responses to that pristine vision. As European power in India and Africa hardened into paternalism and a degree of contempt for their peoples and cultures, the English and Portuguese languages took on a carapace which obscured the dangerous excitement of those original encounters. In Portugal, long before it was appropriated by Salazar's *estado novo* as national propaganda, *The Lusíads* was employed to bolster a bruised national pride. Even today, in post-revolution Portugal, the quincentenary of the *descobrimentos* does not envisage that there is much to be 'discovered' by Portugal, only by other nations learning of her past greatness. Meanwhile, it is instructive to contrast English translations of *The Lusíads* over a similar period. The first, Richard Fanshawe's version of 1655, still makes a splendid read. Though its language has dated, it retains a sweetness and a bustling, grotesque energy which conveys better than any version since that this voyage was an intellectual as well as physical adventure. He takes some liberties, usually in pursuit of rhymes, but in one respect his version is truer than any subsequent translation: the people the Portuguese encounter in Africa and India are, as in the original, consistently called 'people' (*gente*).

By contrast, William Atkinson's prose version of 1952 has the virtues of complete clarity and much greater accuracy. Yet, in a curious manner, the imaginative power of *The Lusíads* seems to embarrass him. His introduction comments curiously on the 'pedantry' of Camões's classical references, on his 'abuse of epithet and adverb', and on 'the ever-recurring problem, in a historical-geographical narrative, of versifying the essentially prosaic'. It has to be said that Atkinson's rendering of the African and Indian dimensions of *The Lusíads* is little more than a tissue of colonial-settler platitudes.

At issue here is not intelligence or scholarship but over-familiarity, so that Camões's most recent English editor can suggest in all seriousness that he need never have left Portugal to find the materials for his epic.[1] Camões has not been fortunate in finding editors and translators who have themselves crossed the equator. Yet the constant weaving of his historical sources with the demands of the epic form and with personal thought and fresh observation are the very substance of *The Lusíads*.

Consider, for instance, a very minor episode, stanzas 62–4 of canto 5, when the navigators put ashore at São Braz, near Mossel Bay on the South African coast. This is their second encounter with a group of Africans, and it is, incidentally, fascinating to compare how different translators address the task of describing their hosts: for Fanshawe they are 'The people that this country did possess'; for the eighteenth-century William Mickle, celebrating British commercial power, they are 'the tenants of the coast'; Atkinson calls them 'the natives here'; while for the South African poet Guy Butler they are 'the nation', as though da Gama was welcomed on the beach by a delegation from the ANC.

Camões includes the episode partly because it features in the historical record which he follows with great respect. His sources are not entirely consistent, one speaking of 'some treachery' and 'two bombards' being fired, another of 'gentleness' with dancing and feasting. He selects the details which suit his purpose: that the people were similar to those previously encountered at St Helen's Bay, that they traded sheep but not their cattle, which they valued too highly to barter, that their women rode on large oxen, and that among them were some skilled in playing a kind of flute. Poetically the episode forms a pastoral counterpoint to the terrifying grandeur of the encounter with Adamastor at the Cape of Good Hope, an instance of Camões's mastery in varying the subject-matter and tone. But his additions are significant. Twice he emphasizes the humanity written in 'their smiling faces'.

[1] Frank Pierce (ed.), *Luís de Camões, Os Lusíadas* (Oxford, 1973), p. x.

Where the source speaks of them 'conversing with our people by signs', Camões shows the frustration of being unable to communicate, and of having to separate without exchanging words. Where the source talks of 'playing and dancing' and 'a kind of pastoral flute', Camões knows that these songs have words sung 'sweetly and in harmony', and he adds the intriguing comment, 'whether rhymed or in prose we could not gauge'. It is Camões the poet, interested in other people's poetry, who notes a problem which still preoccupies students of African oral performance, namely, that the borderline between poetry and prose is unfixed and uncertain.

The Lusíads is packed with such moments when personal experience and alert enquiry combine with an imaginative reinterpretation of his sources to cast a patina of freshness over the text.

Above all else, however, *The Lusíads* is an epic. History supplies its heroes (the Portuguese) and its subject-matter (da Gama's voyage to India in 1497–8). The poet's experience of the same voyage over half-a-century later supplies a thousand intimate touches. But Camões's main concern is to dramatize the significance of that original voyage as an event transcending history, redefining the course of human affairs in the divine plan.

The opening line ('Arms are my theme, and those matchless heroes') deliberately modifies the beginning of Virgil's *Aeneid* ('Arma virumque cano'), and throughout *The Lusíads* Camões makes reference to the episodes, the machinery, and the shaping of Virgil's epic. He begins *in medias res* with the Portuguese already in the Mozambique Channel (appropriately, for this was the part of the voyage where no one had preceded them). This allows for a long internal narrative as da Gama, imitating Aeneas' account of the Trojan War to Queen Dido of Carthage, gives the Sultan of Malindi a long lesson in Portuguese history. The retrospective is balanced by the glimpse of heroes yet to be born and the vision of a glorious future, granted to Aeneas by his father Anchises in the underworld, and to da Gama by Tethys in canto 10. Finally, passing over many more minor episodes and verbal echoes, there is the machinery of the gods and goddesses, of which more in a moment.

There are problems in this for the modern reader. Few of us share the extent and depth of Camões's knowledge of the classics, and the pleasures of *recognition*, that agreeable Renaissance game of spotting how the poet has adapted a favourite passage from a classical author and refurbished it to serve a contemporary purpose, plays little part in our reading. Some of Camões's references are so erudite, not to say arcane, as to function effectively as riddles. How many of us know that 'the bright lover of the adulterous Larisseian' refers to Apollo and his affair with Coronis of Larissa, and that Camões is describing, with appropriate wit, dawn breaking over the Isle of Love? It is difficult to render this without clogging the verse itself (or the foot of the page) with laborious explanations.

Riddling, however, and the sophisticated pleasures of recognition, point to something more interesting than dogged imitation of a classical model. The point is made baldly and literally by da Gama, who insists to the Sultan of Malindi (canto 5, stanzas 86–9) that his voyage is greater than those of Ulysses and Aeneas. His professional scorn for Ulysses for forgetting his crew-mates on the island of the Lotus Eaters, and for Aeneas, for losing even his helmsman on a calm night, is reinforced by the contrast he draws between those shore-hugging Mediterranean voyages and the vast uncharted oceans on which the Portuguese have ventured. Moreover, he says, his story is true: theirs is myth, and 'My own tale in its naked purity | Outdoes all boasting and hyperbole'. For this, if for no other reasons, Camões is not bound by his Virgil, whose language and devices are constantly being subverted and transcended.

Nowhere is this more clearly demonstrated than in what has long been the most controversial feature of *The Lusíads*, namely, Camões's use of the classical gods and goddesses. Within a stanza of the first mention of the Portuguese navigators in canto 1, stanza 19, a debate is raging on Mount Olympus about the wisdom of letting them proceed. Jupiter has resolved that they shall be granted a safe harbour on the coast of Africa to refit their ships. Bacchus opposes this, Venus supports it and is backed by Mars. The decision stands and the fleet finds its way, via Mozambique Island and Mombasa, to Malindi. Halfway through the poem, in canto 6, there is a parallel scene, this time in Neptune's underwater palace, when the Portuguese have left Malindi and are on the last stage of their voyage to India. Bacchus is the sole speaker in persuading the gods of the sea to conjure a hurricane and destroy the fleet once and for all. All through the poem Bacchus and Venus intervene. Bacchus, jealous for his shrines in India, stirs up Muslim hatred in Mombasa, deceives da Gama by impersonating the so-called Christians of Prester John, and incites the Muslims of Calicut to prejudice the Samorin. Meanwhile Venus, admiring the Portuguese for their supposed Roman qualities, seduces Jupiter into maintaining his support for them, summons the sea-nymphs to rescue the fleet in Mombasa, summons them again to subdue the hurricane, and rewards the mariners with the delights of the Isle of Love. Yet at no point in the poem does da Gama fail to attribute what is befalling him to the cosmic struggle between good and evil, or neglect to thank Providence for guidance and protection.

What are we to make of this fusing of Christian and pagan myths? One long tradition of commentary on *The Lusíads*, dating from the terms of the official censor's approval of the poem on behalf of the Office of the Inquisition, has been to read all the pagan episodes allegorically, the gods and goddesses featuring as rhetorical vehicles within a Christian scheme of things. Thus, Jupiter doubles up as God, Venus as a guardian angel (or the Blessed Virgin), and Bacchus as Satan. This was the interpretation elaborated with extraordinary ingenuity and learning by the first great commentator on Camões, the Spanish Manoel Faria e Sousa in 1639, in a manner reflecting the inclusiveness of Renaissance scholarship, and in particular its passion for reconciling classical learning with Christian revelation. It is a reading which, suitably modified, continues to find supporters.

Camões, at a key point in the poem (canto 9, stanzas 90–1), dismisses his pagan gods as simply poetic creations, ('Jupiter, Mercury, Phoebus . . . they | Were all composed of feeble human clay). There is no need to accept the suggestion that these lines, which were acclaimed by Faria e Sousa as confirming his schema, were added at the bidding of the Inquisition and should be censored from modern editions. What they declare is amply confirmed by Tethys in canto 10, stanza 82, in words which must be authoritative:

> I, Saturn and Janus,
> Jupiter and Juno, are mere fables
> Dreamed by mankind in his blindness.
> We serve only to fashion delightful
> Verses . . .

Much of our difficulty here lies in that word 'allegory'. Since the eighteenth century most allegorical writing has been political, offering the reader subversive codes, with one-to-one correspondences between the ciphered and the actual events. This is the context in which we enjoy Dryden's *Absalom and Achitophel* and Orwell's *Animal Farm*. Reading *The Lusíads* in this reductive manner involves us in the absurdity of representing Venus's comic-erotic seduction of Jupiter (canto 2, stanzas 33–43) as an intercession by the Virgin Mary. While Bacchus is plausibly cast as Satan, appearing in dreams or in a multitude of disguises (as a long-lost Christian, a Muslim counsellor, as Mohammed himself), Venus is never anything other than the goddess of love, resplendent in her sexiness and expert in all the arts of seduction. It is important to note that the gods and goddesses never accomplish anything. Like the sylphs in Pope's *Rape of the Lock*, they go about their business blissfully unaware that all their efforts amount to nothing. There is no need for the reader to believe that it was Venus who prevented the fleet entering harbour at Mombasa, or Bacchus who called up the hurricane. Da Gama has no difficulty in explaining all that befalls him in terms of a quite different set of beliefs (nor has the modern reader in attributing Portuguese setbacks to a mix of commercial jealousy and natural disasters).

Medieval and Renaissance allegory, however, was less concerned with one-to-one codes and correspondences than with depths and suggestions and ramifications, reinforcing our understanding of the unity of God's creation. Once we accept Camões's gods and goddesses as entertaining fictions, we can see how he has deployed them to achieve a variety of effects which would have been impossible in a more conventional narrative of the voyage. The debates on Mount Olympus and in Neptune's underwater palace allow him to emphasize the significance of da Gama's achievement as a turning-point in human history, comparable to mankind's legendary first voyage in pursuit of the Golden Fleece, or to the attempts by Daedalus and Icarus to fly. Bacchus, admittedly ranting, warns (canto 6, stanza 29) that the Portuguese voyage means the end of religion as he knows it:

> very soon, I promise you,
> Of the vast oceans and the heavenly span
> They'll be the gods, and you and I but Man.

By contrast, Venus's various antics with or without her sea-nymphs, from the striptease before Jupiter to the nuptials of the Isle of Love, make room for poetry of a startling sensuality. There are moments of stylish comedy about all these scenes, for this is a far from solemn epic: Mars giving Jupiter's throne 'such a thwack with his cudgel | The heavens trembled and sheer fright | Momentarily dimmed Apollo's light', or Neptune's nymphs awaiting Bacchus' arrival at his underwater palace, 'Trying to fathom what in heaven had brought a | King of wine to the domain of water', while Triton stands by awaiting instructions, his head crowned with a lobster shell, his naked slimy body crawling with every kind of mollusc and crustacean. Camões's comic relish in these scenes deserves more emphasis that it has received.

Utterly different, at his epic's very heart, is the entirely original myth of Adamastor, the 'Cape of Storms' personified. The emotional force of this former Titan's love for the nymph Doris and the punishment that followed such presumption, is matched by the terrible prophecy of what is to befall Portuguese navigators in these waters, beginning with his vengeance against Bartolomeu Dias who first rounded the cape in 1488. But he stands not only as sentinel over the most dangerous part of the voyage. He marks the boundary between two different visions of Africa, corresponding to two different divisions of the world.

'Ethiopians' is the word used of the peoples encountered by the navigators along the coasts of South Africa and Mozambique. The word means, in its Greek derivation, simply dark-skinned or sunburned, and is related to the myth of Phaethon, Apollo's son, who borrowed the sun's chariot and, startled by the signs of the Zodiac, lost control and steered too close to earth, scorching some of its peoples. Homer, however (*Odyssey*, i. 22–4), had mentioned two kinds of Ethiopians, 'some where Hyperion sets, some where he dawns', giving rise to a distinction increasingly elaborated by classical and medieval geographers. 'Eastern Ethiopia' became the Africa of fable, containing the ancient kingdoms of Nubia, Abyssinia, and Ophir, linked with Moses, Solomon, and Sheba, and the enduring myth of Prester John. 'Western Ethiopia' was the wild, savage Africa bordering the unexplored Atlantic Ocean. To the north, the two 'Ethiopias' were separated by the Sahara Desert; to the south, by a barrier somewhere to the South.

By the time of da Gama's voyage, however, this division was being superseded by another. The west coast of Africa had been navigated and charted. Camões, in canto 5, describes the fleet sailing past capes and islands already 'christened' anew, past 'beaches that are ours' and kingdoms which have been 'brought to faith in Christ'. Some of this detail is anachronistic, giving rise to the comment that Camões seems at times to be describing his own rather than da Gama's voyage. As *The Lusíads* opens, with the navigators already in the Mozambique Channel, the Cape of Storms has come to mark the boundary between the known Africa of the west coast and the unknown Africa bordering the Indian Ocean. Adamastor charges the Portuguese with breaching 'what is forbidden', desecrating 'Nature's secrets', a charge rich in meaning to the Renaissance reader.

Significantly, this is also the boundary between the world where Christianity rules supreme, and the world where the pagan deities believe they hold sway. For there is no mention of Jupiter, Venus, and Bacchus in the long account of Portuguese history occupying cantos 3 and 4, nor in the voyage down the West African coast in canto 5, nor indeed in Paulo da Gama's further discourse on Portuguese history in canto 8. Parallels are frequently drawn with heroic figures of ancient times and these occasionally border on myth. But paganism does not obtrude until the fleet is in the Indian Ocean, provoking the debate on Mount Olympus. Everything Venus and Bacchus do subsequently is confined to Africa and India, and the distinction adds a further dimension to Camões's recourse to the pagan deities.

Camões was—for the point bears repeating—the first major European artist to visit the tropics and the orient. He was thus the first to face the challenge of finding a language and form to give expression to such new experiences. Da Gama's voyage of exploration becomes an extended metaphor for his own explorations in the 'craft' of poetry. By raiding the Latin classics for references associating Bacchus with India and by expanding on Venus' legendary love for islands, Camões was able to invent for himself the rudiments of a 'tradition' which Portuguese exploits could be represented as supplanting. Once embarked on this course, it was surprising how many classical tales could be adapted to his purpose—Phaethon's chariot, the Argonauts and Daedalus, Memnon and Ethiopia, Venus and Cupid hiding as dolphins from the heat of the tropics, and a host of other borrowings from Virgil, Ovid, Horace, and Catullus. His style, or rather his variety of styles, reflects this, mixing Latin or Latinisms with Castilian Spanish and vernacular, sometimes vulgar, Portuguese, in a combination demonstrably his own. The classical authors gave him a framework and a language to stand off from, even as modern authors like Soyinka and Rushdie have given shape to their work by 'writing back' against British myths about the West Indies, Africa, and India.

But the pagan deities gave Camões something more. As the navigators approach Mozambique Island (canto 1, stanza 45), they pass a cape which Camões confidently identifies as 'Prasso', namely Ptolemy's *Promontorium Prasum*, the furthest point south known to the Greeks. No one knows for sure which cape was meant, but by identifying it with Cape Corrientes Camões is making an ideological point: that these sea routes and city states, currently in the possession of Islam and about to become a battleground, were 'colonized' by the European imagination long before the 'Moors' got there.

The most troublesome aspect of *The Lusiads* to the modern reader must surely be Camões's treatment of Islam. Perhaps we should not be unduly taken aback. The ending of the Cold War has reopened a much older wound in human history—that fault line between Christian and Islamic communities which extends from northern Asia to the west coast of Africa. Fears of Islamic fundamentalism, especially in southern Europe, have led to suggestions that it should be targeted as NATO's newest (or oldest) enemy, while our airports and borders bristle with immigration patrols. In the sixteenth century the Turkish Empire was Europe's rival super-power. The Crusades had ended in catastrophe with the fall of Constantinople in 1453. Though the loss of Christianity's eastern capital was partly offset by the capture of Granada in 1492, the Turks were secure in their occupation of Athens and the Balkans and were advancing in the Middle East and North Africa. The destruction of the Turkish fleet at the Battle of Lepanto occurred while Camões was putting the finishing touches to *The Lusiads*.

Even in this context, Camões's hostility is disturbing. Muslims are consistently presented as *astuto, falso, enganoso, malicioso, pérfido, sábio, sagaz, torpe,* and *gentes infernais.* The only *fiel* Muslim is Monsayeed from Morocco, who turns Christian after helping da Gama escape from Calicut. Yet these adjectives, together with the fact that Camões consistently labels all Muslims as 'Moors', suggest a great deal.

Camões was well informed about Islam and was perfectly aware of its scope and its divisions: the first suspicion of the Sheikh of Mozambique when he comes to inspect the Portuguese fleet is that they must be Turks, whom he regards as hostile. The label 'Moors' insists on two things. It declares that Islam is a single and united enemy; and it identifies the Swahili traders of East Africa and the Muslim rulers of the Persian Gulf, Turkey, and parts of India, with the Muslim Berbers driven out of Portugal during the twelfth to fourteenth centuries. This is the principal theme of canto 3, as da Gama narrates events from the Battle of Ourique (1139) to the Battle of the River Salado (1340), including sieges such as the capture of Lisbon (1147) and of Silves (1189) with the assistance of English and German knights *en route* to the second and third Crusades. The capture of Ceuta in Morocco, Portugal's first overseas possession, was an extension of the same campaign, followed by the earliest voyages down the West African coast in an effort to take 'the Moors' in the rear.

Yet not long before, in the tenth and eleventh centuries, students had been flocking to Muslim Andalusia—to read Aristotle in Arabic with commentaries by Averroes, to study Galen, to learn the use of the astrolabe, to benefit from the new mathematics (since the reign of Henry I, our chief tax collector has been known as chancellor of the exchequer: the reference is to the abacus, the chequered cloth, which made it possible to calculate in tens and units). Andalusia was a centre of learning in all its branches, the civilized heart of the medieval world, a place of culture and architectural splendour, and of greater religious tolerance than any society which followed. It is this that makes Camões's adjectives interesting. Earlier translators had little difficulty in rendering them as 'wily, cunning, dissembling, treacherous, deceitful', and so on, and these are legitimate synonyms. But they also suggest intellect, subtlety, learning, diplomacy—all the provocations of *culture* and *sophistication* to a young, emerging nation, conscious of destiny and flexing its muscles. Self-assertion is less offensive in the relatively powerless than in the powerful, and Camões's hostility to Islam is still infused with the determination to cast off an alien yoke.

The Lusiads, then, belongs with the *Song of Roland,* the epic of *El Cid,* and more directly, Dante's *The Divine Comedy,* in claiming the spiritual, cultural, and intellectual initiative for Europe after a long period during which Islam has been in the ascendancy. As with Dante, Virgil becomes Camões's guide to the origins of the new Christian humanism, in terms of which Portuguese revelations about the size and wealth of our planet can be comprehended. It is no accident that this vision of Europe's significance, and of Portugal's place as the crown on the head of Europe, should have come to Camões in India. No one can speak with assurance of what was passing through his mind during his long sojourn in the orient. Our only source is his poetry, and any conclusions will follow from how that poetry, including his many lyrical poems, is interpreted. The intuition that has guided this present translation is as follows: that during his years in Goa, Macau, and Mozambique, Camões 'discovered' two things.

First, he learned what it was to be Portuguese, to come from a landscape whose towns and rivers he loved, whose plains and castles were haunted by the ghosts of warriors who had fought for this territory, whose provinces were part of Christendom and the Holy Roman Empire but were emerging as a 'state', and whose people were learning loyalty to a concept of nation which transcended loyalty to kings. Secondly, he learned to celebrate what the Portuguese had given to the world with the pioneer voyages of the fifteenth century, culminating in the voyage to India, in revealing the planet's true dimensions, its wealth, and its multitudes of peoples. It was the former of these ideas which was prophetic, taking wing after the restoration of Portuguese independence from Spain in 1640. The latter, Camões's celebration of the newness of the world, was a theme that required, and requires, constant rediscovery.

Needless to add, it is not necessary to accept either of these propositions to enjoy this magnificent poem. Camões calls his heroes 'sublime'. The sublime is not easy to render in modern English, but I hope I have done enough to give an inkling of the great sweep of Camões's narrative, with its endless variety of incident and description, its openness to the wonders of the natural world, its relish of the differences between human societies, its tragedy, its eroticism, its humour, its episodes of pastoral, its nostalgia for that golden age before men first fitted sails to wood and took to the sea, and underlying all, its note of elegy for achievements already fading, already requiring the pageantry of poetry's surprise.

TRANSLATOR'S NOTE

Most English translators of *The Lusíads*, from Richard Fanshawe (1655) to Leonard Bacon (1950), have attempted to reproduce Camões's *octavos*. I respect their efforts, and have a deep affection for Fanshawe who first taught me to love Camões and whose version still best captures the intellectual vitality of the original. J. J. Aubertin's version of 1884 is both skilfully rhymed and extremely accurate. His exuberant claim that he has written as Camões would have written had he been writing English *ottava rima* is justified—so long as we add the rider that his imagined Camões spoke English as a second language. Many a time I have copied out a felicitous phrase only to realize, in the act of writing, that this is not English—rather, an uncanny approximation of English to Portuguese.

For it is an illusion to believe that the verse form of Camões's epic can be replicated in English. Portuguese is an inflected language and its sentences are shaped differently. Nouns and verbs may be widely separated; adjectives follow (or may precede) nouns and adverbs their verbs. One among many consequences of this is to triple at a stroke the rhymes available, so that what is fluid and direct in Portuguese involves, in English, too many inversions of the natural word order to be a satisfactory rendering of the ease and lucidity of Camões's diction. A further distinction is the prevalence in Portuguese of feminine rhymes. What looks on the page like a replication of Camões's poetic forms sounds rather different when read aloud.

It is a question, too, of syntax. English is balder, more direct than Portuguese. Time and again, rendering stanzas of *The Lusíads* into rough and ready English, I have found myself with feet or whole lines to spare, needing padding to restore the shape of the original. This, too, violates both the precision of the Portuguese (for Camões is not prolix) and the natural vigour of any English verse which respects the sinews of the language.

At least two of my predecessors have responded to this problem by abandoning *ottava rima*. William Mickle's best-selling version of 1776 is written in heroic, not to say triumphalist, couplets, piling antithesis on antithesis. William Atkinson's Penguin Classic of 1952 is composed in an academic prose laced with Shakespearian echoes. Both obscure the architecture of *The Lusíads*, its shaping and pacing, substituting rhythms wholly alien to the original. Hence my compromise, for all translations involve painful choices. I have respected the eight-line units of the original text with its formal closes. But, in ambition at least, I have adopted a diction and prosody free to reflect the subtle modernity of Camões's style.

The translation was undertaken with the assistance of a substantial grant over two years from the Calouste Gulbenkian Foundation. I am also grateful to Helder Macedo, who first championed the notion of an untrammelled, un-rhymed *Lusíads* and who has been a consistent well-wisher. I am deeply in debt to a dear friend, Hélio Osvaldo Alves, who has translated my own poems and who, on Station B in Coimbra, encouraged me to proceed by declaring roundly: 'I don't feel I'm missing my *octavos*.' Towards the opposite end of the process, Tom Earle intervened with an equally decisive phrase, correcting one of my couplets with the comment: 'Not very poetic but it's what it means.' With this, and a hundred-and-one other suggestions, he led me to curb elaborations arising from my own fifteen years in the tropics, and to recognize that Camões's virtues are better served by a translation erring on the side of plainness. The faults and failings that remain are, of course, my own.

I have used the text of *Os Lusíadas* edited by Hernani Cidade in his *Luís de Camões: Obras Completas* (Lisboa, 1947), vols. iv and v.

SELECT BIBLIOGRAPHY

Works

Luís de Camões. *Obras Completas*, com prefácio e notas do prof. Hernani Cidade. 5 vols. (Lisbon, 1947).

Frank Pierce (ed.), *Luís de Camões, Os Lusíadas* (Oxford, 1973).

Translations

Luís de Camões, *The Lusiads in Sir Richard Fanshawe's Translation*, with an introduction by Geoffrey Bullough (London, 1963).

Os Lusíadas de Luis de Camões, translated by J. J. Aubertin (London, 2nd edn., 1884).

The Lusiads of Luís de Camões, translated by Leonard Bacon, with an Introduction and notes (New York, 1950).

Luís Vaz de Camões. *The Lusiads*, translated by William C. Atkinson, with an Introduction (London, 1952).

Luís Vaz de Camoens: The Lusiads canto 5, translated by Guy Butler, in M. van Wyk Smith (ed.), *Shades of Adamastor: Africa and the Portuguese Connection: An Anthology of Poetry* (Grahamstown, South Africa, 1988).

Luís de Camões: Epic and Lyric, translated by Keith Bosley, illustrated by Lima de Freitas (Manchester, 1990).

Background and General Studies

Note: among the best general essays on Camões and the world of the Portuguese voyages are William Atkinson's, Leonard Bacon's, Geoffrey Bullough's, Frank Pierce's, and M. van Wyk Smith's introductions to the editions and translations listed above. Bacon's annotations in particular are a constant delight.

A. F. G. Bell, *Luís de Camões* (Oxford, 1923).

C. R. Boxer, *The Portuguese Seaborne Empire* (London, 1969).

Richard Fletcher, *Moorish Spain* (London, 1992).

W. Freitas, *Camões and his Epic. A Historic, Geographic and Cultural Background* (Stanford, 1963).

W. Storck, *Luis de Camoens Leben*, trans. from the German as *Vida e Obras de Luís de Camões*, by C. M. de Vasconcelos (Lisboa, 1897).

On *The Lusiads*

Norwood H. Andrews Jr., 'An Essay on Camões' Concept of the Epic', *Revista de Letras*, 3 (1962), 61–93.

C. M. Bowra, 'Camões and the Epic of Portugal', in *From Virgil to Milton* (London, 1945), 86–138.

Hernani Cidade, *Luís de Camões: o Épico* (new edn., Lisboa, 1986).

Fidelino de Figueiredo, 'Ainda a epica Portuguesa', *Estudios Hispánicos: Homenaje a Archer A. Huntingdon* (Wellesley College, 1952), 155–70.

A. Bartlett Giamatti, 'Camões', in *The Earthly Paradise and the Christian Epic* (Yale, 1969), 210–26.

Edward Glaser, 'Manuel de Faria e Sousa and the Mythology of "Os Lusíadas"', *Miscelanea de Estudos a Joaquim de Carvalho, Figueira da Foz*, 6 (1961), 614–27; and ' "Se a tanto me ajudar o engenho e arte": The Poetics of the Proem to *Os Lusíadas*', *Homenaje al Prof. Rodriguez-Monino* (Madrid, 1966), i. 197–204.

Jorge Borges de Macedo, '*Os Lusíadas' e a Historia* (Lisboa, 1979).

Helder Macedo, *Camões e a Viagem Iniciática* (Lisboa, 1980) and '*The Lusíads*: Epic Celebration and Pastoral Regret', *Portuguese Studies*, 6 (1990), 32–7.

Frank Pierce, 'The Place of Mythology in *The Lusíads*', *Comparative Literature*, 6 (1954), 97–122.

António Salgado Júnior, *Os Lusíadas e a Viagem do Gama* (Porto, 1939).

António José Saraiva, *Estudos Sobre a Arte d'Os Lusíadas* (Lisboa, 2nd edn., 1995).

R. M. Torrance, ' "Se Fantàsticas São / Se Verdadeiras": The Gods of the Lusíads on the Isle of Love', *Modern Language Notes*, 80 (1965), 210–34.

R. M. Walker, 'An Interpretation of the Role of the Supernatural in *Os Lusíadas*', *Revista Camoniana*, 1 (1964), 83–93.

CHRONOLOGY OF
LUÍS VAZ DE CAMÕES

1524/5   Born, probably in Lisbon, possibly in the Mouraria district, son of Simão Vaz de Camões, a ship's captain who drowned off Goa, and Ana de Sá. A direct ancestor, Vasco Lopes de Camões, was from Galicia in Spain, but moved to Portugal in 1370, serving under King João I and becoming known as a minor poet. A grandfather married a distant relative of Vasco da Gama, who died 1524.

c.1539   Develops deep knowledge and love of Italian, Spanish, and Latin (but not Greek) literature, probably at Portugal's national university, based from 1537 at Coimbra.

c.1543   In Lisbon, mixing on the fringe of the court with others of the minor aristocracy, writing poetry and comedies and, according to legend, involved in a hopeless love affair with Caterine de Ataide, following a glimpse of her in church on Good Friday, 1544.

1546   Exiled from Lisbon, perhaps by choice, perhaps by royal decree for amorous causes.

1547   Joins the garrison in Ceuta, Morocco, as a common soldier. Sees action, losing his left eye, and gaining a lasting respect for and hostility towards Islam (the 'Moors').

1549   Back in Lisbon, possibly in the train of Afonso da Noronha, newly appointed Viceroy of India.

1550   Enlists for India on his father's guarantee but does not sail. Described in the document as 'squire' with a red beard.

1552   (June) Arrested for brawling during the Corpus Christi procession. Jailed, then released on payment of fine and undertaking to proceed to India as a soldier.

1553   (March) Sails for India on board the *São Bento*, the only ship of four to arrive safely that year.

1553–6   Engaged in expeditions on the Malabar coast of India and in the Red Sea and along the Arabian and East African coasts.

1556   His satiric comedy *Disparates na India* ('The Follies of India') performed in Goa. Appointed Trustee for the Dead and Absent in Macau, and spends up to a year visiting Malacca and the Moluccas *en route*.

1559   Dismissed following 'an unjust mandate' and recalled to Goa. Shipwrecked in the mouth of the Mekong River in Cambodia and swims ashore, clutching 'these cantos' (evidently *The Lusiads*), but losing all other possessions.

1561–7   In Goa. Jailed on charges, eventually quashed, arising from his post in Macau. Jailed again for debt.

1563   First publication, the dedicatory poem to Garcia da Orta's *Colóquio dos simplese drogas e cousas medicinais*, a study of medicinal plants, published in Goa.

1567   (Sept.) Borrows money for a return passage as far as Mozambique. Stranded there, he compiles his *Parnasso de Luís de Camões*, 'rich in learning, doctrine and philosophy' (stolen and now lost).

1569   (Nov.?) Two friends, Heitor de Silveira and the historian Diogo de Couto, offer a passage to Lisbon on the *Santa Clara*.

1570   (April) Disembarks in a plague-bound Lisbon, after an absence of seventeen years.

1572   *The Lusiads* published, with the approval of the censor of the Holy Office as containing 'nothing scandalous nor contrary to faith and morals', Camões granted tiny royal pension for 'the adequacy of the book he wrote on Indian matters'.

1578   (August) King Sebastião killed and the flower of Portugal's nobility destroyed at Alcácer-Kebir following Portugal's disastrous invasion of Morocco.

1580   (10 June) Dies. The Portuguese throne passes to Spain for sixty years.

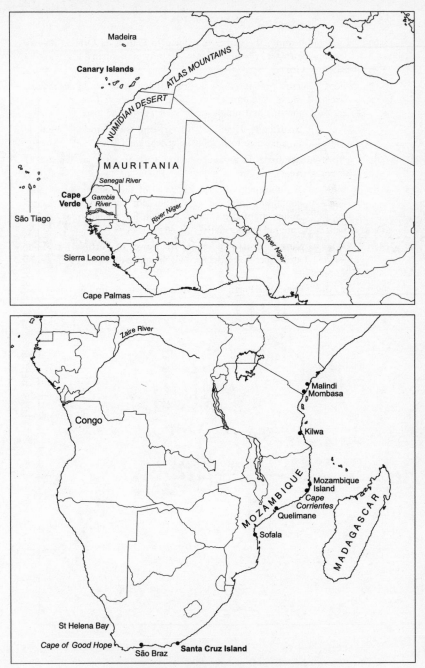

Map 1A:Places mentioned in Canto 5
Map 1B:Places mentioned in Canto 1,2, and 5

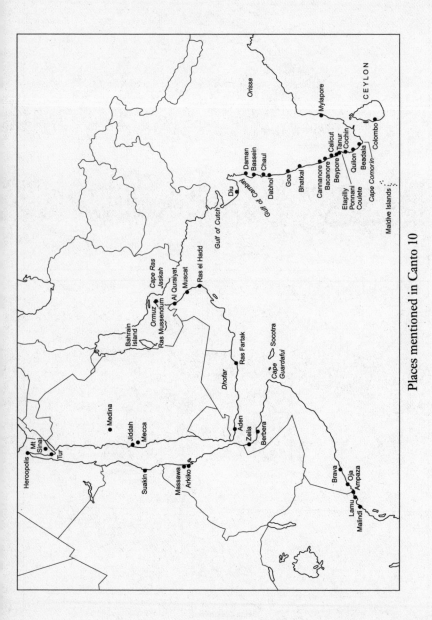

Places mentioned in Canto 10

THE LUSÍADS

Canto One

1   *Arms are my theme,* and those matchless heroes*
     Who from Portugal's far western shores
     By oceans where none had ventured
     Voyaged to Taprobana* and beyond,
     Enduring hazards and assaults
     Such as drew on more than human prowess
     Among far distant peoples, to proclaim
     A New Age and win undying fame;

2   *Kings likewise of glorious memory*
     Who magnified Christ and Empire,
     Bringing ruin on the degenerate
     Lands of Africa and Asia;
     And others whose immortal deeds
     Have conquered death's oblivion
     —These words will go wherever there are men
     If art and invention steer my pen.

3   *Boast no more about the subtle Greek*
     Or the long odyssey of Trojan Aeneas;
     Enough of the oriental conquests
     Of great Alexander and of Trajan;
     I sing of the famous Portuguese
     To whom both Mars and Neptune bowed.
     Abandon all the ancient Muse revered,
     A loftier code of honour has appeared.

4   *And you, nymphs of the Tagus, who*
     First suckled my infant genius,
     If ever in my rustic verses
     I celebrated your companionable river,
     Return me now a loftier tone,
     A style both grand and contemporary;
     Be to me Helicon. Let Apollo choose
     Your waters as the fountain of my muse.

5   *Fire me now with mighty cadences,*
    Not a goatherd's querulous piping
    But the shouts of a battle trumpet,
    Stirring the heart, steeling the countenance;
    Give me a poem worthy of the exploits
    Of those heroes so inspired by Mars,
    To propagate their deeds through space and time
    If poetry can rise to the sublime.

6   *And you, my boy King,* guarantor*
    Of Portugal's ancient freedoms,
    And equal surety for the expansion
    Of Christendom's small empire;
    You, who have the Moors trembling,
    The marvel prophesied for our times,
    Given to the world, in God's eternal reign,
    To win for God much of the world again.

7   *You, tender and green sapling*
    Of that tree more precious to Christ
    Than any other Western lineage,
    Whether in the French or Roman line
    (Witness your scutcheon, visibly
    Stamped with the victory at Ourique,*
    When Christ bestowed, as emblems to emboss,
    The five wounds he suffered on the cross);

8   *You, mighty King, on whose India*
    The new-born sun directs his first beam,
    Shines on your palace in mid-hemisphere,
    And casts his last ray on the Brazils;
    You, to whom we look to yoke and humble
    Arabia's wild horsemen, infidel
    Turks, and India's sons and daughters
    Who yet drink the Ganges' sacred waters:

9   *Descend a little from such majesty,*
    For I see on your youthful countenance
    Already inscribed that maturity
    You will bear to eternity's temple;
    Bend those royal and benign eyes
    Earthwards, and behold this loving tribute;
    The most valiant deeds of modern times
    Given to the world in sure, well-cadenced rhymes.

10 *You will witness a love of country, not*
  Driven by greed but true and enduring,
  For it is no unworthy reward to be famed
  Writing in praise of my native land.
  Observe: you will see names exalted
  Of those of whom you are supreme lord,
  And you can judge which is the better case,
  King of the world or king of such a race.

11 *Observe, it is not for counterfeit*
  Exploits,* fantasies such as muses
  Elsewhere have dreamed or invented,
  That you will hear your people acclaimed.
  Historic deeds such as theirs
  Transcend fables, and would eclipse
  Boiardo's Orlando, and Ariosto's too,
  Even if all they wrote of him were true.

12 *Instead, I give you* Nuno Álvares*
  Who showed country and king such service;
  It would take Homer's lyre to commend
  Sufficiently Egas Moniz and Fuas Roupinho;
  For France's twelve peers, I give you
  The twelve of England led by Magriço,
  And likewise Vasco da Gama, whose genius
  Snatched renown from wandering Aeneas.

13 *If you are looking for stature equal*
  To Charlemagne or Julius Caesar,
  Consider Afonso the first whose lance
  Eclipsed all foreign reputations;
  Or João the first whose reign bequeathed us
  The security of his great victory;
  Or the second João, honourably spurred,
  Or the fourth or fifth Afonso, or the third.

14 *Nor will my lines leave uncommemorated*
  Those who in the lands of the Dawn*
  Bore their arms with such excellence
  Your standard was always victorious:
  Matchless Pacheco, and the fearsome
  Almeidas, whom the Tagus still laments,
  Albuquerque the fierce, Castro the brave,
  And others whose exploits have survived the grave.

15   *While I celebrate these I say nothing*
     Of you, great King, not presuming so far;
     Take up the reins of your kingdom
     To furnish matter for another epic.
     Let the world tremble as it senses
     All you are about to accomplish,
     Africa's land and Oriental seas
     The promised theatre of your victories.

16   *On you, the fearful Moor has his eyes*
     Fixed, knowing his fate prefigured;
     At a glimpse of you, the unbroken
     Indian offers his neck to the yoke;
     Tethys, Neptune's bride, has prepared
     The world's green oceans as a dowry,
     Holding your youth and beauty in such awe
     She hopes to win you for her son-in-law.

17   *There gaze down from Mount Olympus*
     Your two grandsires,* famous in their day,
     —One for the golden peace of his reign,
     The other for his bloody battles.
     Both look to see resurrected in you
     Their times and heroic works, keeping
     In earnest of their true paternity,
     Your place in the temple of eternity.

18   *But while your long reign passes slowly*
     Matching your people's dearest wish,
     Look kindly on my boldness so
     This epic may become your own.
     You will watch, cutting the salt seas
     Portuguese Argonauts,* who will see in turn
     They are watched over by you. Be ready
     To hear your name invoked in jeopardy.

19   They were midway on the wide ocean
     Cleaving the ever-restless waves;
     The billowing wind blew gently,
     The sails of the ships were concave;
     White spume was whipped backwards
     As the mighty prows sped on
     Cutting the sacred waters of the deep,
     Where the cattle of Proteus* never sleep;

20 When the gods* on radiant Olympus,
From where the human race is governed,
Were assembling in glorious council
To decide the future of the Orient.
They advanced across the lovely
Spangled Heavens, treading the Milky Way,
Summoned on Jove the Thunderer's decree
By Atlas' winged grandson, Mercury.

21 They left the managing of the seven
Spheres* deputed them by the Supreme
Power who governs, by thought alone,
The skies, the earth, and the raging seas.
An instant brought together those
From the frozen Arctic or the South
Pole, or living at Earth's remotest ends
Where dawn breaks or where the sun descends.

22 Jove was present in all his majesty
On a throne of crystal stars, shaking
The thunderbolts forged by Vulcan,
His demeanour stern and dominating;
His countenance glowed with a grace
Such as could render a man immortal,
His sceptre and his crown made radiant
By gems like diamonds, but more brilliant.

23 On glittering thrones inlaid with gold
And pearls, but lesser than Jove's,
The other gods took their seats
As reason and good order ordained
(The venerable well to the fore,
The juniors accepting their station);
Then Jove spoke, making his purpose known
With gravity and menace in his tone:

24 —'Immortal tenants of the glistening,
Star-bearing poles and bright heaven,
There cannot have passed from your thoughts
The strength and courage of the Portuguese,
And now it is common knowledge
What the Fates have in store for them,
Conquests which recall the ancient hour
Of Syrian, Persian, Greek, or Roman power.

25 'You have already witnessed how,
    Ill-equipped and hopelessly outnumbered,
    They broke the Moors' army at Ourique,
    Freeing both banks of the sweet Tagus;
    Again, at Aljubarrota* they gained
    Heaven's favour against feared Castile,
    Afterwards, returning to their halls
    With wagonloads of trophies for their walls.

26 'I say nothing, gods, of those earlier
    Days when, under Viriathus,* in their
    Struggle with the might of Rome,
    They achieved such great laurels;
    I pass, too, over the compelling time
    They chose for themselves as leader
    Sertorius,* that rebellious foreigner
    Who feigned he took his counsel from a deer.

27 'Now you can watch them, risking all
    In frail timbers on treacherous seas,
    By routes never charted, and only
    Emboldened by opposing winds;
    Having explored so much of the earth
    From the equator to the midnight sun,
    They recharge their purpose and are drawn
    To touch the very portals of the dawn.

28 'They were promised by eternal Fate
    Whose high laws cannot be broken,
    They should long hold sway in the seas
    Where the sun makes his purple entrance.
    They have endured a winter's voyage;
    Their people are driven and exhausted;
    It seems no more than justice would require
    Soon they should gain the East of their desire.

29 'And since, as you have witnessed,
    They have encountered in their passage
    Such hazards, such skies and latitudes,
    Such raging, repellent winds,
    I resolve they shall be welcomed
    On the African coast as friends,
    And, having re-equipped their weary fleet,
    Embark once more to make their quest complete.'

30   These were Jupiter's pronouncements
      And in due order the gods replied,
      Differing in their judgements,
      Attending to, or advancing reasons.
      But it was Bacchus who dissented*
      Most from Jupiter's edict, well aware
      His own powers in India would cease
      If such men came there as the Portuguese.

31   He knew it was fated there would come
      From Iberia, over the high seas,
      An invincible people to subjugate
      All his India's foaming coastline,
      And with fresh victories would dwarf
      Legends, whether his own or others.
      Deeply it stung him he should forfeit fame
      There in the very cradle of his name.

32   He believed himself India's conquerer,
      And neither Fate nor circumstance
      Could silence the praises of those poets
      Who drank the waters of Parnassus;
      Now he feared his eminence sunk
      In a black urn in those waters
      Of the oblivion nothing can withstand
      If the navigators ever reached that land.

33   Against him spoke the lovely Venus,
      Favouring the people of Portugal
      For her love of the Roman virtue
      She saw resurrected in them;
      In their stout hearts, in the star
      Which shone bright above Ceuta,*
      In the language which an inventive mind
      Could mistake for Latin, passably declined.

34   This stirred the Cytherean,* and more
      Deeply since fate clearly had in mind
      That wherever these warrior people
      Roamed, her rites would be respected.
      So, one god fearing to lose prestige,
      The other ambitious for her altars,
      Obdurately, they pressed their different ends,
      Both in turn supported by their friends.

35 As when the cold north or wild south
    Winds rip through the dark depths
    Of forests, tearing off branches
    With headlong violence, while every
    Valley and mountain reverberates
    With the tumult of driven leaves:
    Such was the furious debate that rolled
    Round sacred Olympus as the gods brawled.

36 But Mars, who of all the parties
    In the wrangle supported the Goddess,
    Whether inspired by his old passion
    Or because the Portuguese deserved it,
    Now hoisted himself to his feet
    With thunder written on his face
    And, in a belligerent gesture, peeled
    Back over his shoulder his massive shield;

37 Raising the beaver* of his diamond-cut
    Helmet, the easier to speak his mind,
    He planted himself glowering
    And implacable before Jupiter,
    Giving the adamantine throne
    Such a thwack with his cudgel
    The heavens trembled, and sheer fright
    Momentarily dimmed Apollo's light;

38 And he spoke: 'Father, whose authority
    Everything you created must acknowledge,
    If you really want to protect these
    People whose exploits you so admire
    In their search for another world,
    Stand by your judgement. You ordained
    Their fate aeons ago. That's my advice.
    Close your ears to pedlars of prejudice.

39 'If it were not obvious that good sense
    Has been scuttled by childish fears,
    I'd have expected Bacchus to stand by
    The sons of Lusus,* his old colleague;
    This latest, wicked intrigue springs
    Only from a perverted brain;
    No onlooker's jealousy should thwart
    What men deserve and has the gods' support.

40   'So Father, in your omnipotence,
      Do not be diverted from the course
      You have determined. It's weakness
      To abandon what you've embarked on.
      Send Mercury, who flies swifter
      Than wind or a well-flighted arrow,
      To prepare some harbour where they can meet
      With news of India and refit their fleet.'

41   As he finished, all-powerful Jove
      Inclined his head, consenting
      To what valiant Mars had demanded,
      And showered nectar over them all.
      The gods took their leave, heading
      Along the glorious Milky Way,
      Each making the appropriate salutation
      Before returning to his proper station.

42   While this was debated in the bright
      Mansion on Mount Olympus, the men of war
      Had cut the seas and were already
      There where the south meets the Orient
      In the channel between Madagascar
      And Mozambique:* the sun was in Pisces,
      That torrid zone where even gods retreat,
      Taking refuge as dolphins* from its heat.

43   Gently the breeze transported the ships
      As if Heaven was at last their ally,
      The elements serene, the horizon showing
      Not one cloud nor any hint of danger.
      They had rounded Cape Corrientes,*
      Ancient Africa's southern boundary,
      When unknown islands swam into their reach
      With waves breaking restlessly on the beach.

44   Vasco da Gama,* the stalwart commander
      Who had given himself to this enterprise
      From motives of pride and honour
      And whom fortune always favoured,
      Saw no reason to make landfall
      On islands which looked uninhabited;
      He resolved to sail past, but his intent
      Was swiftly countermanded by the event.

45   On the instant from the island nearest
The main,* there came in close company
Several small feluccas skimming
The wide bay under their broad sails.
Our people were overjoyed and could only
Stare in excitement at this wonder.
—'Who are these people?' they kept exclaiming,
'What customs? What beliefs? Who is their king?'

46   Their craft, as we could see, were built
For speed, being long and narrow;
Their sails were made of a canvas
Skilfully fashioned from palm leaves;
The people were of the authentic colour
Brought to the world's tropic regions,
When Phaethon* steered Sun's chariot too low
(His sister wept as he splashed into the Po).

47   Their garments were of pure cotton
With vivid stripes on a white ground;
Some fastened above the hips, others
In elegant fashion under one shoulder;
From the waist upwards they were bare;
They were armed with daggers and long knives;
Their heads were turbaned: as the boats came near
They blew on tuneful horns, strange to our ear.

48   Waving their arms and cloth they beckoned
The Lusitanian mariners to heave to;
But our swift prows were already tacking
To run in under the islands.
Soldiers and seamen pulled together
As if here was our destination;
Yards struck, the sails furled aft and main,
The sea exploded around our anchor chain.

49   Even as we were mooring, these strange
People were shinning up the ropes.
They came smiling, and courteously
Our great captain greeted them;
He ordered tables to be spread at once
With foaming bowls of Bacchus' liquid;
Phaethon's scorched Muslims drank their fill,
Relishing the vintage, spreading goodwill.

50   As they ate contentedly, they began
     Questioning in the Arab language,
     —'Where are you from? What do you
     Want? What oceans have you crossed?'
     The powerful Lusitanians replied,
     Conscious of the need for diplomacy:
     —'We are Portuguese from the Occident;
     We seek the passage to the Orient.

51   'We have navigated every ocean
     Between the Antarctic and the Great Bear;
     We have rounded the coast of Africa
     Seeing strange lands and new constellations;
     But our mighty King is so amiable,
     So loved by all, that in his service,
     With cheerful faces we'd adventure on
     Those darker waters of Lake Acheron.*

52   'At his command, we have wandered
     Seeking the land drained by the Indus;
     For this, we have sailed remote oceans,
     Crossed only by the ugly sea-calves.
     Now it is right we should learn
     From you, if honesty prevails here,
     Who you are? Where in the world you dwell?
     And what portents of India you've heard tell.'

53   —'We' (one of the islanders responded)
     'Are not of this place or superstition;
     Those who belong here are suckled by Nature
     Without religion or understanding.
     We are of the sure Faith, taught us
     By Him who is in Abraham's direct line,
     The one Lord* the world respects as true,
     By father Gentile and by mother Jew.

54   'This insignificant island we inhabit
     Happens to have the safest harbour
     Of the whole coast, wherever waves break
     From Kilwa to Mombasa or Sofala.
     We seized it only for this, living
     Here as though we were the natives;
     So, to round off all of which you speak,
     This tiny isle is known as Mozambique.

55   'And now, since you have voyaged so far
      Seeking the Indus and its parched banks,
      Accept from us a pilot to reveal
      The correct course across the ocean.
      Meanwhile, it is proper you should have
      Provisions from land and that the Sheikh
      Governing here should greet you with all speed,
      And furnish you with everything you need.'

56   With these words, the Muslims returned
      With all the company to the boats,
      Taking leave of the captain and the crew
      With every refinement of courtesy.
      Just then, Phoebus in his crystal chariot
      Plunged the bright day underwater,
      Giving way to his sister Moon to keep
      The broad world glimmering in his sleep.

57   Night passed in the weary fleet
      With a strange, unlooked-for joy
      That they had found, in such a remote place,
      The very news they had sought so long.
      Each within himself meditated
      On these people and their strange ways,
      And how believers in so false a creed
      Through so many lands could spread their seed.

58   On Neptune's glistening waves the moon's
      Clear light lay resplendent;
      The stars consorted with the heavens
      Like a meadow pricked with daisies;
      In their dark lair, the angry winds
      Lay still after their journeying;
      While throughout the whole fleet every crew
      Kept the due watch each was accustomed to.

59   But as soon as dappled Aurora
      Shook out her beautiful tresses,
      Opening a red door in the quiet sky
      To rouse Hyperion's son* from his sleep,
      The crew brightened every deck
      Of the fleet with flags and bunting,
      To welcome with ceremony and good cheer
      The island's governor who now drew near.

60   He approached in high good humour
      To review the nimble Portuguese ships,
      With fresh supplies from land, assuming
      They must be those uncultured Turks
      Who, from their home by the Caspian Sea,
      Had set out to conquer all Asia,
      And by fate's decree had even overcome
      The imperial city of Byzantium.

61   The captain welcomed with open pleasure
      The Sheikh and all his attendants,
      Making him a gift of rich fabric
      Carried for just such occasions;
      He offered preserves and strong spirits,
      A drink new to him, which made him merry;
      The Sheikh received it all as due his rank
      (Doubly pleased with what he ate and drank).

62   The Portuguese mariners climbed
      The shrouds, gazing down and marvelling
      At manners and fashions so exotic
      And the language so baffling and intricate.
      But the shrewd Sheikh was also puzzled
      By our skin, our clothes, and the powerful fleet,
      Till in a torrent of questions he remarked
      Perhaps it was from Turkey we embarked.

63   And he added that he required to see
      The books of our laws, commandments, or faith,
      To judge if they matched his own
      Or were Christian, as he now suspected;
      Above all else he examined and noted,
      He implored our captain to offer him
      Some demonstration of what arms we bore
      In the event we found ourselves at war.

64   Our valiant captain replied through one
      Well versed in the difficult language:
      —'I will give you, Sir, an account
      Of myself, our faith, and the arms we carry.
      I am not of that land or that lineage
      Of those wretched people from Turkey.
      I am a European warrior;
      I seek the famous lands of India.

65   'My faith is in Him whom all powers,
      Temporal and spiritual, obey,
      He who created the whole universe,
      And all things, living or inert,
      Who underwent disgrace and insult,
      Suffering unendurable and unjust death,
      But who descended from the heavens to earth
      To raise us mortals to our heavenly worth.

66   'Of this God-Man, the sublime and infinite,
      Ours is not a religion of the book,
      There being no need to convey on paper
      That which subsists in my very soul.
      If, as you said, you want to see weapons
      I can satisfy this desire of yours;
      But view them as a friend, for well I know
      You'll never wish to see them as a foe.'

67   With these words, he ordered the waiting
      Soldiers to uncover their arsenal;
      Coats of armour, flashing breastplates
      Of close-knit mail or laminated,
      Shields with their various coats of arms,
      Cannon-balls, muskets of well-tempered steel,
      Longbows, halberds bristling with spikes,
      Quiverfuls of arrows, trusty pikes.

68   The fire bombs were brought, and with them
      The sulphur pots so noxious;
      But he would not allow Vulcan's sons*
      To ignite their dreadful cannon,
      For with people so few and so faint-hearted,
      It was no part of valour or breeding
      To display what dire force he could rely on,
      Or in sheep's company to act the lion.

69   But now from all the Sheikh was shown,
      And all he recorded with a sharp eye,
      Suspicion took root in his heart,
      And his thoughts became malevolent;
      Nothing showed in his face or gestures
      As, behind a cheerful mask, he continued
      Treating them with gentle condescension,
      Until he could act out his true intention.

70 Pilots, the captain now asked of him,
   To guide the ships' course to India;
   He promised a generous reward
   To anyone who took on the task.
   The Sheikh acquiesced, but with such hot
   Poison coursing through his veins
   He wished, instead of pilots for our way,
   To furnish us with death that very day.

71 Such was the fury and the malice
   Directed suddenly at the strangers,
   As he realized we followed the truths
   Revealed us by the Son of David!
   It is an eternal conundrum,
   Unfathomable by human thought,
   That those closest to God will never be
   Lacking in some perfidious enemy!

72 At last, with his whole retinue,
   The politic Sheikh took leave of the ships
   With exaggerated courtesies
   And for everyone a two-faced smile.
   Their craft cut the narrow
   Stretch of Neptune's domain until,
   Danced ashore by an obsequious throng,
   The Moor was back where such arts belong.

73 Now from his bright ethereal home
   Bacchus, who was born from Jove's thigh,*
   Seeing the Sheikh vexed and offended
   By his encounter with the Portuguese,
   Began to devise some stratagem
   Which would destroy them utterly
   And, while this was hardening in his brain,
   He mused upon his grievances again:

74 —'Fate has already settled* what great
   Conquests and superfluous renown
   Will be won by the Portuguese
   Over the warrior peoples of India.
   Must I alone, son of the supreme
   Father and so abundantly endowed,
   Must I stand idle while another's name,
   Puffed up by Fortune, puts my own to shame?

75   'Once in the past, the gods allowed
      Philip's precocious boy,* Alexander,
      To bully this region so adroitly
      Everything passed under his yoke;
      Must I be silent while Fate bestows
      On so few men such skill and daring
      That I, like Macedonia and Rome,
      Must yield to Portugal the victor's palm?

76   'It shall not be! Before this captain
      Has ventured anywhere, so subtle
      A trap will be conjured for him
      He'll never clap eyes on his Orient.
      I'll descend to earth and manipulate
      The indignation of the Muslims;
      In every undertaking of this type
      The time for action's when the time is ripe.'

77   With these words,* and almost insane
      With anger, he plunged to Africa,
      Taking human features and travelling
      By Cape Corrientes* known of old;
      And the better to weave his clever
      Plot, he adopted the appearance
      Of a Muslim well known in Mozambique,
      Mature, wise, and a favourite with the Sheikh;

78   And entering to speak with him, at a time
      And hour appropriate to his deception,
      He spun the tale that the newcomers
      Were brigands and that all along
      The coastline where the people
      They had pillaged lived, rumour
      Ran wild that wherever their pirate ships
      Anchored, 'peace' was the first word on their lips.

79   —'Much more is reported,' he ranted,
      'Of these bloodthirsty Christians.
      There's hardly a sea they have not looted
      Burning everything in their sight;
      Far away, they conceived this present
      Conspiracy against us, in sum,
      To steal our goods and trample on our graves,
      And take our wives and children as their slaves.

80 'I know, however, that at first light,
The captain plans to take on water,
Bringing with him a small army
For a bad conscience makes one wary;
You can easily wait in silent ambush
Secretly with your armed men;
They will come not suspecting any trap
And, to conclude, will fall into your lap.

81 'And even if this manœuvre fails
To defeat or dispose of them totally,
I have thought of another contrivance
Which will give you satisfaction.
Send them their pilot, but one
Skilled in acting, and adroit enough
To guide them to some port where they can be
Destroyed, routed, killed, or lost at sea.'

82 As soon as he had spoken, the Sheikh,
Who was experienced in such business,
Hugged his shoulders warmly, showing
His gratitude for such advice;
Immediately, he set in motion
Everything necessary for war,
Preparing for the Portuguese such slaughter
The beach would flow with blood instead of water.

83 Meanwhile, to spring his second trap,
He arranged to send to the ships as pilot
A shrewd and experienced Muslim
To whom the affair could be entrusted;
He told him to go with the captain,
Voyaging by such coasts and seaways
That if ambush failed, on some other shore
He would shipwreck and trouble them no more.

84 Apollo's burning rays had already
Walked the mountain tops of Arabia,
When da Gama and his men prepared
To land to replenish their water.
The men in the boats so bore themselves
As if a plot were already suspected,
As in truth they could easily surmise,
For the heart's intuition never lies.

85   In fact, the captain had already sent
      A message that morning, asking
      For the pilot and been answered
      Brusquely, which put him on his guard.
      For this, and because he knew the risk
      Of trusting in a dangerous rival,
      He set out well provided, but bold,
      With no more men than three boats could hold.

86   Then the Muslims came down to the beach
      To prevent us taking on water, some
      Armed with shields and assegais, some
      With bent bows and poisoned arrows,
      Waiting as our soldiers approached.
      Many others were hidden in ambush;
      And to lull suspicion, as a further ploy,
      A group stood out in front as a decoy.

87   All along the white sand beach
      The fearsome Muslims were gesticulating
      With cowhide shields and glinting spears,
      Taunting the mighty Portuguese;
      These were far too spirited to endure
      Such dogs baring their teeth,
      Descending on the beach in such a burst
      No one knew afterwards which man was first.

88   As in the bloody bullring a lover,
      Proud that his radiant lady is watching,
      Doesn't wait for the bull but confronts him,
      Posing, whistling, stamping, and halloing,
      But on the instant the terrible beast,
      Bellowing, blinded by sheer
      Rage, drops his horns in a lightning spurt
      Tossing, goring, and trampling him in the dirt,

89   So from our boats the fusillade began
      In murderous volleys. Lead balls dealt
      Death, the screams were inhuman,
      The shocked air boomed and hissed.
      Then the Muslims' courage broke
      As their blood congealed with panic;
      Those hidden in ambush could be seen to fly,
      While those upon the strand were the first to die.

90   The Portuguese were relentless, pursuing
     Victory with destruction and death,
     Bombarding, burning, and looting
     The exposed, unstockaded village.
     By now, the Sheikh regretted the skirmish
     He had thought to carry off lightly;
     Old men and women with their babes lamented,
     Cursing war and damning him who sent it.

91   The Muslims shot arrows as they fled,
     But uselessly in their fear and haste,
     Flinging rocks and sticks and pebbles,
     The very weapons of desperation.
     Abandoning the island, most
     Fled to the mainland in their terror,
     Taking refuge in the narrow waterway
     Which separates the island in the bay.

92   Some crammed in overloaded dugouts;
     Some tried swimming and were swept
     Under the breakers, swallowing water,
     And were spewed out by the sea in turn.
     The repeated cannonade shattered
     The brittle boats of these uncivil people,
     And so the Portuguese dealt finally
     With their small-minded spite and treachery.

93   They returned in victory to the fleet
     With the spoils of battle and rich plunder,
     And went to take water at their will
     Without objection or any resistance.
     But the Mohammedans were dismayed,
     Their initial hatred being rekindled;
     And, harrowed that their losses were so huge,
     Found comfort in their second subterfuge.

94   The governor of that abject island
     Dispatched envoys to sue for peace,
     The Portuguese not knowing under
     The flag of truce he was plotting war;
     For the promised, but deceitful pilot
     With treachery stamped on his heart,
     Whose task was to steer them to their death,
     Was offered as the pledge of his good faith.

95   The captain was now more than eager
     To return to his proper business,
     With calm weather and the right winds
     For his search for the longed-for India.
     He received the pilot sent him
     Gladly and, with a politic message
     To the Sheikh, thrust the island from his mind,
     Spreading his canvas to the monsoon wind.

96   With this leave-taking, the mighty fleet
     Ploughed Amphitrite's* gentle waves,
     Escorted by the faithful nereids,
     Sweet and delightful companions.
     The captain, who had not yet tumbled
     To the design the pilot was weaving,
     Plied him with fresh questions thick and fast
     About India, and all the coasts they passed.

97   But the pilot, fertile in invention
     As malevolent Bacchus inspired him,
     Plotted death, enslavement, or shipwreck
     Before the Portuguese could reach India.
     Describing the Indian harbours,
     He answered openly all he was asked,
     And confident these answers were sincere,
     The stalwart people saw no cause for fear.

98   Then, subtly as when Sinon to the Trojans
     Sang the praises of the Wooden Horse,
     He let slip that close by, on an island,
     Lived an ancient race of Christians.
     The captain, who was listening intently,
     Rejoiced so greatly at this news
     He offered there and then a king's bribe
     To conduct us to this lost Christian tribe.*

99   Now what the credulous Christian begged
     Was precisely what the pilot sought,
     For the island, in truth, was peopled
     By Muslims, followers of vile Mohammed.
     There he saw his plot maturing
     With strength and numbers far
     Greater than Mozambique's, the island's fame
     There being widespread. Kilwa is its name.

100 Joyfully the fleet changed course,
But Venus, the goddess from Cythera,
Seeing them veering from their proper tack
And sailing to unseasonable death,
Could not permit the people she loved
To perish in so remote a place
So summoned opposing winds, to amend
The bearing plotted by their dangerous friend.

101 At this, the astute Muslim, unable
To carry through his first plan.
Devised a second pernicious scheme,
Still constant to his purpose,
Proposing that, since hostile currents
Had balked their forward progress,
There was another island occupied
By Christians and by Muslims side by side.

102 Even with these words he was lying,
Obeying the instructions given him,
For no Christian people dwelt there,
Only those who worshipped the prophet.
The captain, trusting him in everything,
Asked to be guided there instead,
But Venus, restraining them once more
From crossing the bar, the fleet stood off shore.

103 A tiny channel divided the island
From the continent of Africa;
But there could be seen a magnificent
City with many noble edifices
Marking the whole curve of the bay,
A landmark visible for many miles,
And ruled by a king of great antiquity;
Mombasa* it is named, both isle and city.

104 The captain had at last dropped anchor,
And was strangely elated at the prospect
Of meeting the baptized Christians
The false pilot had invented.
Boats came from the shore with greetings
From the king who already knew of them,
For Bacchus had prepared him long before,
Taking the disguise of the other Moor.

105   The welcome they brought was friendly
In form, but poisonous in its matter,
For its intentions were hostile
As the aftermath would reveal.
O great and grave dangers!*
O the vicissitudes of life's journey!
That wherever a people place their trust,
The little they rely on turns to dust.

106   On the sea, such storms and perils
That death, many times, seemed imminent;
On the land, such battle and intrigue
Such dire, inevitable hardships!
Where may frail humanity shelter
Briefly, in some secure port,
Where the bright heavens cease to vent their rage
On such insects on so small a stage?

Canto Two

1   As the time came for the brilliant star
    Which separates the hours to reach
    His longed-for and lingering horizon,
    Hiding from man his celestial
    Fire in the underwater refuge slid
    Quietly open by the God of Night,
    The Mohammedans were making their way
    To the ships, then anchoring outside the bay.

2   In them was one who came entrusted
    With further diplomatic menace, saying
    —'Valiant captain, who has split
    Neptune's salty domain in two,
    The Sultan who rules this island,
    Advised of your coming, is overjoyed;
    To receive you is his heart's desire,
    Embrace you, and supply what you require.

3   'And because of his profound longing
    To greet one whose fame has gone before,
    He begs you, have no misgivings,
    Enter the bay, you and your fleet;
    And because you bring from a troublesome
    Voyage a crew jaded and infirm,
    He suggests, replenish them here on land;
    Anything that allures is his to command.

4   'If you come hoping for merchandise,
    The riches of the sumptuous Levant,
    Cinnamon, cloves, ardent spices,
    Or potent, health-giving drugs,
    Or if you hope to find precious stones,
    The exquisite ruby, the precise diamond,
    If these are the luxuries you treasure,
    Here is your journey's end, by any measure.'

5 Courteously, the captain responded,
Thanking the Sultan for his words,
But adding that now the sun had descended
He would not comply by risking the bar;
However, as soon as daylight showed
A safe passage for the fleet,
He would cross without hesitation since
Nothing less was due to so great a prince.

6 Then he asked if there really were
Christians as the pilot had claimed;
The alert messenger did not blink
But assured him most were believers;
So by such means his heart was cleared
Of calculation and foreboding,
And our captain was gently led to quell
All lingering doubts about the infidel.

7 Even so, from among those prisoners
On board, sentenced for gross crimes
So their lives could be hazarded
In predicaments such as these,
He sent two of the cleverest, trained
To spy on the city and defences
Of the resourceful Muslims, and to greet
The famous Christians he so longed to meet.

8 With them he sent to the Sultan gifts
In the hope his apparent benignity
Would stay tender and unsullied
Though, in truth, all was the reverse.
Meanwhile, the dangerous ambassadors
Had re-embarked and crossed the tide way
And, with compliments on their smiling lips,
Welcomed ashore the convicts from the ships.

9 After they had presented to the Sultan
With due ceremony the gifts they bore,
They toured the city, but observed
Much less of it than they had hoped,
For the cautious Muslims were reluctant
To let them see all they desired:
Where malice rules, it's natural to fear
Everyone's motives must be similar.

10 But Bacchus, the twice-born,* whose
Countenance shone with perpetual youth,
The same god who wove the fictions
To bring about the fleet's destruction,
Had again taken on human form,
This time in the habit of a Christian
And, in one of the mansions, he had arrayed
A gorgeous altar where on his knees he prayed.

11 There was depicted the Holy Ghost
Painted as a white dove fluttering
Down from on high to that matchless
Phoenix, Mary the chaste Virgin;
There too was pictured the sacred company
Of the twelve apostles, open-mouthed
As, with tongues of fire, the Holy Ghost
Schooled them in languages at Pentecost.*

12 The two friends were conducted where
Bacchus had raised this forgery,
And they fell on their knees, truly
Touched by the God who rules the world.
Semele's son hovered like a priest,
Scattering the sweetest incense
Of Arabia; and thus, when he was through,
The false god was worshipping the true.

13 The Christian convicts were sheltered
For the night hospitably, with every
Scrupulous attention, unaware
Of the fraud practised on their faith;
But as soon as the glittering sun's
Rays lit up the earth, at the very
Instant when over the horizon rolled
Apollo with his countenance of gold,

14 Messengers left the shore with the Sultan's
Renewed invitation to enter harbour,
And with them the men the captain had sent
To whom the Sultan had been so gracious;
And so da Gama, once more assured
That no danger was in the offing,
And that Christians were waiting in that city,
Turned his prows towards the salt estuary.

15   Those sent to spy said they had seen
     Sacred altars and a holy priest;
     It was there they lodged, and slept
     Through the long hours of darkness;
     In the Sultan and the people, they found
     Only generosity and contentment
     There was, in all conscience, nothing to fear
     About courtesies so open and sincere.

16   At this, the noble da Gama received
     Gladly the Muslims who came on board;
     So easily can a trusting soul
     Be taken in by appearances.
     The decks filled with the unbelievers,
     Abandoning the boats which brought them,
     Quietly happy that within the hour
     The Portuguese would fall into their power.

17   Secretly, those on the shore prepared
     Weapons and ammunition so the moment
     The ships anchored in the river
     They would launch a bold assault;
     By this stratagem they were determined
     The sons of Lusus would all be killed,
     As on the unsuspecting they would wreak
     Vengeance for what was done in Mozambique.

18   The stubborn anchors were hauled up,
     The sailors chanting as is their custom;
     Under foresails alone, they turned
     In the wind to where the bar was marked.
     But Venus of Ericina,* who watched
     Tirelessly over the Portuguese heroes,
     Observing the ambush set so secretly,
     Sped swifter than an arrow from heaven to sea.

19   She summoned Nereus' white daughters
     And all the forces of the blue ocean,
     Who obeyed her because she herself
     Had her birth in the salt waves;
     And announcing to them why she had come,
     She led the entire company
     To place their lovely bodies as obstruction
     Between the ships and imminent destruction.

20   They sped across the water, lashing it
     To foam with their silver tails;
     Cloto was breasting the billows
     More impetuously than usual;
     Nisa leapt; Nerina flung herself
     Headlong over the crests, while
     The undulating breakers took alarm
     At the reckless nymphs, and ducked away from harm.

21   Vehement and lovely in her anger,
     Venus rode on a triton's shoulders;
     He did not resent her sweet weight,
     Proud of so beautiful a burden.
     Arriving quickly where the stiff wind
     Was swelling the sails of the warlike fleet,
     The nereids dispersed and without delay
     Circled the light ships as they gathered way.

22   The goddess placed herself with others
     Directly before the flagship's prow,
     Blocking the way* to the bar as the wind
     Gusted, swelling the sails in vain;
     She leaned her soft breasts against the hard timbers,
     Forcing the powerful warship back;
     Other nymphs to port and starboard lifted
     And clear of the dread bar the vessel shifted.

23   As ants,* wise to the coming of winter,
     Lift and carry back to their nest
     Objects beyond all proportion to their size
     As they struggle to lay in store;
     Wearily they labour, displaying
     Powers that seem incredible;
     So toiled the nymphs to snatch and defend
     The Lusitanians from a hideous end.

24   By sheer effort they drove the ship
     Back, in spite of the mariners, who cursed
     As they re-set the sails, wrenching
     The rudder from starboard to port;
     On the stern poop, the shrewd bo'sun
     Shouted in vain about a huge reef
     Directly in their path which if they hit,
     Head-on or glancingly, the hull would split.

25   The rough sailors chanted as they
      Hauled and sweated in rhythm;
      The pandemonium shocked the Muslims
      Who imagined it was some war cry;
      Not knowing the cause, or what
      To make of the uproar, they assumed
      The Portuguese realized what was planned
      And that swift retribution was at hand.

26   To a man, they launched themselves
      Into the light boats which had brought them;
      Some crashed headlong in the water;
      Some chose to escape by swimming;
      From both sides men jumped, driven
      By terror of what they imagined,
      Much preferring the hazards of the sea
      To the hands of their affronted enemy.

27   As in a pond* deep in the countryside,
      Frogs, those one-time people of Lycia,
      If they happen to be out of the water
      When they sense someone approaching,
      From here, there, and everywhere plop
      Back where they feel safest,
      Dissolving in the element they know,
      But above the surface their heads still show;

28   So the Muslims scampered; and the pilot
      Too, who took the ships into danger,
      Believing his plot was discovered,
      Fled by jumping in the brackish water.
      Meanwhile, to avoid hitting the reef
      Where they would lose their dear lives,
      The flagship cast anchors fore and aft,
      And the crew struck sail in the other craft.

29   Watching this, bemused by the Muslims'
      Strange actions and the pilot's
      Equally precipitate flight, da Gama
      Understood what had been planned;
      And seeing there were no hostile
      Winds nor any opposing current
      To obstruct them in their passage ahead,
      He took it for a miracle, and said:

30 —'O rare, unlooked-for deliverance!
O clear, self-evident miracle!
O treachery, baffling but manifest!
O false and malignant people!
What man, however diligent,
Could keep malevolence at bay
If the Immortal Guardian on high
Did not watch over frail humanity?

31 'Plainly, Providence has shown us
There is no safety in these ports;
Visibly has been exposed the fraud
Practised on our good faith;
But since neither long experience
Nor wit can be our salvation,
Do not, O Sacred Guardian, hide your face
From those whose only harbour is your grace!

32 'And being so moved with compassion
For this wretched, wandering people,
Knowing that only your Divine pity
Preserved us from such wicked foes,
Now in your wisdom, be our pilot
To some haven truly secure,
And the India we seek, at last unveil,
For only in Your service do we sail.'

33 Overhearing this pious prayer,
Venus, in all her beauty, was touched
And, parting from the nereids who
Were saddened seeing her go so soon,
Already she was among the bright
Stars, already in the third heaven,
Passing swiftly and only pausing where
Jupiter had his home in the sixth sphere.*

34 She arrived panting from her journey,
Looking so flushed and radiant
The stars and heavens and surrounding
Air and all that saw her loved her;
From her eyes, where Cupid had his nest,
Flashed such a generous warmth
The earth's frozen continents caught fire
And both ice caps burned like Africa.

35   And to further entice the Father
Who always loved and esteemed her,
She displayed herself* as she once did
To Paris* in the forests of Mount Ida.
Had Diana,* when glimpsed by Actaeon,
Looked half so lovely in the clear water,
Never would he have been torn asunder
By his hounds, but perished of sheer wonder.

36   With careful carelessness, her gold hair
Tumbled on her white shoulders;
As she moved, her nipples trembled
As if Love was playing there invisibly;
From her immaculate waist shot the flames
With which Cupid sets hearts smouldering,
While hot desire wove its lustful eyes
Closer than ivy round her marble thighs.

37   With sheerest silk she hid those parts
Normally veiled by modesty,
Though not so demurely as to hide
Or quite reveal her mount of lilies,
But using the barrier of transparency
To fire lust with redoubled ardour.
Vulcan raged with jealousy, while Mars'
Rekindled passion* shook the furthest stars.

38   And selecting for her angelic face
A smile transfused with sadness,
Like a woman ill used in the courtly
Game by an inattentive lover,
Laughing and complaining at the same
Instant, torn between joy and anguish,
The goddess, unequalled in the arts of love,
Less sad than tender, made her speech to Jove:

39   —'I always imagined, mighty Father,
That in matters I have most at heart,
You would be loving and considerate
Even if something weighed to the contrary;
Now I find you angry, without my
Deserving it or having wronged you,
So let Bacchus go ahead with his plot;
Misery, I am resigned, must be my lot.

40 'These my people, for whom I shed
Tears I find were shed uselessly,
Have been led by my love into danger
Because you oppose me so much;
Imploring you, weeping on their behalf,
I struggle against my peace of mind.
Because I love them, they are rejected;
So let me hate them, then they'll be protected.

41 'Let them perish at those brutes' hands
Since I . . .' At this, tenderly,
She bathed her countenance in tears
Like dew-drops on a new-blown rose.
She struggled, as if her lips
Could not utter the pitiful words,
Then tried again; but Jove the Thunderer
With all his authority prevented her.

42 Touched by those tender protestations
That would have moved a tiger's heart,
With a countenance such, as when turned
Downwards, brightens the darkest skies,
He dried her tears and kissed her face,
Embracing her flawless bosom
So fervently that had they been in private
Another Cupid* might have been arrived at.

43 As he pressed her lovely face to his,
She increased her tears and sobbing
As a child, scolded by its nursemaid
Weeps the more for being comforted;
So to quieten her tormented spirit,
He began to unfold to her the future,
And, by her arts, was driven to relate
All that lay hidden in the womb of fate.

44 —'My lovely daughter, do not fear
For the safety of your Portuguese,
Nor that anything weighs more with me
Than those sovereign, tearful eyes;
I promise you, daughter, you will see
The Greeks and Romans far outshone
By what people of Portuguese descent
Will accomplish throughout the Orient.

45   'Though Ulysses* could talk his way
     Out of slavery on Calypso's island,
     Though Antenor breached the Adriatic
     To the source of of the River Timavus,
     Though devout Aeneas steered safely
     Between Scylla and Charybdis,
     Your greater navigators will unfold
     New worlds to the amazement of the old.

46   'You will see, my daughter, castles,
     Cities, ramparts all built at their hands;
     Even the tough, formidable Turks
     You will see consistently routed;
     The independent kings of India
     Will be subject to the king of Portugal,
     Bringing, when all falls under his command,
     A better dispensation to that land.

47   'You will see him, who is persevering
     In his intrepid search for India,
     Strike fear into Neptune himself
     In a dead calm without a breath of wind,
     A miracle* never before witnessed,
     The ocean quaking spontaneously!
     Such strong people! Such bold expedients!
     To terrorize the very elements!

48   'You will see the island* which denied them
     Water become one day a fine port,
     Where the Indian fleet on the long voyage
     From the west can recover and refit.
     All that coastline, which even now
     Wove its deadly plots, will submit,
     Acknowledging by their annual levies
     Their powerlessness against the Portuguese.

49   'You will see* the famous Red Sea
     Turning yellow from sheer fright;
     You will see the great kingdom of Ormuz
     Twice captured and subdued;
     There you will see the furious Moor
     Transfixed by his own arrows,
     For whoever denies your people will curse
     Their resistance has only made things worse.

50 'You will watch them, in mighty Diu,
    Be invincible through two sieges;
    There they will show their calibre
    In outstanding feats of arms;
    Great Mars will swell with envy
    At the ferocity of the Portuguese,
    While the defeated Sultan, facing death,
    Will damn Mohammed with his final breath.

51 'Goa, you will see, seized from the Muslims
    And come in the fullness of time to be
    Queen of the Orient, raised up
    By the triumphs of her conquerors.
    From that proud, noble eminence,
    They will rule with an iron fist
    Idol-worshipping Hindus, and everyone
    Throughout that land with thoughts of rebellion.

52 'You will see them hold with the tiniest
    Garrison the fortress of Cannanore;
    You will see the powerful and populous
    City of Calicut laid waste;
    In Cochin, you will see Pacheco Pereira,
    That matchless hero, prove himself;
    No poet ever praised a victory
    So deserving of eternal glory.

53 'Not even in the seas at Actium,* during
    Rome's civil war, were witnessed
    Such flames, such hotly contested lines,
    When bold Augustus conquered Antony,
    Faithless in glory as he returned
    From the Orient and the Nile
    And from Afghanistan, laden with spoils,
    Though himself caught in Cleopatra's coils,

54 'As the very ocean boils with the fires
    Ignited by your people, battling,
    Taking both Hindu and Muslim captive,
    Subduing the different nations,
    Conquering the Golden Chersonese,*
    Venturing as far as remote China
    And the most distant isles of the Orient,
    Until every sea-way is subservient.

55   'In this way, my daughter, they will show
      Superhuman fortitude, never matched
      From the sea which drinks the Ganges
      To the Atlantic in the far west,
      Or from the northern passage to the Straits
      Named for Magellan,* who deserved better,
      Never, though the world resurrect its dead
      In search of braver men or better led.'

56   With these words, Jove dispatched
      Divine Mercury down to the earth,
      His mission to find a harbour the fleet
      Could approach without forebodings,
      And to prevent da Gama lingering
      Further in treacherous Mombasa,
      To convey to him in his dreams which port
      Would offer the tranquillity he sought.

57   The God from Cyllene* set off at once;
      With his winged feet he descended to earth;
      He bore in his hand the magic wand
      Which brings sleep to tired eyes;
      With it, he recalls from the underworld
      Sad souls, and harnesses the winds;
      With his usual winged helmet on his head,
      Malindi* was the port to which he sped.

58   With him he took Rumour to proclaim
      The rare worth of the Portuguese,
      For reputation constrains respect
      And he who has it, is cherished.
      And so were the people made receptive
      By the legend of da Gama's true fame.
      In no time, all Malindi longed to see
      What kind of men these Portuguese might be.

59   From there, Mercury flew to Mombasa
      Where the ships rode warily at anchor,
      And warned our people to abandon
      That dangerous bar and dissembling land,
      For numbers and skill could achieve
      Little against such hellish designs,
      Nor subtlety nor courage ward off harm,
      Had not heaven itself raised the alarm.

60   Night was now half-way down its road;
     The stars in the heavens with their
     Borrowed light illumined the broad world,
     And sleep was the crew's sole pleasure.
     The illustrious captain, worn out,
     By the anxieties of a night watch
     Was giving his weary eyes a brief respite
     (Others remained on watch throughout the night),

61   When Mercury appeared to him in a dream
     Urging: 'Fly! Fly! Lusitanian
     From the plot the king is weaving
     To put an end to you all. Fly!
     The wind and the heavens favour you;
     The weather is calm, the ocean still;
     Just along the coast is another king
     Honourable, powerful and welcoming!

62   'What awaits you here is the reception
     Cruel Diomedes* offered travellers,
     Feeding the people who were his guests
     To his dreadful, flesh-eating horses;
     What awaits you is the human sacrifice
     Busiris* made of his visitors.
     Your fate will be no different if you pause;
     Fly! Fly these ruthless, barbaric shores!

63   'Sail further along the coast; there,
     Near to the point where the burning sun
     Makes night and day equal,* you will find
     A different, more honourable country;
     A king there, greeting your joyful
     Fleet with many acts of friendship,
     Will secure you as his guests and provide
     For India a skilled and faithful guide.'

64   So Mercury spoke, and the vision
     Astonished the captain, who awoke,
     Seeing a ray of divine light
     Striking through the thick darkness;
     And understanding it was a sign
     Not to remain in that evil place,
     With recharged spirit he ordered the bo'sun
     To spread all sails and head for the ocean.

65 —'Let out sail to the winds,' he cried,
    'Heaven favours us and God has sent them;
    I have seen a messenger from on high
    Who looks kindly on our passage.'
    At this there rose the bustle
    Of the mariners on this side and that,
    Hauling the anchors, chanting as a team,
    With just that show of muscle they esteem.

66 Even as the anchors were being raised,
    The Muslims down in the darkness
    Were secretly trying to cut the cables
    To wreck the ships on the sand-bar;
    But the Portuguese with lynx-like
    Eyes were keeping constant vigil,
    And hearing all the sudden to-and-froing,
    The Muslims scattered, but flying, not rowing!

67 Soon the sharp prows were cleaving
    The silver highway of the seas;
    The light monsoon breezes blew
    With their safe, persistent pressure;
    The sailors talked of the perils
    They had passed, for tension eases
    Slowly from the mind when mere chance contrives
    To bring us through great hazards with our lives.

68 The hot sun had circled the earth once
    And another day begun, when they saw
    Two ships on the horizon cruising
    Peacefully in the pleasant winds.
    They could belong only to the Muslims
    So they set sail to give chase.
    At this the first, not waiting to see more,
    Turned tail and headed for the nearest shore.

69 The second showed no such resource
    But was captured by the Lusitanians
    Without any martial gestures
    Or any thunder from Vulcan's cannon;
    The crew being only a handful, timid
    And lacking spirit, offered
    No resistance; but had any the heart
    It could only have been futile on their part.

70 Da Gama's desire being to obtain
A guide to the India of his ambition,
He hoped to find one among these Moors
But was doomed to disappointment,
No one managing a word of where
In the wide world India might be;
But they all said Malindi was the port
He'd obtain for sure the pilot that he sought.

71 They praised the Sultan's munificence,
Generous disposition, honest heart,
And breadth of vision and humanity,
All qualities compelling respect.
The captain took this as the truth,
Confirming Mercury's message
As he slept, and so the armada sped
Where the Muslims pointed and the dream had said.

72 It was the happy time of the year
When the Sun was entering Taurus,*
When Jupiter loved Europa,
And flowers adorn the horn of plenty;
The speedy sun which circles the earth
Restores the memory of that day
When Christ, who is Lord of every nation,
Rose to put His seal on all creation;

73 Malindi* could be seen on the horizon
As the fleet entered the wide bay,
Bedecked with colourful banners
As befitted Holy Easter Sunday;
Flags were unfurled, the standard flew
Its purples visible from afar;
Timbrels clattered, drums banged a refrain;
So they approached in happy martial strain.

74 People crowded Malindi's beaches
Coming down to stare at the happy fleet,
People more open and more humane;
Than any in the countries left behind.
The Portuguese ships moored before them,
The heavy anchors taking grip,
And one of the captives was dispatched to bring
Their landfall to the notice of the king.

75   The Sultan already knew that nobility
      Was the mark of the Portuguese,
      Being proud it was his harbour
      The courageous people had put into;
      And with the true, honourable spirit
      That distinguishes generous hearts,
      He welcomed them to the comforts of the shore;
      Everything in his realm was theirs, and more.

76   Such genuine tributes, such sincere
      Promises with not a hint of duplicity,
      The Sultan pledged the noble knights
      Who had crossed such lands and seas;
      Yet for all he sent, woolly sheep,
      Domestic fowl, the ripest, choicest,
      Most succulent fruits of the season, still
      His gifts could not exhaust his generous will.

77   The captain received with great joy
      The happy envoy and his message,
      And made the Sultan a further present
      Brought with him for just such occasions:
      Scarlet cloth, its colours flaming,
      Rich, delicately branching coral,
      Which grows on the sea-bed in spongy gardens,
      Till in the broad light of day it hardens.

78   He also sent one, skilled in diplomacy,
      To seal with the noble Sultan a pact,
      Inviting him not to take it amiss
      That he did not disembark at once.
      The adroit ambassador left for the shore
      Seeking an audience with the Sultan
      And, with a skilful rhetoric taught him
      By subtle Minerva,* he besought him:

79   —'Sublime king, to whom was delegated
      By the supreme Justice on pure Olympus
      The governance of a splendid people,
      And no less loved by them than feared;
      As a strong refuge more secure
      Than any throughout the Orient,
      We have sailed far to find you, in our need
      Of the assistance we know is guaranteed.

80 'We are not pirates who, coming upon
   Undefended, unsuspecting cities,
   Commit massacre by fire and sword
   To rob people of what they treasure,
   But we have voyaged from proud Europe,
   Crossing the wide seas in search
   Of India's opulent and spacious land,
   Obedient to our great king's great command.

81 'In what age were there such hard hearts,
   Such bad faith and barbarous manners,
   Not only to deny us harbours
   But even the asylum of desert sands!
   What minds are so given to suspicion,
   Or are so afraid of such a few,
   That with armed contrivance, cunningly deployed,
   They should labour to see us all destroyed?

82 'But you, on whom we may surely depend
   For true friendship, O benign king,
   Securing the sure help which once
   Shipwrecked Ulysses* found in Alcinous,
   We have journeyed safely to your port
   Steered by the divine helmsman;
   In guiding us to you, God has made it clear
   How generous is your heart and how sincere.

83 'Do not think, O King, that if our captain
   Has not disembarked to attend on you,
   Or do you service, it is because
   He suspects you of double-dealing;
   You should know it is all done
   In obedience to his royal master,
   Who strictly ordered him never to be caught
   Away from his fleet, at any beach or port.

84 'And because it is the vassal's duty
   To be ruled, as limbs must be, by the head,
   Do not, as a king, question why
   No one disobeys his king;
   But he undertakes that the story
   Of your nobility and great kindness
   Will be told by him and his, unstintingly,
   As long as rivers press on to the sea.'

85 So he spoke, and all the company,
   Talking naturally among themselves,
   Were full of praise for those who had passed
   Such constellations and such seas;
   And the illustrious Sultan pondered
   Da Gama's great devotion to duty,
   Deeply intrigued, and marvelling as he thought
   Of the king so much obeyed so far from court.

86 And with a face full of smiles, he responded
   To the envoy who had also impressed him,
   —'Remove all fear from your heart,
   And banish all suspicion.
   The world holds you in such esteem
   For your worth and achievements,
   They must be strangely lacking in respect
   Those people, who desired to see you wrecked.

87 'As for your men not stepping ashore
   To observe the normal courtesies,
   It weighs on me a little strangely,
   But I place more value on obedience.
   If their instructions will not permit it,
   Nor am I willing that spirits
   So loyal should be forced to feel contrition,
   Simply to countenance my own ambition.

88 'However, when crystal daylight dawns
   On the world, I with my dhows
   Will go to visit the mighty armada
   I have desired many days to see;
   And having long been buffeted by the seas,
   By the raging winds, and the long journey,
   Here you will be given in honest guise
   Your pilots, munitions, and fresh supplies.'

89 As he finished Apollo, Latona's son,
   Plunged in the sea, and the messenger
   With his cheerful news returned
   In his tiny boat to the fleet.
   All hearts were were filled with joy
   They had at long last encountered
   Firm news of their yearned-for destination,
   And spent the night in raucous jubilation.

90 There was no shortage of fireworks,
  Imitating the quivering comets;
  The bombardiers did their office,
  Blasting land and waves and sky;
  It was like the Cyclops* at the smithy
  As the firebombs were exploded,
  While the crew's voices, shrill with vehemence,
  Shook the heavens, strumming their instruments.

91 On the shore, they responded at once,
  With rockets leaping and whistling;
  Burning wheels spun in the air;
  Hidden sulphur powders exploded;
  Shouting rose to the night skies;
  The sea was lit up by flames and the land
  No less, as if both sides were emulating
  The other party in their celebrating.

92 But soon the restless stars revolved
  To awake mankind to its labours,
  And Memnon's* mother, bringing light,
  Put an end to the longest dream;
  The shadows were slowly withdrawing
  From the dew-drenched flowers of the fields,
  When the Sultan embarked in full array
  To review the armada anchored in the bay.

93 There came behind, crowding the beaches,
  A happy multitude, eager to watch;
  They wore purple tunics with wide sleeves
  The finely woven silk gleaming.
  In the place of warriors' assegais
  Or bows shaped like the horned moon,
  They wielded coconut branches on high
  Like the green palms of a Roman victory.

94 A large and lavish dhow, with awnings
  Draped with multicoloured silks,
  Conveyed the Sultan of Malindi, along
  With the nobles and lords of his kingdom;
  He came gorgeously attired,
  After their fashion and style of beauty;
  On his head was a turban finely rolled,
  Embroidered splendidly with silk and gold;

95   His robe was of the finest damask,
And dyed the Tyrian* purple they admire;
His glittering collar, prized yet more
For its workmanship than its gold,
Was refulgent with diamonds;
In his belt was a richly carved dagger;
Gold and pearls, to make ornament complete,
Studded the velvet slippers on his feet.

96   An attendant with a silk umbrella,
Raised high on a gold-draped pole,
Prohibited the hot sun from burning
Or discomforting the great Sultan.
Music was in the prow, in sharp
Unrhythmic blasts, harsh to our ears,
From instruments like trumpets, but half bent
Like bows, cacophonous and discordant.

97   No less resplendent, the Lusitanian
Took to the boats and left the fleet
To meet the Malindian on the water
With a noble and distinguished retinue.
Da Gama was dressed in Iberian style
Though his cloak, of Venetian satin,
Was of French cut and in his favourite
Deep vermilion such as all men covet;

98   His sleeves were slashed with gold buttons,
Which dazzled as they caught the sun;
His soldierly breeches were embroidered
With the same metal, so hard to obtain;
And likewise pointed with gold were
The delicate fastenings of his doublet;
He wore his gold sword in the Italian way;
His cap's feather slanted eloquently.

99   Those in his company were arrayed
In matchless purples, or in other varied
Eye-catching colours as befitted
The different styles of their dress.
Together their clothes blended
To such a lovely graduated
Enamel, as may be seen in the brilliant bow
Of the lovely nymph Iris,* and all aglow.

100   Sweet trumpets filled the air with sound
      Animating men's happy spirits;
      The boats of the Muslims crowded the sea,
      Their awnings trailing in the water;
      The gunners fired their dreadful cannon,
      Blotting out the sun with smoke:
      Blast followed on blast, becoming so fierce,
      The Muslims clapped their hands across their ears.

101   Boarding the captain's boat, the Sultan
      Raised him up in his arms;
      While he, with the courtesy due to a king,
      Welcomed him as his rank required;
      The Sultan noted his dress and style
      With admiration and wonder,
      As one struck to his soul by the idea
      Of voyaging from so far to India.

102   And with munificent words he offered
      Anything his kingdom might supply,
      And that if he lacked provisions
      He should assume them already furnished;
      He said more, that without seeing them
      He knew of the Lusitanian people,
      For he had learned already of the long wars*
      Fought by the Portuguese against the Moors.

103   All Africa, he said had resounded
      With the great deeds they had performed
      In winning for themselves the crown
      Of the kingdom of the Hesperides;*
      With many fine words, he expressed
      Less what the Portuguese deserved
      Than what had reached Malindi by report;
      So da Gama responded in this sort:

104   —'O generous king,* unique in showing
      Compassion to the Lusitanian people,
      Who through so much misery and danger
      Have tested the mad fury of the seas;
      That Almighty, Divine Providence
      Who turns the heavens and rules mankind,
      Will more reward you than is in our power
      For receiving us at this place and hour.

105   'You alone, of all Africa's peoples,
       Welcomed us from the ocean in peace;
       In you, from the dreadful winds of Aeolus,*
       We found benign, sincere harbour;
       As long as the Great Pole herds the stars
       And the sun gives light to the world,
       Wherever glory and whatever fame
       Accrues to me, I'll keep alive your name.'

106   At this, the boats were manœuvred
       To review the fleet as the Sultan wished;
       They circled the ships one by one
       To observe and take note of everything;
       Once more cannon thundered to the heavens,
       And the fleet fired a broadside;
       Once more the trumpets rang out in salute;
       The Muslims with their slughorns followed suit.

107   But after the generous Sultan had studied
       All there was to be seen, and finding
       The unaccustomed conjunction of noise
       Not only a surprise, but intimidating;
       He asked for quiet and to drop anchor
       From the light craft carrying them,
       To talk at leisure with the great da Gama
       On matters which he knew only by rumour.

108   The Sultan took delight in conversing
       On different topics, questioning
       Now about the famous, splendid battles
       Fought with the followers of Mohammed,
       Now about the many different peoples
       Who lived in farthest Hesperia,
       Now about those lands which are our neighbours,
       Now of the watery highway of our labours.

109   —'But first of all, most valiant captain,
       Tell us (he said) clearly and plainly,
       With due regard for order, of your land,
       Clime, and where in the world you dwell;
       And also of your ancient lineage,
       And the origin of so powerful a kingdom;
       List all your battles from the earliest days,
       Which knowing not, I know deserve all praise.

110 'And tell us, too, of the long circuit
You have made across the angry oceans,
What outlandish customs you have seen
In this uncivil Africa of ours;
Tell us, now the horses of dawn
With their golden bridles are hauling
The sun's glittering chariot from the east;
The winds are sleeping, and the waves have ceased.

111 'The fullness of the hour is matched
By the depth of my desire to hear you,
For who does not know by report
Of the matchless works of the Portuguese?
We Malindians are not so remote
From the bright sun's beaten track,
That you should consider us too uncouth
To take the measure of so great a truth.

112 'The proud Titans* fought in vain
Against pure radiant Olympus;
Pirithous and Theseus ventured crassly
In the dark and fearful realm of Pluto.
But if such feats had been accomplished,
The tasks of assaulting the Heavens
Or Hell were no more hard or various
Than combating the angry seas of Nereus.

113 'Herostratus set fire to Diana's temple
Built by subtle Ctesiphon,* solely
To be known throughout the world
And remembered by the human race.
If the desire for fame can lead
To such sacrilege and atrocity,
How much better to hold in memory
One whose deeds are worth eternal glory.'

Canto Three

1   *Now it is for you, Calliope,* to teach me*
    What famous da Gama told the Sultan;
    Inspire living song and a godlike voice
    In this mortal heart, your devotee.
    Nor should Apollo,* inventor of healing,
    By whom, lovely lady, you bore Orpheus,
    Squander again the devotion he owes
    On various Daphnes, Clyties, or Leucothoes.

2   *O Nymph, give effect to my ambition*
    To match what the Portuguese deserve;
    Let the world see that the Tagus
    Sparkles with the waters of Parnassus;
    Come down from the Muses' mountain,
    For already I feel Apollo's baptism;
    Denying me, you may appear afraid
    I'll leave revered Orpheus in the shade.

3   All those present were waiting eagerly
    For what the great da Gama would say,
    When, losing himself a little in thought,
    He raised his eyes and spoke:
    —You command me, O King, to describe
    My people's long descent, yet this is no
    Extraneous tale you ask me to begin,
    But the glories of my own kith and kin.

4   To praise the achievements of another
    Is customary and to be desired,
    But my praise of my fellow countrymen
    Will sound, I fear, all too unconvincing;
    And I know whatever time I take
    Will be all too short to tell you all;
    But you have asked and your command is chief;
    I will against my will, and I'll be brief.

5 I speak, moreover, from a compulsion
   To keep to the strict path of truth,
   For on such deeds, the more I dwell
   The more will be left unsaid.
   But so that due method may prevail
   In my account of what you wish to know,
   First I will describe that distant shore,
   And after I will talk of bloody war.

6 Between the tropic governed by Cancer,
   The bright sun's most northern track,
   And that region shunned for cold
   As much as the equator is for heat,
   Lies noble Europe, confronting both
   The Arctic and the Occident. To north
   And west the Atlantic is its boundary,
   And to the south the Mediterranean sea.

7 In the far east where the sun rises
   It borders Asia, but is skirted
   By the cold and winding River Don
   Which runs down into the Sea of Azov,
   And by the turbulent Aegean Sea
   Where warrior Greeks once held sway,
   But of triumphant Troy in all her glory
   The sailor sees only a memory.

8 In the uttermost north, close beneath
   The Polar Star, are the alps named
   Hyperborean,* after the wind
   Which rages there unremittingly.
   Apollo's rays which kindle the world
   Are so attenuated in their power,
   Snow-drifts linger year-long on the mountains;
   The sea is ice-bound, frozen too the fountains.

9 Here there live in vast numbers
   Scythians,* who long ago fought a war
   With the rulers of ancient Egypt
   Over the origins of the human race;
   So far were both sides from the truth
   (So prone to error is the human mind),
   On a matter that need no further task us
   Than the biblical city of Damascus.

10   Within this region are to be found
      Ice-bound Lapland, bleak Norway,
      And Scandinavia, that peninsula
      Whose Goths once conquered Italy;
      Beyond it, there opens a channel
      To the vast inland Baltic Sea,
      Navigable when not in winter's chains
      By Prussians, cold Swedes, and chilly Danes.

11   Between this sea and the Don live
      Strange peoples: Ruthenians, Moscovites,
      And Livonians, once called Sarmatians;
      In the Black Forest mountains are Poles.
      The German Empire rules as its subjects
      Bohemians, Hungarians, and Saxons,
      Together with various tiny riverine
      Dukedoms on the Elbe, Danube, Ems, and Rhine.

12   Between the lower Danube and the famous
      Strait which Helle* named with her life,
      Live the sturdy Thracians in a land
      Which Mars has made his own.
      But the mountains beyond in the Balkans
      Have fallen to the Turks; and even
      Byzantium has suffered the same fate
      To the great shame of Constantine the Great!*

13   Next is Macedonia whose people dwell
      By the cold waters of the River Vardar;
      And then you, O most splendid nation,
      With your polity, genius, and daring,
      Who fostered eloquence and the loftiest
      Ideals, O lucid Greece,
      Touching the sublime in hexameters,
      Not less inspired in war than in letters.

14   Next the Dalmatians, and in that gulf
      Where Antenor* once built Padua,
      Noble Venice floats on the waters
      —So great from such low beginnings.
      From here extends a long peninsula,
      To which many nations were subject;
      An exalted people, imposing accord
      No less by genius than by the sword.

15   Neptune's kingdom all but surrounds it,
      With Nature's bulwarks on the fourth side;
      And dividing it the Apennines,
      Mark the scenes of glorious battles;
      Today, Rome's power is in decline,
      It is home to the Keeper of the Keys,*
      No longer boasting Empire as its merit:
      So God rains blessings on the poor in spirit!

16   Beyond Italy lies Gaul, made known
      World wide by Caesar's conquests;
      It is watered by the rivers Seine,
      The Rhone, the Rhine, and the Garonne;
      In the south rises that mountain range
      Named from the buried nymph Pyrene,*
      Which once caught fire, or so the tale is told,
      And its rivers ran with silver and pure gold.

17   Here is encountered noble Iberia,
      The head, as it were, of all Europe,
      Whose dominion and unique glory
      Has seen many turns of Fortune's wheel;
      But never by force or treason could
      Fate's fickleness stain her honour,
      Nor rob her of her daring, nor disgrace
      The warrior virtues bred by such a race.

18   She confronts Mauretania, where
      The Mediterranean is almost closed
      At the strait, which famously takes its name
      From the last labour* of Hercules.
      Iberia, too, is all but an island,
      But its greatness is of several nations
      Each one of them so noble and so blessed
      That each in turn believes it is the best.

19   Here is Aragon, which gained renown
      For conquering turbulent Naples;*
      Here Navarre, and the Asturias, once
      Bulwark against the Muslim people;
      Here wary Galicia, and peerless
      Castile, ordained by her planets
      Spain's deliverer and her rightful lord,
      With León, Seville, and Granada all restored.*

20   And here, as if crowning Europe's
       Head, is the little kingdom of Portugal,
       Where the continent ends and the sea begins,
       And where Phoebus reclines in the ocean.
       By Heaven's will she prospered
       Against the unworthy Mauritanians,
       Driving them out; and in their hot garrison
       In Africa has not ceased to harass them.

21   This is my blessed home, my earliest love,
       Where, if Heaven allows my safe return
       With this task at last accomplished,
       I will be content to breath my last.
       She was named Lusitania, so it's said
       From Lusus* or Lysa, thought to be
       Bacchus' sons, or members of his band,
       The very first to cultivate this land.

22   Here the shepherd was born whose very name,
       Viriatus,* bears witness to his manhood,
       Whose fame none could overcome,
       Nor even Rome's power undo him.
       Meanwhile Time, which consumes its children,
       Conspired she should, by the will of Heaven,
       Play a part in the world, and in a word
       Become a great kingdom. Hear what occurred:

23   There was a king in Spain, by name Alfonso,*
       Who took battle to the Saracens
       So ruthlessly and with such skill
       Many lost their land and their lives.
       The story of these exploits flew
       From Gibraltar to the Caspian mountains,
       And many knights came flocking in their pride,
       All ready to be martyred at his side.

24   For they burned, more than for fame,
       With an inward love of the Faith;
       They came from various kingdoms
       Leaving their homes and native shores.
       Afterwards, when they had given proof
       Of highest merit in splendid deeds,
       Alfonso swore on his illustrious sword
       Such services should gain their due reward.

25 Of these, Henrique* (younger son, it's said,
Of a well-attested king of Hungary),
Was given Portugal as his portion,
Then little valued by the world;
But as a further sign of deep regard,
The king offered the young Count
His daughter, the Princess Teresa's hand,
Holding through her the power in that land.

26 Afterwards, he gained many victories
Over the heirs of the Ishmaelites,*
Capturing much neighbouring territory,
Fulfilling his great heart's urge;
As reward for these excellent deeds,
God on high soon granted him
A son, to whose illustrious hand would fall
The destiny of warlike Portugal.

27 Long before this, Henrique had been
At the conquest of the Holy City,*
And had seen the sands of Jordan
Where God's own flesh was baptized;
(This was when Godfrey of Boulogne
Completed the conquest of Judaea,
And many who had fought in these campaigns
Returned from their crusade to their domains).

28 Reaching the end of his long life,
And driven to the fatal necessity,
The great Hungarian, full of honours,
Returned his soul to Him who gave it.
There remained his son, still a tender
Youth, but one in whom the father,
Unrivalled in the world, was resurrected:
From such a father no less was expected.

29 But the old legend—perhaps untrue;
From antiquity nothing is certain—
States that his mother,* seizing the state,
Was not averse to a second wedding.
Disinheriting her orphaned son,
She insisted that in Portugal
Authority descended through her name,
Her marriage being its source and only claim.

30   Prince Afonso (for so he was named
     After his grandfather), found himself
     Powerless in the lands his mother
     And her consort ruled and devoured;
     But his martial instincts were aroused
     And, picturing the realm already his,
     He took only a short time to reflect,
     And as swiftly put his thoughts into effect.

31   So at Guimarães* the battlefield where
     She, so unlike a mother, denied
     Her son her love and his inheritance,
     Was steeped in the blood of civil war.
     Ranged against him in the field,
     She could not see how much she erred
     Against God, against maternal duty,
     Beset by the temptations of her beauty.

32   O cruel Procne! O witch Medea!*
     Who avenged on your own blameless sons
     The crimes committed by their fathers,
     Witness Teresa's double guilt!
     Sheer lust and naked greed
     Are this crime's commonest causes:
     Scylla murdered her father for the one;
     Teresa on both accounts attacked her son.

33   But the fair prince won the field
     Over his stepfather and wicked mother;
     And at a stroke the whole realm,
     Which had fought against him, was his;
     But anger overcame his judgement
     When he made fast his mother in chains;
     Honour your parents is the fifth commandment,
     And God was storing up due punishment!

34   Proud Castile came to her aid
     Against the outnumbered Portuguese
     To avenge the affront to Teresa,
     But Afonso was undaunted by any task.
     In fierce battle, his stout heart,
     So far retaining Heaven's help,
     Not only held his own in the fierce fight,
     But put his rugged enemy to flight.

35   Soon afterwards, the strong prince
      Was besieged by overwhelming numbers
      In Guimarães, for so the angry
      Castilian looked for redress;
      But, at the risk of a terrible death,
      Faithful Egas,* his tutor, rescued him,
      When all else had otherwise despaired,
      Given he found himself so ill-prepared.

36   For the loyal servitor, knowing
      His prince unable to oppose,
      Pledged his word to the Castilian
      That Afonso would make his obeisance.
      The enemy raised the fearful siege
      Trusting the advice of Egas Moniz,
      But the young prince, fired by ambition,
      Was too proud to offer his submission.

37   When the appointed time approached,
      And the king of Castile was waiting
      For the prince to show obedience
      And vow to accept his mandate,
      Egas, finding himself perjured,
      As Castile could never have foreseen,
      Resolved with his person to remove the stain
      Of the promise he had sworn to in vain,

38   And with his sons and wife he departed
      To redeem his honour along with them,
      Shoeless and in rags, in such fashion
      As would move more to pity than anger.
      —'If you wish, great king, to avenge yourself
      For my rash confidence,' he vowed,
      'I stand here before you, ready to comply
      With my life for the pledge that proved a lie.'

39   'You see before you the innocent lives
      Of my blameless sons and my consort,
      If great and generous hearts take
      Pleasure in destroying the weak;
      You see, too, my hands and delinquent tongue.
      On them alone exact your revenge;
      Take Sinis* as your merciless model,
      Or Perillus with his horrid brazen bull.'

40   As before the axe the condemned man,
      Supping already his cup of death,
      Puts his throat on the appalling block
      And anticipates the dread blow:
      So Egas before his indignant master
      Waited in resignation; but the king,
      Rejoicing in such rare integrity,
      Forgot his anger and inclined to pity.

41   O Portuguese honour, so scrupulous
      In a matter of trust and duty!
      What more did Zophyrus do, slashing
      His face, slitting his nostrils?
      —To win Babylon for his Darius,
      Who sighed a thousand times to have
      Zophyrus* home and whole would please him more
      Than Babylons captured by the score.

42   But now Prince Afonso was marshalling
      The prosperous Portuguese army
      Against the Moors who possessed the lands
      Beyond the clear, delightful Tagus;
      Already the proud army, full of fight,
      Was drawn up in the plain of Ourique,*
      Confronting the Saracen enemy,
      Though weaker far in men and weaponry.

43   In none other he placed his trust
      Than almighty God who rules the Heavens,
      For so few were the men of Christ
      That for each the Moors had a hundred;
      Judge whether by worldly standards
      It was more foolhardy than brave,
      With such a tiny army to take on
      Such cruel odds as a century to one.

44   Five Moorish kings were the enemy
      The foremost of whom was named Ismar;
      All of them tried and tested in war
      Where they won their fame and pre-eminence;
      In their ranks were warrior women,
      Like the handsome and powerful queen
      Who rescued the Trojans, Penthesilea,*
      And her legendary Amazons of Asia.

45 Dawn with its cold and serene light
   Had driven the bright stars from the pole,
   When the Cross of the Son of Mary
   Was revealed to Afonso, inspiring him;
   He fell on his knees before the vision
   And fired by overwhelming faith,
   'To the infidels, the infidels', he implored,
   'Not me who know your infinite power, O Lord!'

46 At this miracle the Portuguese
   Were inflamed, raising on their shields
   As their rightful king this excellent
   Prince whom they loved from the heart;
   And there before the great host
   Of the enemy, they shook the heavens
   So the clouds re-echoed: 'Hail, hail, all
   Hail Afonso, true king of Portugal!'

47 As a fierce mastiff in the mountains,
   Spurred on by the shouts of peasants,
   Will attack a full-grown bull who trusts
   In the power of his dreadful horns;
   Now it snaps at his ear, now at his flank
   Yelping, more agile than strong,
   Until grappled by the throat and held fast,
   The bull's strength ebbs, collapsing at last:

48 So the new king, his courage blazing
   With God's and his people's favours,
   Fell on the barbarians, rampant
   At the head of his inspired army.
   The infidels rose up in alarm,
   Clanging their armour, shouting to their men,
   Grabbing their bows and lances, to the roar
   Of sounding brass in the tumult of war.

49 As when a fire, kindled in the scorched
   Plains (and fanned by whistling
   Boreas), is spread by the wind
   And sweeps through the undergrowth;
   A group of shepherds taking sweet rest
   After their morning's labours are roused
   By flames crackling in the dry foliage,
   And round up their flock and fly to the village:

50   So the startled Moors snatched up
     Their weapons hastily and at random;
     They did not turn, but stood their ground
     Launching their terrible cavalry.
     Without flinching, the Portuguese met them,
     Impaling them through their hearts;
     Some fell half dead, while the survivors ran
     Calling aloud for help from the *Koran*.

51   Dreadful encounters took place there
     So that even the mountains shuddered,
     While the battle horses careered
     Madly, disfiguring the earth;
     Ferocious blows were dealt out;
     War engulfed the whole plain;
     But the Portuguese hacked and chopped with flail-
     ing swords, shattering harness, mesh and mail.

52   Heads went rolling on the battlefield,
     Arms, legs, anonymous, without feeling,
     And the entrails of others, palpitating,
     Their faces bloodless, and numb.
     By now, the enemy had lost the day;
     The rivers ran with shed blood
     While the earth changed colour, as the serried
     Meadow of white and green turned bloody red.

53   So the Portuguese emerged victorious
     Gathering a rich prize of trophies;
     Three days the great king stayed in the field
     Where the Spanish Moors were broken.
     It was here on the proud white buckler,*
     In cruciform as the stamp of victory,
     That five shields in heavenly blue were embossed,
     One for each of the five kings who had lost;

54   And on these five shields he painted
     Thirty pieces of silver, God's ransom,
     Written testimony, in distinct colours,
     To the One by Whom he was favoured;
     On each of the five blue shields
     Of the cross, five silver coins were painted,
     And in order that the number should suffice
     The five coins in the middle counted twice.

55   Enough time passed to fix this huge
      Victory in time, when the noble king
      Captured Leiria, which had been taken
      Earlier by the now defeated Moors.
      And jointly he subdued the forts
      Of Arronches* and noble Santarém,*
      Ancient Roman town, where the Tagus flows
      Serenely through fertile water meadows.

56   And soon after, to these noble towns
      He added Mafra* and, near the ancient
      Promontory of the Moon, brought
      Cool Sintra* under his mighty arm,
      Sintra where every pool and stream
      Has nymphs hidden in its waters,
      Fleeing in vain from Cupid's tender fires
      While the cold depths burn with their desires.

57   Then you, most noble Lisbon,* princess
      Without peer among the world's cities,
      Named for her founder, that coiner of words
      Through whose cunning Troy was burned;
      You, to whom vast oceans bow, bowed
      Then to the might of the Portuguese,
      With the help of two mighty armadas
      Descending from the north as crusaders.

58   For there were passing from the Elbe
      And the Rhine, and from snow-bound Britain,
      Many knights with the holy ambition
      To destroy the might of the Saracens;
      Anchoring in the pleasant Tagus,
      They joined forces with great Afonso,
      Whose fame persuaded them to change their plan,
      So the patient siege of Lisbon began.

59   Five times the moon had been reborn
      And five times shown her full face,
      When the breached city yielded
      To the hard encircling armies.
      It was a battle so bloody and ferocious
      As to test the uttermost resolve
      Of the victors, relentless and daring,
      And of the vanquished, at the last despairing.

60 And so, at last, Lisbon was captured
    Which had never in former times
    Surrendered, not even to the armies
    Of the Vandals* from the north,
    Whose conquests spread such terror
    From the Ebro to the Tagus
    And to the Guadalquivir, that they came
    To bequeath to Andalusia its name.

61 What city anywhere had the strength
    To stand against those mighty forces
    Whose fame was already widespread
    If Lisbon could not resist them?
    All Estremadura* was now theirs,
    And Óbidos, with Torres Vedras,
    And gentle Alenquer, soothed by the moans
    Of fresh waters humming among the stones.

62 And you, too, lands of the Alentejo*
    Famed for your hectares of Ceres' corn,
    You surrendered your castles and armies
    To the power not to be resisted;
    Moorish peasants, skilled husbandmen
    Of the fertile soils, you soon discovered
    Elvas, Moura, Serpa, and your forsaken
    Alcácer do Sal had all been taken.

63 And even that noble city, once seat
    Of the rebel hero Sertorius,
    Where today the glistening waters flow,
    Sustaining the land and the people,
    On the aqueduct with its thousand
    Towering arches, even Évora yielded*
    To the strategy and daring of peerless
    Gerald, who of fear itself was Fearless.

64 Then Afonso, who never knew repose,
    Packing his short life with achievement,
    Rode on to Beja* to take bloody
    Vengeance for the sacking of Trancoso;*
    The city could not long resist him
    And, no sooner had it surrendered,
    Our angry troops were as good as their word
    Putting every living creature to the sword.

65   Captured in the same campaign were
     Sesimbra* with its fishing grounds,
     And Palmela where, by good fortune,
     He massacred a powerful army
     (The town bated its breath, the hillside
     Witnessed) hurrying to its relief
     By the flank of the mountain, unaware
     Of the catastrophe lurking for them there.

66   It was the towering King of Badajoz,
     With four thousand fierce horsemen,
     And innumerable foot, garnished
     With gold, and the accoutrements of war.
     But as in the month of May, a bull
     Rampant, jealous for his cows,
     Catching a passer-by's scent, will stampede
     And trample him in his blind, brute need:

67   So Afonso fell on them as they passed
     Heedlessly, dropping from nowhere
     To wound and kill and devastate;
     The Moorish king fled panic-stricken;
     His army, matching his sudden terror,
     Sought only to follow his tracks,
     Those who achieved such splendid devilry
     Being no more than just sixty cavalry.

68   Seizing the occasion of this victory,
     The great and tireless king gathered
     From throughout the entire kingdom
     Those most experienced in conquest.
     He laid siege to Badajoz,* quickly
     Gaining his ambition, fighting
     With such skill and such ferocity and zest,
     It soon yielded along with all the rest.

69   But almighty God who so long withheld
     The punishment due to him, perhaps
     Allowing an interval for repentance,
     Or for reasons beyond men's knowledge,
     Although He had guarded the king
     Through all vicissitudes, His will
     No longer protected Afonso's gains
     From his mother's curse whom he kept in chains.

70 For there in the town he had besieged,
    He was himself trapped by the Leónese,
    Because the conquest he had made
    Belonged to León and not Portugal.
    His stubbornness cost him dearly,
    As so often happens, for riding out
    He broke his leg on the city's iron gates
    And ended León's prisoner and Fate's.

71 O great Pompey, grieve no longer*
    To see your famous deeds in ruins,
    Nor that just Fate should grant
    Victory to Caesar, your father-in-law;
    Though none could tell, from the Black Sea
    To Aswan with its vertical sun,
    Or from Arcturus to the hot equator
    Where the fear of Pompey's name was greater;

72 Although rich Arabia and the ferocious
    Heniochi and Colchis, of the golden
    Fleece and the Cappadocians
    And Judaeans, God's chosen people,
    Together with the gentle Sophenians
    And the cruel Cilicians, and Armenia
    Where the Tigris and Euphrates both rise
    On Mount Ararat, there in paradise;

73 Although at last your conquests extended
    From Asia to the Atlas Mountains,
    Do not be astonished that the field
    Of Thessaly witnessed your defeat;
    Behold proud, triumphant Afonso,
    Surrender all and be taken,
    Humbled by those engines of God's ire,*
    His daughter's husband and his wife's sire!

74 Ransomed at last from his Divine
    Chastisement, the sublime king
    Was besieged at Santarém* by the Saracens,
    But presumptuously and in vain;
    Afterwards, from the sacred Cape
    Which has long been named by its saint,
    He brought to Lisbon's most holy altar
    The relics of St Vincent, blessed martyr;

75 And to continue his life's mission,
   The old man sent his powerful son
   Well furnished with men and arms
   To fight for the lands beyond the Tagus.
   Sancho,* a strong and spirited lad,
   Marched at once and made the waters
   Of the Guadalquivir, which washes Seville,
   Run red with the blood of the infidel.

76 And spurred on by this victory,
   The youth did not rest while he foresaw
   A further triumph just as damaging,
   Over the enemy besieging Beja,
   Nor did the happy prince take long
   To accomplish all he had hoped.
   Faced with such losses, the Moors were dismayed,
   Contemplating how they might be repaid.

77 They came together* from the Atlas Mountains*
   Which Medusa petrified long ago;
   And from Cape Spartel and Mauretania,
   Once home of the giant Antaeus;*
   The King of Ceuta made one with them
   While yet others assembled with their arms,
   To the sound of trumpet and raw tuba,
   From all the ancient kingdom of Juba.

78 In command of this vast company,
   Emir Al-muminin invaded Portugal;
   He led thirteen Moorish kings of note,
   All subject to his sceptre;
   And doing whatever harm he could
   In whichever towns he could harm,
   He advanced to Santarém to surround
   Dom Sancho, ill-prepared for what he found.

79 The Emir launched a furious assault,
   Deploying a thousand tricks of battle;
   But his battering-rams, hidden mines,
   And catapults counted but little,
   For Afonso's son lacked none of his father's
   Strength, valour, and resourcefulness;
   On all sides there was the same persistence,
   The same resolve, the same stubborn resistance.

80   Meanwhile, the old man, now compelled
      By years of labour to retirement,
      Was living in Coimbra, where the meadows
      Are made green by the River Mondego,
      But learning that his son was besieged
      In Santarém by the infidel,
      He rode out as when he first won his spurs,
      No less alert for his advancing years.

81   With his famed men, all veterans,
      He went to his son's rescue and, as allies
      They speedily laid waste the Moors
      With the customary Portuguese ferocity;
      The whole battle meadow was littered
      With caps and various mantles
      Of horses and bridles, helmets and swords,
      All now abandoned by their former lords.

82   Those who survived did so in flight
      From the field and from Portugal too;
      Only Emir Al-muminin did not leave
      For life itself had abandoned him.
      To the One who permitted this victory
      They made thank-offerings without measure;
      In so great a triumph, visibly God's
      Favour was decisive, and not the odds.

83   Having accomplished so many victories,
      Aged Afonso,* the illustrious prince,
      Who had conquered all before him,
      Was at last conquered by time;
      Sickness with its chill hand
      Took firm hold of his weakened frame,
      And so his years, so many yet so few,
      Paid to the gloomy goddess Nature's due.

84   The high headlands mourned him
      And the tears of the forlorn rivers
      Swamped the newly planted fields
      With the floods of desolation.
      Eternally, so far had spread
      The story of his valiant deeds,
      His stricken land will call out in its pain
      'Afonso, O Afonso', but in vain.

85   Sancho, strong youth, who continued
    Matching his father's bravery,
    As he had proved, while he yet lived
    When the Guadalquivir ran with blood,
    And when he destroyed the hosts
    Of the Muslim king of Andalusia,
    And again at Beja when those who laid
    Presumptuous siege felt the power of his blade,

86   When later he was raised to the throne,
    And had reigned only a few years,
    He invested the city of Silves*
    Where the Moors tended the fields.
    He was helped by the valiant knights
    From German ships which were passing,
    Furnished with men and weapons, to reclaim
    The holy city of Jerusalem.

87   They were sailing with reinforcements
    For red-beard Frederick Barbarossa,
    In his sacred venture to regain
    The city of Our Lord's passion,
    After Guy de Lusignan with his people
    Had surrendered to great Saladin;
    For Guy had camped in a plain without water,
    And his men perished more of thirst than slaughter.

88   But Sancho asked the splendid fleet,
    Already committed to holy war
    And driven to port by contrary winds,
    For support in his own campaign;
    Thus as had happened to his father
    When he took Lisbon, in the same crusade,
    With the help of Germans, Silves was reduced
    And its people tamed, or killed if they refused.

89   Having taken from Mohammed so many
    Trophies of battle, he could not allow
    The Leónese to live peaceably
    In a land accustomed to fighting,
    Until the splendid frontier city*
    Of Tuy came under his firm yoke,
    And many neighbouring towns in that campaign
    Fell to you, Sancho, and to your domain.

90   But struck down amid such triumphs
      By grim death, he was succeeded
      By his only son, esteemed by all,
      The second Afonso* and the third king.
      During his reign, Alcácer do Sal
      Was captured finally from the Moors
      Who paid due penalty for having dared
      To reconquer a town they should have spared.

91   After Afonso's death, there succeeded
      Sancho the second,* callow and remiss,
      Whose negligence was so extreme
      He was ruled by those he ruled.
      Putting favourites first, he lost favour,
      Forfeiting his kingdom to another,
      Because his sole concern in every crisis
      Was to pacify his court in all its vices.

92   This Sancho was never so depraved
      As Nero, who bedded a youth as though
      A woman, and later committed
      Incest with his mother Agrippina;
      Nor so cruel to his subjects
      That he set his own city ablaze;
      Nor so evil as Heliogabalus;
      Nor effeminate like King Sardanapalus;

93   Nor were his people oppressed
      As was Sicily by its tyrants;
      Nor did he devise like Phalaris
      New methods of inhuman torture;
      But the proud nation, accustomed
      To kings who were sovereign in everything,
      Would not obey him, nor indeed consent
      To a king who had not proved Most Excellent.

94   So his brother,* the Count of Boulogne,
      Governed in his stead and became
      King, when in his customary,
      Leisurely manner, Sancho died.
      This one, named Afonso the Brave,
      Having secured the kingdom, set out
      To extend it, his appetite for glory
      Cramped by so confined a territory.

95   Of the lands of the Algarve which were
      His by his marriage, he recaptured
      The greater part, expelling the Moors
      Who had lost their instinct for battle.
      So at last, his warrior virtues made
      The sons of Lusus free and sovereign;
      The Moors' defeat was absolute through all
      The land assigned by fate to Portugal.*

96   Then after him came King Dinis,* noble
      And worthy heir to brave Afonso,
      For with his fame he overshadowed
      The munificence of Alexander;
      With him the happy kingdom flourished
      (He presided over a golden age)
      With order, constitutions, and sound law,
      Beacons in a land reprieved from war.

97   He was the first to make Coimbra
      A city devoted to Minerva,
      Tempting the Muses down from Helicon
      To tread the meadows of the Mondego.
      Great Apollo established there
      What Athens herself had most cherished,
      The evergreen gown and gold-embroidered hat,
      Those laurels of the baccalaureate.

98   King Dinis rebuilt our noblest towns,
      Securing citadel and fortress,
      Reshaping, as it were, the whole kingdom
      With great edifices and high walls;
      But after harsh Fate had snipped
      The thread of his diminished days,
      He left a son, Afonso the Fourth,
      A disobedient prince, but a king of worth.

99   In his heart he had always harboured
      Serene contempt for Castilian pride,
      For it is not for the Portuguese
      To tremble before those who outnumber them;
      Nevertheless, when an army of Moors*
      Disembarked to retake Iberia,
      And approached Castile, intending to invade,
      It was proud Afonso's part to rush with aid.

100 Never did Semiramis* with her Assyrians
  So choke the plains of Hydaspes,
  Nor Attila,* who terrorized Italy,
  Calling himself the scourge of God,
  March at the head of so many Goths
  As now, with stupendous forces,
  The fierce Saracens camped in the meadow
  Lying alongside the River Salado.

101 Seeing this vast, unassailable army,
  The proud King of Castile feared
  Much more than his own demise,
  A second conquest of Christian Spain,
  And to beg support from the mighty
  Portuguese, he sent as envoy
  His dear consort, the beloved daughter
  Of the same king she needed to support her.

102 As the ravishing Maria entered
  Her royal father's splendid palace,
  Her countenance was lovely, but overcast,
  And tears welled in her eyes;
  On her shoulders, white as ivory,
  Her angelic hair tumbled loose,
  As encouraged by her father's joyful tones
  She sobbed out this appeal, between moans:

103 —'The multitudes of Africa, as many
  As live there, strange and terrible people,
  Are brought by the great king of Morocco
  To take possession of noble Spain.
  Such a conjoined force has never been
  Since the salt seas first washed the shore;
  They bring such ferocity in their wake,
  The living tremble, and the dead quake!

104 'He whom you gave me as husband,
  Trying to defend his terrified country
  With his tiny army, stands naked
  Before the full weight of the Moorish sword;
  And if you do not reinforce him,
  You will see me forfeit him and the throne,
  To be a widow, obscure and distressed,
  Unhusbanded, unkingdomed, dispossessed.

105   'Therefore, O King, at whose name the very
       Rivers of Morocco freeze for fear,
       Delay no more! Help, and quickly,
       The wretched people of Castile.
       If it is a father's clear, true love
       I read in your bright countenance,
       Go in speed, my father, go in speed,
       Lest you arrive too late for those in need.'

106   Fearful Maria used just such a tone
       As Venus had used, when pleading sadly
       With Jove her father, begging favours
       For Aeneas her son, as he ploughed the seas,
       Stirring in the god such pity, he laid
       Down his dreadful thunderbolts,
       Acquiescing, as if it were as naught,
       In everything his weeping daughter sought.

107   Then at Évora the squadrons gathered,
       The men's armour, lances, spears,
       And swords flashed in the brilliant sunlight;
       Horses whinnied in their harness;
       Sonorous trumpets rang out
       To men long accustomed to peace,
       To seize their glistening weapons and follow,
       The summons echoing from every hollow.

108   Proudly in their midst and escorted
       By every mark of royalty, rode
       Valiant Afonso, his neck towering
       High above all other warriors,
       Putting spirit, by sheer example,
       Into anyone fearful of the outcome.
       So he crossed into Castile with his serene
       And elegant daughter, its noble queen.

109   United on the plain of the Salado
       The two Afonsos, at length, confronted
       Such a multitude of the infidels
       Plain and mountain could not hold them.
       Not a man was so strong or valiant
       As not to anticipate defeat,
       Did he not discern at every stride
       Christ was the comrade fighting at his side.

110   The Ishmaelites* were as if laughing
     At the Christians' puny forces,
     And were sharing out estates
     Between the factions of their army;
     In the same manner as they pretended
     To the illustrious name of 'Saracen',
     So already they were claiming title
     To Spain in their arrogant recital.

111   As when the robust and brutal giant,*
     Whom King Saul judiciously feared,
     Seeing the harmless shepherd before him
     With stones as his only visible weapon,
     With proud, boastful words he insulted
     The slight youth, dressed in his rags,
     Who whirled the catapult, opening his eyes
     To the power of Faith, more potent than size;

112   In the same manner the Moors insulted
     The Christian armies, not realizing
     They were backed by the might of Heaven
     To which Hell yields with its horrors.
     At this, the Castilian with good tactics
     Turned his fury on the King of Morocco,
     While the Portuguese, with reckless ardour,
     Charged point-blank at the King of Grenada.

113   Then swords and lances clanged against
     Coats of armour, in a grim tattoo!
     Men cried out, following their faith
     Some to 'Mohammed', others 'Santiago'.*
     Screams rent the skies from the wounded,
     Who created with their shed blood
     A filthy lake, in which others who had found
     Refuge from the clash of iron lay drowned.

114   The Portuguese took the battle so
     Impetuously to the Moors of Grenada,
     That in a trice they routed them,
     Armour and numbers availing nothing.
     Pausing from such a cheap triumph
     The bold victors were not satisfied,
     But rushed to reinforce the brave Castilian,
     Who was himself fighting the Mauretanian.

115 The molten sun was drawing near
The home of Tethys* and just beginning
His last descent when the evening star
Brought to a close that memorable day,
When the massed regiments of the Moors
Were destroyed by the two kings,
With greater carnage than any victory
Yet recorded in the world's memory.

116 Roman Marius* did not kill a quarter
Of those who died in this rout
When he forced his army to drink water
Running with the blood of the enemy;
Nor Hannibal, from his cradle
Ancient Rome's most bitter foe,
When triumphing at Cannae he gathered
Six gallons of gold rings from the dead.

117 Though you, Emperor Titus, dispatched
To the underworld yet more souls,
When you destroyed in Jerusalem
The people stubborn to their ancient rite,
It was Heaven permitted this,
And not the might of your armies;
For so was prophesied in the Ancient Word,
And afterwards confirmed by Christ our Lord.

118 Riding in triumph from such a victory,
Afonso returned to Portuguese soil,
To secure as much fame with peace
As he had gained in the rigours of war;
But now the tragic history* unfolded
Of her whom men disinterred from the grave
And, in a pitiful and macabre scene,
Only after her death was enthroned as queen.

119 You alone, you, pure love, whose
Raw power drives human hearts,
You alone encompassed her murder
Like some perfidious enemy.
When they say, cruel love, your thirst
Is never quenched by grief's tears,
The truth is it suits your nature more
To drench your harsh altars in human gore.

120 You were living safely, lovely Inês,
   Enjoying the sweet fruits of youth,
   In that soft deception of the soul
   That fortune never indulges long;
   In the Mondego's responsive meadows
   With tears welling in your lovely eyes,
   To mountains and fresh lawns you would impart
   The one name that was written in your heart.

121 Such yearning for your Prince was matched
   By his own heart's vivid memories,
   Bringing you constantly to his eyes
   When parted from your beauties;
   By night, in sweet deceitful dreams,
   By day, in images which soared,
   Whatever struck his mind, or caught his sight,
   Became instant mementoes of delight.

122 All matches, all alliances
   With princesses, women of beauty,
   He spurned, for pure love can accept
   No substitute for the adored face.
   Studying these effects of love,
   Aged Afonso, who took a king's account
   Of the people's muttering, and the strange life
   Of his son who refused to take a wife,

123 Plotted to release the son held captive,
   By dispatching Inês from the world,
   Believing that only with innocent blood
   Could he quench the flames of desire.
   What cruel madness could contrive
   That a sharp sword which had borne the brunt
   Of the Moors' onslaught should turn its weight
   On a lady, so refined, so delicate?

124 They dragged her, the vile beasts,
   To the king, who was disposed to mercy;
   But the mob with false, passionate
   Arguments insisted on her death.
   She, with sad and piteous cries
   Of anguish, and of yearning,
   Less for her death than for leaving forlorn
   Her dear prince and the two sons she had borne,

125 Lifted up to the crystal heavens
Eyes that were brimming with tears
(Her eyes because her hands were tied
By one of the churlish warders).
Then, gazing at the little ones
She so loved, and held so precious,
But whose destiny as orphans looked sealed,
To their obdurate grandfather she appealed:

126 —'If once upon a time brute animals,
Naturally cruel from their birth,
Or wild birds, whose only instinct
Is hunting on the wind for their prey,
If these could pity little children,*
Such as Semiramis, reared
By doves, or the gentle she-wolf famous
For giving suck to Romulus and Remus,

127 'Then you, with your human face and heart
(If it can be human to slaughter
A defenceless woman, solely for yielding
Her heart to the prince who won her),
You must feel for these tiny children
If not for my unmerited death;
Pity their plight and pity my anguish, since
You are not troubled by my innocence.

128 'If you knew how to kill with fire
And sword when you defeated the Moors,
Discover now how to be merciful
To one whose death is undeserved;
But, if my innocence must be punished,
Put me in sad, perpetual exile,
In the glaciers of Scythia, or placed
Endlessly weeping in Libya's burning waste;

129 'Send me where ferocity belongs
Among lions and tigers; and I will see
If there exists among them that mercy
Absent from the hearts of men.
There, yearning with my whole soul
For the one I truly love, these
Whom you see before you, his creation,
Will be their sad mother's consolation.'

130   The kindly king was moved by her speech
And wished to have her pardoned,
But the headstrong mob and her destiny
(Which overruled) would not be denied.
The men at hand for this fine deed
Drew their swords of well-tempered steel,
And take note, those who performed the butchery
Were honourable knights, sworn to chivalry!

131   As when the lovely girl, Polyxena,*
Her aged parent's one remaining joy,
Was sentenced by the ghost of Achilles
While harsh Pyrrhus prepared his sword;
She, with eyes calm as the air
As patient as a lamb, fixed them
On her mother, and knowing Achilles' price,
Went uncomplaining to the sacrifice:

132   So confronting Inês, the brute killers,
In that neck of alabaster, which sustained
The very features which transfixed
The prince who afterwards made her queen,
Plunged their swords, as the white
Flowers she had watered with tears
Weltered in blood, lost in their delirium
To any thoughts of the punishment to come.

133   Well might the sun have refused to dawn
On this dreadful day, as when Apollo
Turned from the grim table of Thyestes
When Atreus* served him his own sons!
Only the hollow valleys could hear
Faintly from her bloodless lips,
The name 'Pedro', the last thing she would say,
Echoing, echoing, until it died away.

134   Like a daisy, plucked before its time
For its white and lovely petals,
Maltreated in the frivolous hands
Of a maiden weaving a chaplet,
The scent fades and the colours wither:
So it was with the pale maiden,
So from her lovely face the roses fled,
The bloom of life expired, she was dead.

135   The nymphs of Mondego long remembered
      That dark death with mourning,
      And their tears were transformed
      To a fountain in eternal memory;
      Its name, 'the Loves of Inês',
      Who wandered there, still endures.
      Fortunate the flowers that bloom above
      Such waters, such tears, telling of Love!

136   Little time passed before Pedro
      Was avenged* for this mortal injury,
      When ascending the kingdom's throne
      He laid hands on the assassins,
      Helped by that other Pedro, the Cruel;
      Enemies together of human life,
      Their pact was as brutal as when Augustus
      Conspired with Antony and Lepidus.

137   Known as the Chastiser, he came down hard
      On thieves, murderers, and adulterers;
      Fiery-tempered, his greatest pleasure
      Was imposing the severest punishments;
      But he protected the cities justly
      From all the arrogance of the nobles;
      He brought more thieves to harsher penalties,*
      Than Theseus did or wandering Hercules.

138   From just and rigorous Pedro sprang
      (Witness Nature's strange contradictions!)
      Gentle Fernando,* lazy and negligent,
      Who left the borders defenceless;
      At which the King of Castile, seeing
      The land unguarded and exposed,
      Brought it close to complete devastation;
      So a weak king weakens the strongest nation.

139   This was either clear punishment
      For the sin of seizing Leonor Teles
      From her husband, and marrying her
      Deluded by her appearance;
      Or perhaps it was that the heart
      Given over to lust gets its deserts,
      Becoming pliable—they are not wrong
      Who claim rutting emasculates the strong.

140   Lust always has the consequences*
       God has dealt out to so many:
       Such as those who stole the lovely Helen,
       Or Appius, as Tarquinius witnessed.
       For what else was King David condemned?
       Or for what else the illustrious tribe
       Of Benjamin? What schooling could be plainer?
       For Sarah, Pharaoh, Shechem, for Dinah.

141   And to show how an infatuation
       Makes idiots of the mightiest,
       Take Hercules, turned transvestite
       While his Omphale wore his skin and club.
       Mark Antony's fame was overshadowed
       By his obsession with Cleopatra,
       And you, too, Hannibal when you betrayed
       Your lust for the Apulian peasant maid.

142   Yet what man could for long avoid
       The gentle web which love spins,
       Between human roses and driven snow,
       Gold hair and translucent alabaster?
       Or who be unmoved by the pilgrim beauty
       Of a face such as might be Medusa's,
       Transfiguring every heart she inspires
       Not to stone but volcanic desires?

143   Or take the case of a confident look,
       An open, gentle, angelic face,
       With the power to transform nature,
       Who could take arms against her?
       Rightly acquitted is Fernando
       By those experienced in love;
       While those who are the most disposed to blame
       Were never touched by fantasy or flame.

Canto Four

1   After the dark hours of tempest,
    Blank night, and the screaming wind,
    Morning dawns serene and clear
    With hopes of reaching harbour safely;
    Sunlight dissolves the thick gloom
    Dispelling every foreboding:
    So it happened, like the turning of the tide,
    For Portugal when King Fernando died.

2   For if our people longed for a hero*
    To avenge the crimes and insolence
    Of those who had so much prospered
    From Fernando's languor and neglect,
    Soon afterwards, they obtained him
    In João the First of the House of Avis,
    Of distinction, with abilities to spare,
    And (though a bastard) Pedro's rightful heir.

3   This was ordained by Divine Heaven,
    Which spoke its will by many signs,
    As when in Évora an infant girl,*
    Too young for speech, uttered his name,
    Raising herself and her voice in the cradle,
    As the voice of the Heavenly Will,
    —'Portugal, Portugal', she lisped, lifting
    Her baby hand, 'For Dom João! Our new king!'

4   But warped by the hatreds of those days
    The people of the kingdom committed
    Absolute and outright cruelties,*
    Indiscriminately on all sides;
    They killed the friends and family
    Of the adulterous count, and of the queen
    Who, when Fernando died, turned even more
    Unashamedly and obviously a whore.

5   The count at last was put to the sword
    Dishonourably, in her very presence,
    Many others joining him in death,
    For the fire, once lit, raged and spread;
    Lisbon's bishop, despite his order,
    Was hurled, like Hector's son, from a tower;
    He found in rank and sanctuary no retreat;
    His abused corpse was left naked in the street.

6   It put in history's long shadow
    The savagery which Rome witnessed,
    At the hands of cruel Marius*
    And ferocious Sulla after he had fled.
    For Leonor now revealed to the world
    Her infatuation with the dead count,
    And caused Portugal and Spain mutual slaughter
    By insisting the true heir was her daughter.

7   Beatrice was the daughter married
    To Juan of Castile, who claimed the throne,
    And was said to be Fernando's child,
    If that tale is to be believed.
    Castile upheld it, declaring roundly
    The daughter should succeed the father,
    And from all the different nations of Spain
    Assembled his troops* for this new campaign.

8   They came from Burgos which (perhaps)
    Derives its name* from ancient Brigo,
    The land Fernán González and El Cid
    Won back from the Moorish occupation.
    Nor did fears dissuade those men
    Who spend laborious days hoeing
    The plains of León, and who in previous wars
    Had proved superb fighting against the Moors.

9   Vandals,* confident in their ancient
    Valour, came together from Seville,
    That capital city of Andalusia
    Which is washed by the Guadalquivir.
    And that noble island also rallied,
    Once the Phoenicians' home, their banners
    Woven with the pillars of Hercules,*
    Insignia of the city of Cadiz.

10   They came, too, from the kingdom of Toledo,
Noble and ancient city, where the Tagus,
Descending from the hills of Cuenca,
Makes a calm and reflective curve.
Nor did danger deter those others,
Galicia's tough and pungent peasants,
Taking up arms once more against a foe
Whose staying power they sampled long ago.

11   War's black furies even infected
The people of Biscay, who know nothing
Of polite manners and who bear
Remarks from strangers very ill;
While men from Guipuzcoa and Asturias,
Enriched by their iron mines,
Brandishing to a man their iron swords,
Went to war to assist their overlords.

12   King João, whose strength grew from his heart
As Jewish Samson's did from his locks,
Though his whole army looked very little,
Made preparation with the little he had;
He took opinion of his principal lords,
Not because he lacked an opinion,
But only to sound out his people's thoughts,
Divided as they were between the courts.

13   Those who at heart opposed the common will
Were furnished with their excuses;
For their ancient fortitude had decayed
To an untimely faithlessness,
Putting cold, inert cowardice before
That loyalty which is second nature;
Denying king and country, and if enticed
Would, like Peter, deny their very Christ.

14   But never was this true of mighty
Dom Nuno Álvares;* though he saw
His own brothers in clear opposition
He stood his ground and faced them,
Harshly reproaching the inconstant
Will of these vacillating people,
Fist on sword, much angrier than eloquent,
Barking at land and sea and firmament:

15 —'What? Of the illustrious Portuguese,
    Is there one who is not a patriot?
    What? In this province, princess
    Of warriors everywhere, is there
    Anyone who won't defend it? Who lacks
    The faith, love, spirit, and skill
    Of the true Portuguese? Have you no pride,
    Letting your native land be occupied?

16 'What? Do you call yourselves descendants
    Of those heroes, who under the banner
    Of the valiant and ferocious Henrique*
    Put to flight such a vast army?
    So many flags, so many nations
    Fled that day in such disgrace,
    Seven illustrious counts were brought to book,
    Not to mention all the booty they took.

17 'These, with whom you now have to deal,
    Who are they but those regularly dispatched
    By sublime Dinis and his sublime son,
    Along with your fathers and grandfathers?
    But if pitiful Fernando, with his airs,
    Has so enfeebled the lot of you,
    Our brave new king will stiffen your backbone,
    If men change with whoever's on the throne.

18 'You have such a king! Had you courage
    To match the king you've raised up,
    You could conquer anyone you wished
    Beyond this one here, who's already lost!
    And if this doesn't rouse you
    From the terror oozing from your pores,
    If it's fear makes you flabby and compliant,
    I'll fight alone against the foreign tyrant.

19 'I alone with my men and with this
    (At this, he half unsheathed his sword),
    Will protect from the pernicious enemy
    This land no other has conquered;
    In the name of my king and grieving country,
    And of the chivalry you now deny,
    I'll send not just these Spaniards packing,
    But as many more as come against my king!'

20   As when young Scipio* reassembled
      The young men who fled at Canusium,
      Tattered remnants of Cannae, resigned
      To surrender to Hannibal's army;
      Scipio put spirit in the youths
      Making them swear on his drawn sword,
      Never to desert Rome while they drew breath
      Or when they died to die a soldier's death:

21   So Nuno put stomach in the people
      Who, hearing his last arguments,
      Shook off the chill, urgent fear
      That had gripped their hearts like ice.
      They took to their horses, charging
      Up and down the plain in excitement,
      Twirling their lances, shouting in high fever,
      —'Viva the king! Viva liberty! Viva!'

22   Among the commoners, people applauded
      The struggle to preserve the country;
      Others repaired and polished their weapons
      Long tarnished with the rust of peace;
      Each armed himself as he could, lining
      Helmets, trying on breastplates;
      In a thousand different styles they came clothed
      With emblems and tokens of their betrothed.

23   In the midst of this dazzling company,
      João rode out from cool Abrantes,*
      Abrantes which delights in the fresh,
      Brimming waters of the Tagus.
      Leading the army's vanguard was a man
      Equipped to command the powerful,
      Numberless armies of the Orient,
      Like that which Xerxes* led across the Hellespont.

24   I speak of Dom Nuno Álvares,
      Scourge of the proud Castilians,
      As was fierce Attila* long ago
      First of the French, then the Romans.
      Leading the Portuguese right flank
      Was yet another famous knight,
      An accomplished commander, the zealous
      Mem Rodrigues, of the family Vasconcelos;

25   And on the corresponding flank,
     Antão Vasques de Almada* was captain,
     Who was later made Count of Avranches,
     Commanding the army of the left side.
     Then, bringing the rear guard, could be seen
     The pennant with its shields and castles
     Of João of Avis, every inch a king,
     Making war's burden seem a trivial thing.

26   They thronged Abrantes's city walls,
     Congealed as it were by a joyous fear,
     Mothers, sisters, wives, and sweethearts
     Vowing to fast, and make pilgrimage.
     Soon the martial squadrons arrived
     Before the hosts of the enemy,
     Who greeted them with a tremendous shout,
     Though not a man was not beset by doubt.

27   Trumpets responded with the challenge,
     Piercing fifes and the timbrels;
     Standard-bearers unfurled the banners
     In all their myriad, contrasting colours.
     It was the season when, on the threshing-floors,
     Ceres rewards the workers with grain;
     The sun was in Virgo, the month August;
     Bacchus was trampling out the sweet must.

28   The war trumpet of Castile sounded,
     Horrifying, savage, mighty, and ominous;
     Cape Ortegal* heard it, and the Guadiana
     Turned back upstream for fear;
     The Douro heard it and the Alentejo;
     The Tagus ran anxiously to the sea;
     And mothers clutched their little ones fast
     To their bosoms, hearing the dreadful blast.

29   Many faces were drained of colour
     As their life blood rushed to the heart;
     In great danger, our apprehension
     Far exceeds the danger; or, if not,
     It seems so; for the actual fury
     Of attacking and vanquishing the foe
     Makes us oblivious to the battle cry
     As men lose eyes or arms or legs, or die.

30   So the uncertain battle was joined;
On both sides, the first files advanced,
Some marching in defence of their land,
Others in the hope of winning it;
At once, the great Pereira, overflowing
With valour, surged to the front of the front line,
Hacking until the battlefield was sown
With those who sought to make the land their own.

31   Now the charged air was shrieking
With arrows, darts, and various shot;
Under the hoofs of the foaming
Horses, the earth shook, the valley echoed;
Lances were shivered, and heavy armour
Kept crashing to the ground like thunder,
As the enemy launched their main attack
On Nuno's few, who at first hurled them back.

32   He saw his brothers advance against him,
(Cruel outcome) but was undismayed,
For treason against a king and nation
Is worse than killing a brother;
Of such traitors, many were present
In the front line, fighting cousins
And brothers (terrible contingency),
As in the wars of Caesar and Pompey.

33   O Sertorius,* O noble Coriolanus,
Catiline, and you others of antiquity
Who with sacrilegious hearts became
Enemies of your native land;
If in Pluto's kingdom of shades
You are undergoing retribution,
Tell the dark king that traitors such as these
Have even been found among the Portuguese.

34   Our first ranks broke with so many
Of the enemy coming against them!
But Nuno was there, as a powerful lion
In the mountains above Ceuta
Finds himself surrounded by knights
Going hunting in the plains of Tetuan:
They prod him with spears and he, agitated
Prowls in his rage but is not intimidated;

35   He regards them grimly, but feral
       Instinct and brute fury prevent him
       Retreating, and he charges the thicket
       Of lances even as they press on him:
       So it was with Nuno, as the grass grew
       Dark with Spanish blood, while
       Men of his own, whose manhood he cherished,
       Overwhelmed by sheer numbers, also perished.

36   João knew of the onslaught Nuno
       Was sustaining and, as a wise captain,
       He was everywhere, seeing everything,
       Heartening all with his words and presence.
       Like a fierce lioness, which has whelped
       And ventures out hunting for food,
       While her cubs, left waiting in her lair
       Are stolen by a shepherd from Massylia,*

37   In her furious roaring and rampaging,
       She makes the Seven Brothers* tremble:
       So João, with a few, chosen men
       Came charging to the front line:
       —'O brave knights, o peerless
       Companions, equalled by no one,
       Defend your native soil, you Portuguese!
       On your lances hang all our liberties!

38   'You see me here, your king and comrade,
       Amidst all the weapons and armour
       Of the enemy, I ran to you first.
       Battle on, you true patriots!'
       So spoke the magnificent warrior
       And brandishing his lance four times,
       He hurled it, and it followed from that cast
       That many Castilian knights breathed their last,

39   For with this, his men were fired anew
       With noble shame and fresh resolve,
       Attacking with re-doubled ardour,
       Staking all on the game of war,
       They vied: their swords smoked with blood;
       Their lances pierced cuirass and heart.
       They fought hand to hand, taking and giving
       Blows like men oblivious to living.

40 Many they dispatched* with cold steel
    In their flesh to view the Styx.
    The Master of Santiago died there
    Fighting with tremendous power;
    There died also, causing great havoc,
    The cruel Master of Calatrava;
    While the accursed Pereiras, still apostate,
    Died blaspheming Heaven, and cursing Fate.

41 Many common people of no known names
    Descended along with the nobility,
    To where Cerberus,* with the three jaws,
    Hungers for souls departing this world.
    But then, dishonouring and disgracing
    The pride of the frantic enemy,
    The noble standard of sublime Castile
    Was trampled under the Portuguese heel.

42 At this, battle became massacre
    With deaths, shrieks, blood, and stabbing;
    Such a myriad of people perished
    The very flowers changed colour.
    Even in flight, men died; then the fury
    Dwindled, and lances were superfluous;
    Castile recognized the fates were malign
    Accepted them, and abandoned his design.

43 He withdrew, leaving the field to the victor
    And happy not to have left his life;
    The survivors followed, their fear
    Providing not legs but wings to flee;
    In their hearts' core was the anguish
    Of death and of wealth squandered,
    Of bruises and dishonour, and the deep offence
    That others should triumph at their expense.

44 Some went away blaspheming, cursing
    Whoever was the first to invent war;
    Others blamed that ravenous hunger
    That reckless, insatiable greed
    Which, to possess what is another's,
    Exposes wretches to the pangs of Hell,
    Causes such destitution and deprives
    Of sons, so many mothers; of husbands, wives.

45 Triumphant João remained in the field
  The customary days with great glory;
  And afterwards made pilgrimages
  To honour Him who gave the victory.
  But Nuno, who had no desire
  To be remembered among the people
  Other than as a soldier, and courageous,
  Left for his estates across the Tagus.

46 His fortune favoured him* in a manner
  To give effect to his intentions,
  When the border lands of Andalusia
  Ceded him victory and spoils.
  Soon after, the ancient Bétis flag
  Of Seville and of various other lords
  Were struck down, without the means to fight,
  Unable to resist Portuguese might.

47 Cast down by these defeats, and others,
  The Castilians were in despair,
  Till peace, which the people now desired
  Was granted at last to the vanquished.
  Soon after, it was the Almighty's will
  To bestow the hands of the hostile kings
  On two illustrious, comely, and sovereign
  English princesses,* Philippa and Catherine.

48 But a warrior's heart, attuned to war,
  Is restless without an enemy to harm,
  And having no one to conquer on land,
  He attacked the waves of the ocean.
  João was the first king to set foot
  Beyond his native soil, so Africa
  Should learn in battle how much less sufficed
  The power of Islam than the power of Christ.

49 A thousand swimming birds, spreading
  Their concave pinions to the winds,
  Parted the white, turbulent waves
  To where Hercules set his pillars.
  He seized Mount Abyla and the noble city
  Of Ceuta,* expelling Mohammed,
  And protecting all Spain from any reason
  To fear some Count Julian's further treason.

50 Death could not permit to Portugal
   Many years of so auspicious
   A hero, but elected he should join
   The heavenly chorus of the angels.
   But to safeguard the Lusitanians,
   And extend their kingdom further, God
   Gave in his stead those royal paragons,
   A progeny* of supremely gifted sons.

51 Yet time, which knows no constancy,
   Alternating joy with sadness,
   And good with evil, was not auspicious
   When King Duarte occupied the throne.
   What state was always prosperous?
   When was Fortune for ever fair?
   For in this kingdom with this latest reign
   This law of life applied in all its pain.

52 He saw Fernando,* his saintly brother
   (A prince who aspired to the highest glory),
   Delivered as captive to the Saracens
   To ransom the wretched, besieged people.
   For sheer love of his country
   He passed his life as a slave, adamant
   Ceuta should never be forfeit by the Crown,
   Putting the public good above his own.

53 Codrus,* in order to outwit the oracles
   And defeat the Dorians, killed himself;
   Regulus, so Rome should not surrender,
   Chose to surrender his liberty.
   Fernando, to make Iberia secure,
   Made himself a perpetual hostage!
   Codrus and Curtius were never such,
   Nor did the faithful Decii do so much.

54 But Afonso the Fifth,* unrivalled heir
   (And the bearer of a warrior's name),
   Conquered and trampled the presumption
   Of the barbarians across the strait,
   And would have lived and died victorious
   Had he not ventured into Castile;
   Though Africa would not credit such a thing
   As defeat for so terrible a king.

55   He plucked the apples of the Hesperides*
      Which only Hercules could gather;
      To this day, the brave Moors suffer
      The yoke he placed on their necks.
      He wore the palms and green laurel
      Of victory, for all they hastened
      To strengthen the walls of Alcácer-Ceguir,
      Strong Arzilla, and populous Tangier.

56   For the Portuguese army, accustomed
      To destroy whatever they found before them,
      Smashed the adamantine ramparts
      And captured all three fortresses.
      The knights were heroic, worthy
      Of memorial in the loftiest style,
      While the name of Portugal was once again
      Attested and refined in this campaign.

57   But afterwards, gripped by ambition
      And by power's bitter-sweet glory,
      He laid claim to the throne of Castile*
      By attacking Ferdinand of Aragon.
      From Cadiz to the snow-capped Pyrenees,
      All the proud and various nations
      Flocked together to make common accord
      With Ferdinand alone as their sovereign lord.

58   Reluctant, meanwhile, to laze at home,
      Prince João, Afonso's son, rode out
      To reinforce his ambitious father,
      Which proved no small assistance.
      It happened, his sanguinary father
      Escaped from his predicament,
      Beaten, but with the outcome undecided
      Because the battle's course was divided;

59   For the proud son, a gentle, strong
      And spirited knight, contested
      The field for the entire day
      Doing immense damage to the enemy.
      So it was when Octavius, avenging
      The murder of great Caesar
      Knew defeat, while Antony his ally
      Was victorious on the field of Philippi.*

60 Then, after everlasting night had
    Lodged Afonso in the serene heavens,
    The prince who became ruler
    Was João II and the thirteenth king.
    He, in pursuit of eternal fame,
    Took on a task beyond human ambition,
    To touch the rosy fingers of the dawn,
    The very quest to which I myself was born.

61 He appointed envoys* who passed
    Through Spain, France, and Italy,
    And there in the famous harbour where
    Parthenope* was buried, they embarked
    —Naples, where the Fates are active,
    Making her subject to various peoples,
    But time's fullness has made her great again,
    Under the happy suzerainty of Spain.

62 They crossed the eastern Mediterranean,
    Passing the sandy beaches of Rhodes,
    And headed for the river banks*
    Made famous by the death of Pompey;
    They passed Memphis and the lands watered
    By the floods of the sinuous Nile;
    Beyond Egypt to Ethiopia, where still
    Is maintained the ancient Christian ritual.

63 They parted the waves of the Red Sea
    Where the children of Israel passed on foot;
    Behind them lay the Nabathean hills*
    Named after Ismael's son;
    Then that sweet-smelling region, home
    Of Myrrha,* Adonis' mother, the coast
    Of Arabia the Blessed, skirting those known
    As the Arabias of Desert and of Stone.

64 They voyaged into the Persian Gulf
    Where the Tower of Babel* is still recalled,
    Where Tigris and Euphrates mingle
    Waters from the Garden of Eden.
    They went searching for the sacred spring
    (The tale of which remains to be told)
    Of the source of the Indus, passing seas
    Which, for Trajan, ended all his victories.*

65   They saw unknown and strange peoples,
      Indian, Carmanian, and Gedrosian,
      Studying the different styles and manners
      Each region produces and makes its own.
      But from journeys so long and rigorous,
      It is not easy to come home;
      They died, remaining on that distant strand,
      Eternally exiled from their native land.

66   It appears that bright heaven preserved
      For King Manuel,* with all his merits,
      This arduous venture which stirred him
      To such illustrious, exalted deeds;
      Manuel, who succeeded João
      Both to the kingdom and his exalted quest,
      Was just as eager in his devotion
      To exploring and mastering the ocean.

67   The noble vision of his unique
      Inheritance, from forbears whose constant
      Passion was to enlarge the kingdom,
      Never ceased for an instant
      To dominate his thoughts until once
      Upon a time, when the clear daylight
      Faded, and the glimmering stars began to shine,
      Beckoning to slumber at their first decline,

68   Being stretched out on his golden bed
      Where imaginings can be so vivid,
      His thoughts returning continuously
      To his office and descent and duty,
      His heavy eyelids drooped without
      His heart becoming vacant, for as
      Sleep descended quietly to restore him
      Morpheus,* in various guises, rose before him.

69   First, he dreamed he had been spirited
      Up to touch the first sphere,* and could
      See beneath him various nations
      With many strange and wild peoples;
      But there, close to where the sun rises,
      Straining his eyes in the distance,
      From a range of mountains, ancient and vast,
      He saw two noble rivers tumble past.

70 Wild birds and savage beasts were
All that lived in that towering jungle;
Thick undergrowth and ancient trees
Barred human passage and influence.
Those hard, inhospitable crags
Were visibly a region where,
Since Adam's sin down to the present day,
No human foot had ever found a way.

71 From the rivers, he seemed to see emerge
Two ancients, bending towards him
With slow paces like countrymen,
And of venerable appearance;
Water dripped from their uncombed locks
Making their whole bodies glisten;
Their skin was leathery and cinnamon,
Their shaggy beards dishevelled and undone.

72 The foreheads of both were crowned
With chaplets of grass and nameless fronds.
One seemed more deliberate in his gait
As if he had tramped the further;
And his river with its slower current
Seemed to have come from elsewhere,
Like Alpheus flowing to meet his Arethuse
Underground* from Arcadia to Syracuse.

73 And having the graver bearing of the two,
He spoke up to Manuel from afar:
—'You, to whose crown and kingdom
So much of the world is reserved:
We others, also known to fame
Whose necks were never before yoked,
Counsel you now, the moment is at hand
To accept the tribute* flowing from our land.

74 'I am the famous Ganges* whose waters
Have their source in the earthly paradise;
This other is the Indus, which springs
In this mountain which you behold.
We shall cost you unremitting war,
But persevering, you will become
Peerless in victory, knowing no defeat,
Conquering as many peoples as you meet.'

75   The famous, sacred river said no more
      And both disappeared on the instant.
      Manuel awoke with the thrill of discovery
      And a new direction to his thoughts.
      Now Phoebus stretched his mantle
      Over the dark, sleeping hemisphere,
      And dawn emerged, dipping in her palette
      Of multi-coloured flowers for rose and scarlet.

76   The king summoned the lords to council
      To tell of the figures of his dream;
      The words spoken by the venerable saint
      Were a great wonder to them all.
      They resolved at once to equip
      A fleet and an intrepid crew,
      Commissioned to plough the remotest seas,
      To explore new regions, make discoveries.

77   For myself, though not knowing the outcome
      If what I wanted should ever happen,
      My heart had always whispered to me
      Of some great enterprise of this kind;
      Nor do I know for what intimation,
      Or what confidence he placed in me,
      Manuel the Fortunate laid in these very hands
      The key to this pursuit of unknown lands.

78   And with entreaties and affectionate words
      Which with kings are the more binding,
      He said: 'The price of heroic deeds
      Is great effort and endurance;
      To risk life to the point of losing it
      Is the guarantee of glory;
      The man who is not cowed by abject fears,
      Though life be short, his fame survives the years.

79   'I have chosen you from among all others
      For this enterprise which you well deserve,
      And I know for mine and glory's sake
      You will bear the hazards and hardships.'
      I could bear no more, but: 'Small as it
      Is to endure iron, fire, and snow,
      The more it grieves me, O most noble king
      My life should be so poor an offering.

80 'Command me to such vast labours*
As Eurystheus devised for Hercules:
The Cleonaean lion, the Stymphalian harpies,
The Erymanthian boar, and the Hydra,
Or to descend to the dark and empty shades
Where the Styx flows through Pluto's fields;
The greater danger, the greater daring;
Spirit in this, and flesh, will be unsparing.'

81 The king thanked me with signal favours
And complimented my good will,
For virtue rewarded is redoubled,
And praise encourages great deeds.
On the instant, compelled by love
And comradeship as by desire for glory,
There offered to sail with me* none other
Than Paulo da Gama, my dear brother.

82 Nicolau Coelho also joined me,
A man to endure any labour,
And like my brother, valiant and wise
And a fierce and tested warrior.
I equipped myself with young people
All driven by a thirst for glory;
All spirited and, in fact, so appearing
Simply by the act of volunteering.

83 King Manuel rewarded them generously,
Giving greater zeal to their preparations,
And inspired them with noble words
For whatever hardships might come.
It was as when the Argonauts assembled
To battle for the Golden Fleece
In that prophetic ship, the first to be
Launched by man on the Black (or any) Sea.

84 So at last in Ulysses' famous harbour*
With noble bustle and resolve
(Where the Tagus mingles its fresh water
And white sands with the salt sea),
The ships lay ready; and no misgivings
Subdued the youthful spirits
For the mariners' and soldiers' one desire
Was to follow me through tempest and fire.

85   The soldiers came along the margin
      Clad in various colours and fashions,
      And furnished equally in spirit
      To explore new regions of the globe.
      The powerful ships signalled quietly,
      Their flags rippling in the gentle wind,
      As if confident their tale would never die,
      But live on like *Argo* in the night sky.*

86   Having done everything practical
      To make ready for so long a voyage,
      We prepared our souls to meet death
      Which is always on a sailor's horizon.
      To God on high who alone sustains
      The heavens with his loved presence,
      We asked His favour that He should endorse
      Our every enterprise and steer our course.

87   The holy chapel* from which we parted
      Is built there on the very beach,
      And takes its name, Belém, from the town
      Where God was given to the world as flesh.
      O King, I tell you, when I reflect
      On how I parted from that shore,
      Tormented by so many doubts and fears,
      Even now it is hard to restrain my tears.

88   That day, a vast throng from the city
      (As friends, as family, others
      Only to watch), crowded the shore,
      Their faces anxious and dismayed
      Looking on, as in the holy company
      Of a thousand zealous monks,
      With heartfelt intercessions on our lips
      We marched in solemn file towards the ships.

89   The people considered us already lost
      On so long and uncertain a journey,
      The women with piteous wailing,
      The men with agonizing sighs;
      Mothers, sweethearts, and sisters, made
      Fretful by their love, heightened
      The desolation and the arctic fear
      We should not return for many a long year.

90 One such was saying: 'O my dear son,
    My only comfort and sweet support
    In this my tottering old age, now
    Doomed to end in grief and pain,
    Why do you leave me wretched and indigent?
    Why do you travel so far away,
    To be lost at sea as your memorial,
    And bloated fish your only burial?'

91 Or one bareheaded: 'O dearest husband,
    But for whose love I could not exist,
    Why do you risk on the angry seas
    That which belongs to me, not you?
    Why, for so dubious a voyage, do you
    Forget our so sweet affection?
    Is our passion, our happiness so frail
    As to scatter in the wind swelling the sail?'

92 As these piteous, loving speeches
    Poured from gentle, human hearts,
    The old and the children took them up
    In the different manner of their years.
    The nearest mountains echoed them,
    As if stirred by deepest sympathy,
    While tears as many as the grains of sand
    Rained without ceasing on the white strand.

93 As for us, we dared not lift our faces
    To our mothers and our wives, fearing
    To be harrowed, or discouraged
    From the enterprise so firmly begun,
    And I decided we should all embark
    Without the customary farewells,
    For, though they may be love's proper course,
    They make the pain of separation worse.

94 But an old man* of venerable appearance
    Standing among the crowd on the shore,
    Fixed his eyes on us, disapproving,
    And wagged his head three times,
    Then raising a little his infirm voice
    So we heard him clearly from the sea,
    With a wisdom only experience could impart,
    He uttered these words from a much-tried heart:

95   —'O pride of power! O futile lust
     For that vanity known as fame!
     That hollow conceit which puffs itself up
     And which popular cant calls honour!
     What punishment, what poetic justice,
     You exact on souls that pursue you!
     To what deaths, what miseries you condemn
     Your heroes! What pains you inflict on them!

96   'You wreck all peace of soul and body,
     You promote separation and adultery;
     Subtly, manifestly, you consume
     The wealth of kingdoms and empires!
     They call distinction, they call honour
     What deserves ridicule and contempt;
     They talk of glory and eternal fame,
     And men are driven frantic by a name!

97   'To what new catastrophes do you plan
     To drag this kingdom and these people?
     What perils, what deaths have you in store
     Under what magniloquent title?
     What visions of kingdoms and gold-mines
     Will you guide them to infallibly?
     What fame do you promise them? What stories?
     What conquests and processions? What glories?

98   'And as for you, heirs of that madcap
     Adam,* whose sin and disobedience
     Not only drove us from paradise
     Into this exile and sad absence,
     But deprived us for ever of the divine
     State of simple tranquillity,
     That golden age of innocence, before
     This age of iron experience and war:

99   'Already in this vainglorious business
     Delusions are possessing you,
     Already, ferocity and brute force
     Are labelled strength and valour,
     The heresy "Long live Death!" is already
     Current among you, when life should always
     Be cherished, as Christ in times gone by
     Who gave us life was yet afraid to die.*

100   'Is not the Ishmaelite* close at hand,
With whom you have waged countless wars?
If a fresh crusade is your purpose,
Does he not bow to the faith of Arabia?
If it is land and riches you desire,
Does he not own a thousand cities?
Or if it's fresh battle honours you covet,
Is he not still a formidable target?

101   'You ignore the enemy at the gate
In the search for another so far away,
Unpeopling the ancient kingdom,
Leaving it vulnerable and bereft!
You are lured by the dangers of the unknown,
So history will flatter you, as
"Seigneurs"* (or titles yet more copious),
India's, Persia's, Arabia's, Ethiopia's!

102   'The devil take the man who first put
Dry wood on the waves with a sail!
Hell's fires are too good for him
If the laws I live by are righteous!
And may no solemn chronicler,
No sweet harpist nor eloquent poet*
Commend your deeds or celebrate your fame,
But let your folly vanish with your name!

103   'Prometheus* stole the fire from heaven
Which rages in every human heart,
Setting the world ablaze with arms,
With death and dishonour, and all for nothing!
How much better for us, Prometheus,
How much less harmful for the world,
Had you not breathed into your famous statue
The restlessness that goads mankind to match you!

104   'Unhappy Phaethon would not have crashed
Apollo's car, nor craftsman Daedalus*
Dropped from the sky with his son, naming
The latter a sea, the former a river.
In what great or infamous undertaking,
Through fire, sword, water, heat, or cold,
Was Man's ambition not the driving feature?
Wretched circumstance! Outlandish creature!'

Canto Five

1   As the honourable old man was uttering
    These words, we spread our wings
    To the serene and tranquil breezes
    And departed from the loved harbour;
    And, as is now the custom at sea,
    The sails unfurled, we bellowed:
    'God speed!', and the north winds as usual
    Heard and responded, shifting the great hull.

2   The sun was in Leo,* the ferocious
    Beast of Nemea, slain by Hercules,
    And the world was in the sixth age
    Of its decline since Christ's birth,
    Having witnessed, as custom has it,
    Fourteen hundred journeys of the sun
    Plus ninety-seven, the last still in motion
    When our small armada turned to face the ocean.

3   Little by little our gaze was exiled
    From the native hills we left behind;
    There remained the dear Tagus and green
    Sintra, and on those our sight long dwelt;
    Our hearts, too, stayed behind us,
    Lodged with their griefs in the loved land;
    And when at last all faded from the eye,
    Nothing was visible but sea and sky.

4   We were navigating waters only
    Portuguese had sailed before us,
    Seeing the islands and latitudes
    Plotted by Henry,* our noble prince;
    Off to our left were the mountains
    And towns of Mauretania, once home
    Of giant Antaeus,* while on the right hand
    All was unknown, though rumour spoke of land.

5   We passed the fine island of Madeira*
     Named for its great forests, and known
     More for its name than its ancient past
     For we were the first to people it;
     Though had Venus known it existed,
     Before we revealed it to the world,
     Well might the goddess have forgotten Paphos,
     Cythera, and Gnidus and even Cyprus.

6   We skirted the Numidian desert
     Where the Berber people, who never enjoy
     Cool water, nor green leaves, pasture
     Their cattle, endlessly wandering:
     This land, where ostriches digest
     Iron in their stomachs, bestows no fruits;
     It is a region of the harshest penury,
     Dividing Ethiopia from Barbary.*

7   We crossed the northern limit of the sun's
     Heavenly course at the Tropic of Cancer,
     Where live nations the youthful Phaethon
     Deprived of the brightness of day;
     Strange peoples bathe in the chill
     Current of the dark Senegal River,
     But Asinarius* is never heard
     Since we christened it afresh as Cape Verde.

8   Having passed by now the Canary Islands*
     Once called the Fortunate Isles,
     We sailed on to the Hesperides
     As the Cape Verde islands were known,
     Islands from which our earlier fleets
     Embarked to discover new marvels.
     We made harbour, the winds remaining fair,
     And went ashore to take provisions there.

9   Our landfall was at the island named
     For the warrior saint, Santiago,*
     Who helped the Spaniards to such purpose
     In bringing catastrophe to the Moors.
     From there, so favourable were the north
     Winds, we headed straight for the open
     Ocean, gratified by the interlude
     Of harbour, sweet repose, and fresh food.

10 We crossed the broad gulf,* bypassing
    That huge part of Africa to our east,
    Leaving in our wake the Jalof province
    With its various nations of black people;
    Then Mandingo, that vast country,
    Expert in all the arts of gold
    Where the winding River Gambia reaches
    Down at last to its Atlantic beaches.

11 We passed the islands of the Gorgons,
    Where long ago lived those sisters
    Who, being all but deprived of vision,
    Had one eye which served all three.
    Medusa was she whose locks entangled
    Neptune and drove Athene to revenge,
    And whose head conveyed in Perseus' hands
    Dripped writhing adders on the burning sands!

12 So, with our prows pointing ever south,*
    We thrust deeper into the Atlantic
    Leaving Sierra Leone's lion mountain
    And the cape which we call Cape Palmas.
    Off the River Niger, we distinctly heard
    Breakers pounding on beaches that are ours,
    Then São Tomé, named after him who trod
    With Christ on earth and touched the side of God.

13 There, the mighty kingdom of the Congo*
    Has been brought by us to faith in Christ,
    Where the Zaire flows, immense and brimming,
    A river never seen by the ancients.
    From this open sea I looked my last
    At the constellations of the north.
    For we had by now crossed the burning line*
    Which marks division in the earth's design.

14 Our sailors had discovered long since,
    In that new hemisphere, the Southern Cross,*
    Though those who had not witnessed it
    For a while doubted its existence.
    We saw new heavens, less sparkling
    And, for lack of stars, less beautiful
    Nearing the pole, where no one comprehends
    If a continent begins or the sea ends.

15 By now we had left behind both tropics*
Where Apollo's chariot twice pauses,
Coursing from pole to pole, making
Its contrasting winters and summers;
At times becalmed, at times wracked
By storms whipped up by Aeolus,
We saw both Bears,* for all Juno taught us
Plunging headlong into Neptune's waters.

16 To talk at length of the sea's dangers
As though matters beyond ordinary men,
Sudden, catastrophic thunderstorms,
Bolts setting the atmosphere ablaze,
Black squalls, nights of pitch darkness,
Earth-splitting claps of thunder,
Would be wearisome and a grave error,
Even if my voice could inspire terror.

17 For I saw with my own eyes sights
Which rough sailors, whose only schooling
Is observation and long experience,
Take as knowledge, evident and sure,
And which those with higher intelligence
Who use their skills and learning
To penetrate earth's secrets (if they could),
Dismiss as false or feebly understood.

18 I saw beyond question St Elmo's Fire,*
Which the sailors hold to be sacred,
Manifest at a time of intractable winds,
Of dark tempest and sad wailing.
No less miraculous and astonishing
Was the spectacle of ocean
And cloud, joined by what could only be
A spout sucking up moisture from the sea.

19 I saw it distinctly (and do not presume
My eyes deceived me) rise in the air,
A little vapour and subtle smoke
Rotating a little from the wind's drag;
From there could be seen a tube extending
To the very heavens, but so slender
The eye could scarcely make it out; it seemed
Tenuous as a mist or something dreamed.

20 It went on growing little by little
    To the thickness of a mast-head;
    Though here narrow, and there wider as
    It drew up great gulps of water;
    Its foot undulated with the waves;
    On the top, a black cloud condensed,
    Growing heavier by the moment and sup-
    purating with the huge volume taken up.

21 As a purple leech may be seen swelling
    On the lips of some beast (who casually
    Picked it up from a cool fountain)
    Slaking its thirst with another's blood;
    The more it sucks, the bigger it grows,
    Gorging itself to bursting-point:
    So the swollen, dropsical column swelled
    Together with the black cloud it upheld.

22 Then, sated and replete, it drew up
    The foot it still retained in the sea,
    And drifted away across the heavens
    Spattering the sea with a shower;
    It returned to the water the water it took
    But held back all traces of salt:
    Witness then, experts in nomenclature
    What wonders exist in unlettered Nature!

23 If philosophers of old, who visited
    So many lands to study their secrets,
    Had witnessed the marvels I witnessed,
    Spreading my sail to such different winds,
    What great writings they would have left us!
    What revelations about the heavens,
    What marvellous testimonies to Nature's youth!
    And all without hyperbole. Plain truth!

24 By now the moon at her shifting post
    In the first sphere had five times shown
    Her crescent face, five times her full,
    Since the fleet began our long voyage,
    When from the topmost lookout
    A keen-eyed sailor holloed: 'Land! Land!'
    Impatiently, our people rushed on deck
    All peering eastwards at the tiny speck.

25 Looking at first like clouds, the range
 Of mountains we had glimpsed grew clearer;
 The heavy anchors were prepared;
 As we approached we struck sails;
 Then in order to discover in parts
 So remote, precisely where we were,
 Using the astrolabe,* that instrument
 It took skill and ingenuity to invent,

26 We went ashore* at an open stretch,
 Where our men quickly scattered
 To reconnoitre this welcome land
 Where no one seemed to have ventured;
 But I, eager to know where I was,
 Stayed on the sandy beach with the pilots
 To measure the sun's height, and use our art
 To fix our bearing on the cosmic chart.

27 We found we had long ago left behind
 The southern Tropic of Capricorn,
 Being between it and the Antarctic,
 That least-known region of the world.
 At this, my companions returning,
 I saw a stranger with a black skin
 They had captured, making his sweet harvest
 Of honey from the wild bees in the forest.

28 He looked thunderstruck, like a man
 Never placed in such an extreme;
 He could not understand us, nor we him
 Who seemed wilder than Polyphemus.*
 I began by showing him pure gold
 The supreme metal of civilization,
 Then fine silverware and hot condiment:
 Nothing stirred in the brute the least excitement.

29 I arranged to show him simpler things:
 Tiny beads of transparent crystal,
 Some little jingling bells and rattles,
 A red bonnet of a pleasing colour;
 I saw at once from nods and gestures
 That these had made him very happy.
 I freed him and let him take his pillage,
 Small as it was, to his nearby village.

30   The next day his fellows, all of them
      Naked, and blacker than seemed possible,
      Trooped down the rugged hillside paths
      Hoping for what their friend had obtained.
      They were so gentle and well disposed
      It caused our friend Fernão Veloso*
      To try his hand as anthropologist
      And discover how such people could exist.

31   Trusting to his strong arm, Veloso
      Was too confident he would be safe;
      But after much time had elapsed
      While I watched for some signal,
      I was scanning the horizon anxiously
      For the adventurer, when he appeared
      On the rough track scurrying to the shore
      A great deal faster than he went before.

32   Coelho's* boat was quick to take him
      Off, but before it could make a landing,
      A bold Ethiopian* grappled with him
      To prevent him making an escape;
      More and more came after Veloso,
      By now surrounded and helpless;
      We sprang to the oars but, as we bent our backs,
      There sprang from ambush a battalion of blacks;

33   Countless arrows and stones rained
      On the rest of us in a thick cloud,
      And not tossed to the wind aimlessly
      For it was there I got this leg wound;
      But we, as the aggrieved people,
      Returned so superadded a reply
      It was not just those bonnets that they wear
      Were crimson at the end of this affair!

34   As soon as Veloso was safe and sound
      We rowed quickly back to the ships,
      For, given this people's bad faith
      And brutish lack of courtesies,
      We were not likely to obtain from them
      Any news of the India we desired
      Except that it was many moons away,
      So I ordered full sail without delay.

35 Soon, one of the men said to Veloso
(As everyone was relaxing, laughing):
—'Veloso my friend, that hill's obviously
Better to come down than go up . . .'
—'Absolutely,' said the bold adventurer
'But up there, when I saw so many
Of those dogs approaching, I looked about me,
Knowing you'd be scared to death without me.'

36 He said that as soon as they mounted
The crest, the black men of whom I speak
Refused to let him proceed, threatening
To kill him if he persisted;
When he turned back, they laid an ambush
So when we sought to rescue him,
They could dispatch us to eternity
And rob our corpses with complete security.

37 Five more suns had risen and set
Since we embarked from that beach,
Cutting seas no other nation had braved,
With the winds gusting favourably,
When that night as we kept watch
At the sharp prow and at our ease,
A cloud above the mast loomed huge and high
Blackening out completely the night sky.

38 So fearful it looked, so overpowering,
It put great terror in our hearts;
The dark, invisible waters roared
As if frustrated, pounding on some reef.
'Oh Omnipotent and Sublime,' I cried,
'What demon does this region hold,
Rising before us in this dreadful form
For it seems something mightier than a storm?'

39 Even as I spoke, an immense shape*
Materialized in the night air,
Grotesque and of enormous stature,
With heavy jowls, and an unkempt beard,
Scowling from shrunken, hollow eyes,
Its complexion earthy and pale,
Its hair grizzled and matted with clay,
Its mouth coal black, teeth yellow with decay.

40   So towered its thick limbs, I swear
      You could believe it a second
      Colossus of Rhodes,* that giant
      Of the ancient world's seven wonders.
      It spoke with a coarse, gravelly voice
      Booming from the ocean's depths;
      Our hair was on end, our flesh shuddering,
      Mine and everyone's, to hear and behold the thing.

41   It addressed us: 'O reckless people,
      Bolder than any the world has known,
      As stubborn in your countless,
      Cruel wars as in vainglorious quests;
      Because you have breached what is forbidden,
      Daring to cross such remote seas,
      Where I alone for so long have prevailed
      And no ship, large or small, has ever sailed,

42   'Because you have desecrated nature's
      Secrets and the mysteries of the deep,
      Where no human, however noble
      Or immortal his worth, should trespass,
      Hear from me now what retribution
      Fate prescribes for your insolence,
      Whether ocean-borne, or along the shores
      You will subjugate with your dreadful wars;

43   'No matter how many vessels attempt
      The audacious passage you are plotting,
      My cape will be implacably hostile
      With gales beyond any you have encountered;
      On the next fleet* which broaches
      These turbulent waters, I shall impose
      Such retribution and exact such debts
      The destruction will be far worse than my threats.

44   'Here, in my reckoning, I'll take sweet revenge
      On Dias* who betrayed me to the world,
      Nor is he the only Portuguese
      Who will pay for your foolish persistence;
      If what I imagine comes to pass,
      Year by year your fleets will meet
      Shipwreck, with calamities so combined
      That death alone will bring you peace of mind.

45   'As for your first viceroy,* whose fame
     Fortune will beacon to the heavens,
     Here will be his far-flung tomb
     By God's inscrutable judgement,
     Here he will surrender the opulent
     Trophies wrung from the Turkish fleet,
     And atone for his bloody crimes, the massacre
     Of Kilwa, the levelling of Mombasa.

46   'Another will come,* a man of honour,
     Noble, generous, and a lover
     Bringing with him a beautiful lady,
     Love's due reward for his virtues;
     Vindictive fate will deliver them,
     To these harsh, implacable shores;
     They will have time to contemplate my curse,
     Weathering shipwreck to endure far worse.

47   'They will watch their dear children,
     Fruits of such love, perish of hunger;
     They will see harsh, grasping people
     Tear her clothes from the lovely lady,
     And her body of such crystal beauty
     Exposed to frost and the scorching winds,
     After marching so far in the terrible heat,
     Tramping the rough sand with her delicate feet.

48   'Those who avoid their dreadful fate
     Must witness further sufferings,
     Two hapless lovers falling victim
     To the parched, relentless bush;
     After softening the very rocks
     With tears distilled from grief and pain,
     They lie embraced, their souls already flown
     Their wretched gaol of exquisite flesh and bone.'

49   The fearsome creature was in full spate
     Chanting our destiny when, rising
     I demanded: 'Who are you, whose
     Outlandish shape utterly dumbfounds me?'
     His mouth and black eyes grimaced
     Giving vent to an awesome roar,
     Then answered bitterly, with the heavy voice
     Of one who speaks compelled and not by choice:

50   —'I am that vast, secret promontory
      You Portuguese call the Cape of Storms,*
      Which neither Ptolemy, Pompey, Strabo,
      Pliny, nor any authors knew of.
      Here Africa ends. Here its coast
      Concludes in this, my vast inviolate
      Plateau, extending southwards to the Pole
      And, by your daring, struck to my very soul.

51   'I was one of those rugged Titans*
      With Enceladus, Aegeon, and Briareus;
      I am called Adamastor, and we fought
      With the Shaker of Vulcan's thunderbolts.
      No, I could not hurl mountain on mountain
      But choosing to fight on the waters,
      I was Lord of the sea. Whatever tactic
      Neptune attempted, I was on his track.

52   'Desire for Peleus' immortal wife*
      Entangled me hopelessly in this affair;
      I spurned all heaven's goddesses
      For love of the princess of the ocean.
      My whole being became enslaved
      When I saw her with the daughters
      Of Nereus, advancing naked up the shore
      And to this day there is nothing I want more.

53   'But knowing I could never win her
      With an ugly, swollen face like mine,
      I resolved to seize her by force
      Telling Doris, her mother, of my plans;
      In her fear, the goddess spoke to Tethys,
      But she, practical in her beauty,
      Laughed, "What loves could any nymph devise
      To satisfy a monster of such size?

54   ' "Yet to keep the oceans secure from war
      I will do what's unavoidable
      Though preserving my honour intact."
      This was my go-between's reply;
      I could not tumble to any deceit
      (For who is so blind as a lover?)
      But believed myself blessed and set apart,
      Such hopes and longings quickened in my heart.

55   'Like a poor fool, I abandoned the war,
    And one night, as Doris had sworn
    Tethys approached, with her glorious
    Face and her naked, matchless body;
    Like a madman I ran, with arms
    Outstretched, to her who was my
    Soul's life, heart's joy, body's prayer
    Kissing her lovely eyes, her cheeks, her hair.

56   'But, oh, what words for my chagrin!
    Convinced my beloved was in my arms,
    I found myself hugging a hillside
    Of undergrowth and rough bush;
    I was cheek to cheek with a boulder
    I had seized as her angelic face,
    Unmanned utterly, dumb and numb with shock,
    A rock on an escarpment, kissing rock!

57   'O nymph, loveliest of all the ocean,
    Though my existence gave you no joy,
    What did it cost you to beguile me
    With mountain, cloud, dream, or void?
    I stormed off, all but insane
    With hurt and my humiliation
    To find some world where she would not resort
    Who turned my grief into such splendid sport.

58   'By this time, my Titan brothers
    Had been conquered and expelled,
    Pinned beneath various mountains
    So the Gods could live in peace;
    No hand can prevail against the heaven,
    And I, tormented by my tears,
    Slowly began to feel what heavy state
    Was planned for my audacity by Fate.

59   'My flesh was moulded to hard clay,
    My bones compressed to rock;
    These limbs you see, and this trunk
    Were stretched out over the waters;
    The gods moulded my great bulk
    Into this remote promontory;
    And of all tortures, the most agonizing
    Is that Tethys surrounds me, tantalizing.'

60   So he finished, and sighing dreadfully
     Vanished suddenly from our sight;
     The black clouds dispersed and a resonant
     Moaning echoed over the sea.
     Raising my hands to the sacred chorus
     Of angels, who had long watched over us,
     I prayed to God that He should turn aside
     The evils Adamastor prophesied.

61   By now Apollo's team of four
     Were bringing back the sun's chariot
     And Table Mountain was revealed to us
     To which the giant was transformed.
     At long last, hugging this coast,
     Our prows were pointing eastwards;
     I followed it some miles, and once again
     Turned for the shore and landed with my men.

62   The people who owned the country* here,
     Though they were likewise Ethiopians,
     Were cordial and humane, unlike
     Those others who proved so treacherous;
     They came towards us on the sandy beach
     With dancing and an air of festival,
     Their wives along with them, and they were driving
     Humped cattle which looked sleek and thriving.

63   Their wives, black as polished ebony,
     Were perched on gently lumbering oxen,
     Beasts which, of all their cattle
     Are the ones they prize the most.
     They sang pastoral songs in their own
     Tongue, sweetly and in harmony,
     Whether rhymed, or in prose, we could not gauge
     But like the pipes of Virgil's golden age.

64   These, as their smiling faces promised,
     Dealt with us as fellow humans,
     Bringing sheep and poultry to barter
     For the goods we had on board;
     But as for news of what we sought,
     For all our desire to converse with them,
     Neither with words nor signs could we prevail,
     So we once again raised anchor and set sail.

65 By now we had made a complete circuit
    Of black Africa's coast, pointing
    Our prows towards the equator,
    Leaving the Antarctic in our wake.
    We passed Santa Cruz* where Dias,
    Having rounded the Cape of Storms,
    And planted a memorial column,
    Not knowing of his triumph, turned for home.

66 From here we sailed on many days
    Into both fair and wretched weather,
    Charting a new course on the ocean,
    Swept along only by our hopes,
    At times fighting the sea itself
    As, changing its moods wilfully,
    It conjured up a current of such force
    Our ships could make no headway in their course.

67 So overbearing was its pressure
    It drove us backward in our tracks,
    The whole sea running against us
    Though the breeze was in our favour;
    But at this, the south and south-west
    Winds, as though whipped to anger by
    The sea's challenge, unleashed a furious gale,
    So what dragged the hull was conquered by the sail.

68 The sun dawned on that holy day
    On which three kings from the Orient*
    Came in search of a King, newly born,
    Who is One, and yet Three in One;
    We made landfall once again, among
    Equally gentle people, at the mouth
    Of a river to which we gave the name
    Epiphany, to match the day we came.

69 Once more, we were offered without stint
    Fresh food, and water from the river,
    But no sign of India, for with them
    It was again as if we were dumb.
    Consider, O King, how far we had voyaged
    Encountering only pastoral people,
    Without any precise news, nor the least
    Rumour of what we searched for in the East!

70   Reflect how close by now we were,
      To defeat, emaciated by hunger,
      Exhausted by storms, by climates
      And seas beyond all our experience,
      So weary of promises dashed, so
      Often driven to despair beneath
      Heavens with scarcely one familiar star
      And hostile to the kind of men we are!

71   Our provisions were thoroughly rancid;
      To consume them made our bodies worse,
      While nothing brought any comfort
      In pursuing such fleeting hopes!
      Would you believe that had our company
      Of soldiers not been Portuguese,
      They would have remained so long obedient
      To their king and to me, their king's agent?

72   Do you imagine if I, their captain,
      Opposed them, they would not have mutinied,
      Driven to become pirates out of sheer
      Rage and desperation and hunger?
      Truly, their metal has been tested;
      There is no trial so great could turn
      Such soldiers from their natural qualities
      Of discipline, of being Portuguese.

73   So we left that haven of sweet water
      To resume ploughing the salt seas;
      We stood off a little from the coast,
      Heading out of sight of land
      For the cool, southern breezes
      Might have becalmed us in that bay
      Where the coast turns eastwards to a famous town,
      Ancient Sofala,* where the gold comes down.

74   Once past, however, we swung the helm,
      With a fervent prayer to St Nicholas,*
      Pointing our prow with the other ships
      To where breakers roared on the coast.
      Our hearts were torn with fear and desire,
      Aware of the feeble planks beneath us
      And of hopes thwarted. Then, approaching shore,
      We saw a sight to make our spirits soar.

75   It happened that, being close to land
     So that bays and beaches were visible,
     On a river flowing to the open sea*
     Boats with sails were coming and going.
     Our rejoicing knew no bounds, for
     Surely, coming upon a people skilled
     In the art of navigation, we thought
     They must know of the India we sought.

76   These, too, were Ethiopians,* but seemed
     More in touch with the larger world;
     Some Arabic words* were mingled
     With the language they were speaking;
     They covered their heads with turbans
     Of fine cotton-weave fabric,
     And round their privy parts, as a further clue,
     They wore a length of cotton coloured blue.

77   In the little Arabic they could manage
     And which Fernão Martins spoke fluently,
     They said their sea was crossed and recrossed
     By ships equalling ours in size;
     They appeared from where the sun rises,
     Sailing south to where the coast bulges,
     Then back towards the sun where (as they say)
     Live people like us 'the colour of the day'.

78   So overjoyed were we at meeting
     These people, and even more by their news,
     From the omens we encountered there,
     We named that river the Good Signs,
     And we raised up a stone column
     (We carried a number to mark
     Such places), naming it for St Raphael,*
     Tobias's gracious guide to Gabael.

79   Here we careened the ships, scraping
     The hulls clean of six months' sludge,
     And barnacles and limpets, harmful
     Parasites of an ocean voyage;
     From the friendly people nearby we had,
     In that glad time, every kindness,
     Furnishing our food, and generously,
     Without a hint of guile or treachery.

80   But for all the joy and fervent hope
      That harbour gave us, pleasure was not
      Unsullied, for Fortune, to compensate,
      Struck us with further hardship.
      So serene heaven dispenses;
      We are born with this onerous
      Condition—that suffering is persistent
      While joy, by its nature, is transient.

81   From a disease more cruel* and loathsome
      Than I ever before witnessed, many
      Slipped from life, and in an alien land
      Their bones are forever sepulchred.
      Would any credit without seeing it?
      It attacked the mouth. The gums
      Swelled horribly, and the flesh alongside
      Turned tumid and soon after putrefied.

82   Putrefied with a foetid stench
      Which poisoned the surrounding air.
      We had no learned doctor with us,
      Still less an experienced surgeon;
      But some, with some little knowledge
      Of this art, cut away the rotting meat
      As if they were corpses, for as we said,
      If it remained they were as good as dead.

83   And so in that unmapped wilderness,
      We left, for all eternity, comrades
      Who, in all our trials and misfortunes,
      Had always risked all at our side.
      How simple it is to bury a man!
      Any wave of the sea, any foreign
      Mound, as with our friends, will accommodate
      Flesh, no matter how lowly or how great.

84   So we departed from that estuary
      With great hope and greater grief,
      And hugging the coast we cut the sea
      In search of more certain news;
      We came at length to Mozambique
      Of whose treachery and bad faith
      You, O King, are already a connoisseur,
      Likewise of inhospitable Mombasa.

85   At long last, to this safe anchorage,
   This welcoming harbour which gives health
   To the living and life to the dead,
   God in his mercy piloted us.
   Here, O King, rest after labour,
   Sweet solace and peace of mind
   You provided. Now I lay down my task,
   Having answered everything I heard you ask.

86   Did you think, O King, the world contained
   Men who would tackle such a journey?
   Do you imagine that Aeneas and subtle
   Ulysses ever ventured so far?
   Did either of them dare to embark on
   Actual oceans? For all the poetry
   Written about them, did they see a fraction
   Of what I know through strategy and action?

87   Homer so drank of the Aonian spring,*
   That Rhodes, Smyrna, Ios, and Athens,
   Colophon, Arcos, and Salamis claim
   The honour of being his birthplace;
   Virgil brought fame to all Italy;
   Hearing his exalted voice,
   In pastoral mode, his native Mincius sighed,
   While his epic made the Tiber swell with pride;

88   Let them sing on,* piling praises
   On their more-than-human heroes,
   Inventing Circe and Polyphemus,
   Sirens who make men sleep with song;
   Let them sail under canvas and oar
   To the Cicones, leaving their
   Shipmates in that lotus-befuddled realm,
   Losing even their pilot at the helm;

89   Let them fantasize, of winds leaping
   From wine-skins, and of amorous Calypsos;
   Harpies who foul their own banquets;
   Pilgrimages to the underworld;
   However they polish and decorate
   With metaphor such empty fables,
   My own tale in its naked purity
   Outdoes all boasting and hyperbole.

*

90   All the Malindians were spellbound
     By the eloquent captain's words,
     As he brought to an end his long account
     Of exalted and heroic deeds.
     The king spoke of the high courage
     Of the kings made famous by such wars;
     Of the people he praised their fealty,
     Their strength of spirit and nobility.

91   As they went their ways, they recounted
     The episodes each was most struck by;
     None could take his eyes from the heroes
     Who had rounded such horizons.
     But now Apollo guided the reins,
     Once steered so recklessly by Phaethon,
     To rest in the lovely arms of Tethys,
     And the king's barge returned him to his palace.

92   How sweet is the praise and the glory
     Of our exploits, when it rings true!
     True nobility strives to leave
     A name surpassing the ancients.
     So often it happens that greatness
     Springs from emulation of the great;
     What brave man, committed to what cause
     Will not be given fresh impulse by applause?

93   It was not Achilles' glorious deeds
     Alexander held in such high regard
     But great Homer's harmonious numbers;
     It was these he praised and coveted.
     The fame of Miltiades at Marathon
     Roused Themistocles only to envy;
     Nothing, he said, could give him any pleasure
     Till his own deeds were praised in equal measure.

94   Vasco da Gama laboured to prove
     Those odysseys the world acclaims
     Did not merit as much fame and glory
     As his own, which shook heaven and earth.
     True. Yet only as Emperor Augustus
     Esteemed, honoured, and recompensed
     The Mantuan, could Aeneas' story
     Give resonance and wings to Rome's glory.

95   Portugal has had her Alexander,
       Her Caesar, Scipio, and Octavius,
       But she did not bestow such talents
       As would have made them men of culture.
       Augustus, even when facing defeat,
       Wrote verses, graceful and to the point;
       As Fulvia found,* over her behaviour
       When Antony abandoned her for Glaphyra.

96   Caesar campaigned to conquer France,
       But war did not impede his learning,
       As pen in one hand, sword in the other,
       He equalled Cicero in eloquence.
       It is known of Scipio* he attained
       Great facility in his comedies,
       For even generals may be impressed:
       His Homer was Alexander's head-rest.

97   It is hard to think of a great commander
       Whether Roman, Greek, or Barbarian,
       Who was not also skilled in learning
       Unless, that is, among us Portuguese.
       I cannot admit without reproach
       The reason we have so few poets
       Is that poetry is not an art we love;
       For who can cherish what he's ignorant of?

98   For this, not any fault in nature,
       We have no Virgil nor Homer among us;
       Nor will there be, if this continues,
       Any pious Aeneas or fierce Achilles.
       Worst of all is that harsh circumstance
       Has made each of us in turn so harsh,
       And in matters of genius so remiss
       That, for most of us, ignorance is bliss.

99   Let da Gama be grateful to the muses
       That they love his country as they do,
       Being constrained to honour in poetry
       His title, fame, and exploits in war;
       For in truth, neither he nor his lineage
       Condescend to be Calliope's friend,
       Nor encourage the nymphs of Tagus to trim
       Their cloths of gold and sing instead of him.

100   Sheer sisterly love and the pure desire
To honour with due and measured praise
The achievements of the Portuguese
Are what move the Tagus nymphs;
So let no one with great deeds
In his heart cease to persevere,
Or neglect to keep some lofty goal in view,
Lest he fail to reap the honour that's his due.

Canto Six

1   The Muslim king was at his wits' end
How to entertain the brave mariners,
To gain the Christian king's alliance
And the friendship of such strong people.
He spoke of his grief he was lodged so far
From the abundant lands of Europe,
Lamenting fortune had not placed his villas
Much nearer Hercules' illustrious pillars.*

2   With games, dances, and other pleasures
Very Malindian in their fashion,
And with pleasant fishing excursions
As when the Egyptian beguiled Antony,
Every day the distinguished Sultan
Feasted his Lusitanian guests,
With banquets of game and fowl and fish,
Strange fruits, and many an unknown dish.

3   But the captain, aware he was lingering
Too long, with the fresh winds urging
Departure, and being supplied with pilots
And fresh provisions from the land,
Resolved to stay no longer, having
Much of the silver ocean to travel.
He took his leave of the kindly, generous Moor
Who urged that this new friendship should endure.

4   The Sultan begged further, that his port
Should always be honoured by their ships,
That he wished no less than to offer
Such heroes his throne and his kingdom,
And that while his soul ruled his body,
He would be ready to sacrifice
His country and his life at any time
To a king so good, a people so sublime.

5   With similar ornament, the captain
     Replied then, spreading canvas,
     Set sail once more for the lands of the dawn
     That had so long been his goal.
     In his new pilot* there was no deceit,
     Just an expert knowledge of the course,
     So he cruised now with greater ease of mind
     Than in the latitudes they left behind.

6   They were now in the waters of the orient,
     Crossing the Indian Ocean, glimpsing
     The sun's cradle where it dawns in fire;
     They had all but achieved their purpose;
     But wicked Bacchus,* struck to his soul
     By the good fortune which awaited
     The worthy Portuguese, began to rage,
     Burn, blaspheme, babble, and rampage.

7   He saw heaven was fully resolved
     To make of Lisbon a second Rome;
     He could not halt what was determined
     By that higher, absolute power.
     He abandoned Olympus in desperation;
     He sought help on earth, plunging to the court
     Of the underwater god,* whose devotions
     Govern the activity of the oceans.

8   In the deep chambers of the innermost
     Vaulted caverns where the sea retreats,
     There, whence the waves leap in fury
     When the sea responds to the winds' challenge,
     Is Neptune's home, and the cheerful
     Nereids', and other gods the ocean
     Recognizes, granting its damp deities
     Enough space for their underwater cities.

9   There in the undiscovered depths
     Bacchus found sands of the finest silver;
     He saw, on an open plain, tall towers
     Of pure translucent crystal;
     Though the closer the eye approached
     So much less could it be sure
     If any crystal could be so transparent,
     Or any diamond so clear and radiant.

10 The doors were of gold, richly inlaid
With those pearls that are born in shells,
And were worked with gorgeous carvings
On which angry Bacchus feasted his gaze;
First, he saw in various colours
The confused face of primeval chaos;*
Then the four basic elements, displayed
Going about their tasks, were each portrayed.

11 Highest of all was Fire, sublimity's
Very essence, and self-sustaining;
It has animated all living things
Since Prometheus first stole it.
Beyond, also sublime but invisible,
Was Air, which disperses rapidly,
And in heat or cold displays such acumen
That no part of the globe is left a vacuum.

12 There was Earth, covered with mountains
With green meadows and flourishing trees,
Supplying pasture and sustaining life
For the myriad creatures springing there.
And the bright form was also carved
Of Water, dividing the continents,
Propagating fish of every species,
While by moisture flesh prospers and increases.

13 In another part was depicted the war
The young gods fought with the titans;
Typhoeus* was there, under the mass
Of Etna with its crackling flames;
Neptune was carved there, smiting
The earth* to give primitive man
The warhorse; then Minerva, peacefully,
With her own gift of the first olive tree.

14 Bacchus' rage would not long allow
Such sights to constrain him, bursting
Headlong into Neptune's palace
Who, warned already of his coming,
Was at the portal to welcome him,
Along with a puzzled bevy of nymphs,
Trying to fathom what in heaven had brought a
King of wine to the domain of water.

15   —'Neptune,' he said, 'do not be alarmed
      To receive Bacchus in your kingdom,
      For even the great and powerful
      May be crushed by unjust fortune.
      Summon the sea gods before I say
      More, if you want to discover more;
      Let me tell gods what's about to befall
      Them! Let all hear what threatens us all!'

16   Divining already that this would be
      A weird business, Neptune dispatched
      Triton* to summon the gods who inhabit
      The cold sea between coast and coast.
      This huge, swarthy youth, who took
      Pride in being son of the king
      And of loved Amphitrite, was trumpeter
      To Neptune and underwater courier.

17   The hairs of his beard and the hair
      Falling from his head to his shoulders
      Were all one mass of mud, and visibly
      Had never been touched by a comb;
      Each dangling dreadlock was a cluster
      Of gleaming, blue-black mussels.
      On his head, by way of coronet, he wore
      The biggest lobster-shell you ever saw.

18   His body was naked, even his genitals,
      So as not to impede his swimming,
      But tiny creatures of the sea
      Crawled over him by the hundreds;
      Crabs and prawns and many others
      Which wax with the growing moon,
      Cockles and oysters, and the slimy husks
      Of convoluted whelks and other molluscs.

19   In his hand was a huge twisted conch
      On which he blew a powerful blast;
      The melodious sound was heard booming
      Throughout all the world's oceans;
      At once the company of the gods
      Responded, travelling to the courts
      Of the god who once built the walls of Troy
      (Which the angry Greeks united to destroy).

20 Father Ocean came,* with all the host
Of sons and daughters he had fathered;
Nereus came, married to Doris
Who peopled all the sea with nymphs;
Proteus came, leaving his seals
To graze on the salty pastures,
Though being a prophet, obviously, he
Foresaw what Bacchus wanted in the sea.

21 Tethys was there, Neptune's delicious
Wife, daughter of Earth and Sky,
Her face both serene and happy, and so
Lovely the sea was becalmed in wonder;
She was dressed in a precious gown
Of the finest linen weave, through which
Much of her radiant body was revealed,
For such beauty is not to be concealed.

22 Amphitrite, resplendent as the flowers,
Could not miss such an occasion;
She brought the dolphin which counselled her
To surrender to the love of Neptune.
Each seeming to outshine the sun
With eyes which conquered all they saw,
Two wives together of the same husband
Walked in perfect harmony, hand in hand.

23 Ino who fled from mad King Athamas
And was changed into a goddess,
Brought her son, that lovely infant,
Also numbered among the gods;
He ran along the beach, playing
With the shells which the salt waves
Keep casting up or, if he paused to rest,
Lovely Panopea took him to her breast.

24 And Glaucus, the god who was once human
And by the virtue of a powerful herb
Became a fish, from which disaster
The outcome was his divinity,
He also came, but grieving Circe's
Revenge against the beautiful
Scylla, whom he loved, knowing his love returned,
Changed to a monster by the one he spurned.

25   At last all of them took their seats
In the great hall of the celestial palace,
The goddesses on lavish canopies,
The gods on thrones of crystal;
Neptune, with Bacchus enthroned at his side,
Saluted each in turn, as fumes
Of ambergris were wafted through the air,
Sweeter than all the scents of Arabia.

26   The hubbub of the gods' arrival
And their greetings having subsided,
Bacchus began to unveil the secret
Torment gnawing at his soul.
His face was overcast with cares,
And exposing his heartfelt longing
For their help in devising one last stroke
To put pay to the sons of Lusus, he spoke:

27   —'O Neptune, you who rule by right
The angry seas from pole to pole,
Who confine the peoples of the earth
To their fixed appointed boundaries;
And you, Father Ocean, who envelop
The entire globe, keeping apart
The continents, and with just decrees ordain
Each race must live within its own domain;

28   'And you, gods of the sea, who suffer
No encroachment on your vast kingdom,
Chastising in a manner to suit
The offence, whoever ventures upon it:
Was it folly to take such precautions?
Who can it be has softened hearts
Once determinedly, implacably combined
Against puny and insolent mankind?

29   'You have seen with what presumption
Daedalus assaulted the very heavens;
You observed the Argonauts' mad ambition
To tame the sea with sail and oar;
Then, and daily, you swallow such
Insults, that very soon, I promise you,
Of the vast oceans and the heavenly span
They'll be the gods and you and I but Man.

30 'Consider how this wretched tribe
    Named after one of my former vassals,*
    Has found the courage to dominate
    You, me, and the entire world.
    Look how they dare to plough oceans
    Where even the Romans never ventured;
    Behold the ways they trespass on your realm,
    Breaking your laws wherever they turn their helm.

31 'I bore witness when the Argonauts
    First made a breach in your kingdom,
    How Boreas, and his friend Aquilo,*
    And all the other winds fought back.
    If the winds then felt so affronted
    By that insignificant, daring band,
    Revenge now should provoke you even more,
    So why delay? What are you waiting for?

32 'I don't expect you, gods, to believe
    I left the heavens out of love of you,
    Nor from rage at the wrongs you suffer,
    But for what is being done to me:
    You all remember, when I conquered
    The lands of India in the Orient,
    What honours and eternal fame I won?
    Now with these interlopers, all's undone.

33 'The supreme Lord and the Fates who rule
    The lower world as they see fit
    Are determined to grant still greater fame
    To these ocean-faring heroes.
    Here you see for yourselves, gods,
    How they teach even gods to do wrong;
    It comes to this—the famous and elect
    Are the ones least entitled to respect!

34 'For this reason I abandoned Olympus
    Seeking redress for my injuries,
    To see if the credit I lost in heaven
    May by chance be redeemed in your waters.'
    He wished to say more, but could prevent
    No longer spurting from both his eyes
    Salt, scalding tears of which he was ashamed,
    But at that the gods of water were inflamed.

35   The passion surging through the gods'
Hearts in that instant left no room
For debate nor sober reflection,
Nor could brook a moment's delay.
Furiously, they instructed Aeolus,*
On Neptune's behalf, to unloose at once
His strongest, wildest nor-and-nor-east-galers,
Once and for all to rid the seas of sailors.

36   Proteus sought first to intervene
To declare what he felt on the matter;
And all expected what was to follow
Would be some profound prophecy;
But so great was the momentary
Uproar in the company of the gods,
That Tethys shouted, silencing everyone,
—'Neptune's fully aware of what must be done!'

37   Aeolus in his presumption was already
Releasing winds from his prison,
Goading them on with provocative words
Against the brave and spirited heroes.
Suddenly, the sky was overcast
And gales, which had never blown
With such fury, doubled their force to make
Houses, towers, mountains topple in their wake.

38   But while the gods were at their council
In the watery depths, the weary, happy
Fleet, with calm seas and gentle winds,
Was pursuing its tremendous journey.
It was the time when the light of day
Was furthest removed from the east;
The bells of the first watch* had been reckoned
And men were awakening for the second.

39   They came still weary, drugged with sleep,
Yawning, drooping now and then against
The yards, and all wretchedly dressed
For the chill wind that was blowing;
They could barely force their eyes open,
But rubbing them, they stretched their arms,
Swapping stories and anecdotes to shake
Drowsiness off and keep themselves awake.

40   —'This is tiresome,' said one. 'How better
      To make the hours of this watch pass
      Than with some agreeable tale
      That will dispel the burden of sleep?'
      Leonard,* who was always preoccupied
      With thoughts of some beloved, agreed:
      —'Let love be our theme,' he said. 'Let's dance
      The hours away with the stuff of romance.'

41   —'No,' said Veloso.* 'Gentle topics
      Have no place amid such hardships;
      The work of a ship is too demanding
      For talk of love and such refinements;
      Instead, our story must be of war
      And the fierce heat of battle;
      Grim days await us, hard labour, with groans
      Our only comfort. I feel it in my bones.'

42   All agreed in this and invited Veloso
      To tell whatever tale he pleased.
      —'I will,' he said, 'and let no one complain
      I am dealing in fable or fiction;
      And to learn from me, and it, to behave
      Nobly and with honour, I will speak
      Of courtiers born and raised in Portugal,
      The Twelve of England,* and heroes all!

43   'In the time when King João, Pedro's son,
      Ruled Portugal with a gentle rein,
      After securing peace and freedom
      Against all the plots of Castile,
      Far to the north, in mighty
      Snow-bound England, fierce Discord
      Scattered her evil tares from an iron hand,
      Which brought great lustre to our own land.

44   'It happened once that the gentle ladies
      Of the English court and their noble lords
      Quarrelled with angry words (perhaps
      From conviction, or simply to provoke).
      The courtiers, for whom such badinage
      Signified little, said they would prove
      Honour and fame, being *ad hominem*
      Could not exist in women, as women;

45   'But that any knight with lance and sword
     Who offered to take the ladies' cause
     Would be met in the field or in the lists
     And rewarded with dishonour or death.
     The delicate ladies, unaccustomed
     To such insults, and well aware
     They lacked the strength of body to defend
     Their honour, appealed to relative and friend.

46   'But since their enemies were highly placed
     And powerful in the kingdom, neither
     Relatives nor sweethearts rallied
     To the ladies' side as they should.
     With tears on their lovely faces,
     Such as would rouse the gods in heaven,
     They took their tale of insolence and taunt
     To the Duke of Lancaster, John of Gaunt.

47   'This mighty Englishman had campaigned
     With the Portuguese against Castile
     And knew of their great-heartedness
     And that fortune was their friend;
     He had made trial, too, in Portugal
     Of their romantic dispositions,
     When King João took Philippa as his own,
     Queen of his heart, and partner of his throne.

48   'The Duke could not succour them himself
     For fear of worsening the rancour,
     But he said: "When I asserted my claim
     To the lands and throne of Castile,
     I found in the noble Portuguese
     Such gallantry and daring,
     They are the very knights, upon my word,
     To champion your honour by fire and sword;

49   ' "If, in this affront, you would be served
     Ladies, I will send ambassadors
     Bearing discreet, courtly letters
     Which will make your provocation known;
     If you, on your part, also send
     Messages of love and allurement
     Watered with tears, I do believe that thence
     You'll find your champions and a strong defence."

50 'So the wily Duke counselled them,
　　And named at once twelve strong men;
　　And he advised the ladies to draw lots
　　So each had her knight, they also
　　Being twelve; then finding who had
　　Drawn whom, each in their different styles
　　Wrote to her own hero in Portugal,
　　And all to the King, likewise the Duke to all.

51 'These messages arrived in Portugal;
　　The court was ravished by this novelty;
　　The noble King was first to volunteer
　　But his kingship would not permit it;
　　All the courtiers clamoured as one man
　　To flock to the great adventure,
　　But events favoured only the dozen
　　Fortunate champions the Duke had chosen.

52 'In loyal Porto, the city (as is said)
　　From which Portugal derives her name,
　　He who commands the ship of state
　　Commanded a vessel made ready.
　　Quickly, the twelve equipped themselves
　　With the latest arms and accoutrements,
　　With helmets, crests, mottoes, and devices,
　　Horses, and trappings in countless guises.

53 'Then, obtaining due leave from their king,
　　There sailed from the famous Douro river
　　Those twelve knights picked by the judgement
　　Of the veteran Duke of Lancaster.
　　None of the band differed from his friends
　　In valour or courtly virtues;
　　But one of the dozen, Magriço* by name,
　　Begged to be indulged in a secret aim:

54 ' "My brave companions, I have long desired
　　To visit foreign countries, to view
　　Rivers other than the Douro and Tagus,
　　Other peoples, laws, and customs.
　　Now that the chance presents itself
　　(There being so much to see), I desire
　　To go by land, if this suits everyone;
　　I will rejoin you afterwards in London.

55   ' "Should God, who is final arbiter
       And last resource of all creatures,
       Prevent my keeping the appointed time,
       You will lose little by my absence:
       You will do all that must be done;
       But my intuition tells me neither
       Rivers nor mountains, fortune good or ill,
       Shall obstruct me, for rejoin you, I will."

56   'So Magriço; and, embracing his friends,
       He obtains their assent and departs.
       He goes by Léon and Castile, viewing
       Forts once captured by our armies;
       And Navarre, with the dizzy heights
       Of the Pyrenees, dividing Spain from Gaul.
       Through the cities of France he meanders,
       Lingering in the market towns of Flanders.

57   'But there, from accident or whim,
       He spends many days without proceeding.
       Meanwhile, the eleven of the company
       Had cut the cold seas of the north;
       They reached England's shrouded coast,
       And all made their way to London;
       Each was fêted by the Duke as his guest,
       While the ladies attended and caressed.

58   'The appointed day arrived to enter
       The lists against the twelve English
       In the tourney guaranteed by the king;
       They donned their helmets, greaves, and mail.
       Now the ladies could see for themselves
       The fierce spirit of the Portuguese;
       Their own silks were gorgeous to behold,
       Lit by a thousand precious stones and gold.

59   'But she, to whom had fallen by lot
       The still-absent Magriço, was robed
       As for mourning, having no brave knight
       As her champion in that affair;
       The eleven insisted that their business
       Should be carried through at the English court,
       For the ladies would gain their victory
       Though two of their knights died, or even three.

60   'Raised on high in an open theatre
     Sat the King of England with all his court;
     They were seated, without formality,
     In their groups of threes and fours;
     Never from the Tagus to the Bactrus*
     Did the sun shine on twelve knights
     Who, for valour and strength, could equal these
     English facing the eleven Portuguese.

61   'The horses, champing their gold bits,
     Foamed at the mouth, showing their spirit;
     The sun's rays glanced from the armour
     As from crystal or hard diamond;
     From all sides it was being judged
     An ill-matched and unfair contest,
     Eleven with a dozen; but then a loud
     Buzz of excitement passed across the crowd.

62   'The spectators craned their necks to see
     What was causing the commotion,
     When a knight rode in on horseback,
     Wearing full armour, ready for combat;
     To the king and the ladies, he made salute,
     And joined the eleven, and it was Magriço,
     Embracing each companion as his friend
     And proving he was faithful to the end.

63   'His lady, hearing this was the knight
     Come to champion her name and honour,
     Rejoiced and dressed in a cloth of that gold
     The unworthy prize more than virtue.
     The signal given, trumpets sounded,
     Inciting the warriors to battle;
     At once, pricking their spurs, they loosened rein,
     Aimed their lances, and struck fire from the plain.

64   'The thundering of the horses' hoofs
     Made the whole battle-ground tremble;
     The hearts of all those who were watching
     Thumped with exhilaration and terror.
     One flies rather than falls from his horse;
     One falling to the earth with his horse, groans;
     One's white armour is soaked with bloody spume;
     One whips his horse's flank with his helmet plume.

65 'Some in those lists found perpetual sleep,
    Making an end of life's brief span;
    Some horses went running riderless,
    Some riders staggered without horses.
    English pride was hurled from its throne
    As two or three abandoned the cause;
    Those who returned with their swords to the field
    Encountered worse than harness, mail, and shield.

66 'To expend words on lurid descriptions
    Of frantic blows and terrible thrusts
    Is for poetasters whom we know
    Waste our time with their empty fables;
    Sufficient to end with what is certain
    That, with many resounding exploits,
    To our side fell the palm of victory
    And to the ladies, honour, and glory.

67 'The Duke regaled the victorious twelve
    With feasting and revelry in his palace;
    The lovely company of the ladies
    Kept huntsmen and cooks occupied
    As they sought to give their liberators
    Countless banquets daily, hourly,
    While they were guests in England, until all
    Returned at last to their loved Portugal.

68 'Except great Magriço, whom they report
    Was still ambitious to see the world,
    And remained to render notable
    Service to the Countess of Flanders;
    For being now no longer a novice
    In the lists or open combat,
    He killed a Frenchman, as if his fate was
    To imitate Corvinus and Torquatus.*

69 'Another of the twelve* betook himself
    To Germany and fought a duel
    With a German who, with an underhand
    Thrust, tried to kill him treacherously.'
    Veloso was continuing when the crew
    Interrupted, saying he should not digress
    From the tale of Magriço and his fate;
    The affair of him in Germany could wait.

70 But just then, as they were listening,
The bo'sun who was watching the weather
Blew on his whistle and, springing to life,
The mariners rushed to their posts;
Then, because the breeze was freshening,
He shouted to reef the foretopsails:
'Jump to it,' he said. 'The horizon's shook off
A black cloud there, I don't like the look of.'

71 Scarcely were the topsails taken in
When a sudden, almighty tempest* broke.
—'Strike,' yelled the bo'sun with a great shout,
'Strike,' he bellowed, 'strike the main sail!'
The angry winds give them no time
To react but, smacking the sail head on,
Ripped it to pieces with a clap like thunder
As if the very globe was rent asunder.

72 In the sudden panic and confusion, all
Pierced the heavens with their cries,
For with the tearing of the sail, the vessel
Keeled, shipping torrents of water.
—'Lighten ship,' said the bo'sun at once.
'All together! Everything overboard!
You others to the pumps. Hurry, or down
We go! Look alive! It's pump or drown!'

73 The willing soldiers clambered at once
To man the pumps but as they reached them
The pitching, as dire seas punched
The vessel, hurled them to the deck.
Three mariners, hardened and brawny,
Were not enough to manage the helm;
They fixed block and tackle on either side,
But skill was futile, and their strength defied.

74 The winds could not have been more violent,
Gusting with greater ferocity,
Had they been levelling to the ground
The formidable Tower of Babel.
In mountainous seas which leaped
Higher by the minute, the ship
Wallowed from side to side like a ship's boat,
Astounding everyone she stayed afloat.

75   Paulo da Gama's warship was all but
     Foundering, the mainmast snapped in two,
     And the crew were loud in their cries
     To Him who came to save the world.
     The winds snatched and tossed aside
     Similar prayers from Coelho's caravel,
     Though the bo'sun with foresight had contrived
     To strike sail just as the storm arrived.

76   By now, furious Neptune's waves
     Were piling up to the clouds, then
     Yawning as if to the innermost
     Entrails of the deepest depths;
     Winds from all quarters sought
     To smash the very fabric of the world;
     Blue lightning crackled in the pitch-black night,
     And the whole heavens were ablaze with light.

77   All along the storm-swept coast
     The Halcyon birds* raised their lament,
     Recalling those tears so long ago
     Provoked by the raging waters.
     The lovesick dolphins, all this while,
     Hid in their underwater caves,
     Fleeing the breakers and relentless gale,
     Yet even there they trembled and grew pale.

78   Never was such lightning forged
     Against the overweening Titans
     By the muscular, sooty blacksmith*
     Who wrought Aeneas' shining armour;
     Not even Jove himself hurled
     Such thunderbolts in that deluge
     When survived only Pyrrha and Deucalion
     Who cast stones to fashion women and men.

79   How many mountains were toppled that day
     By the frantic lashing of the waves!
     How many ancient trees uprooted
     By the wind's unremitting fury!
     Those buttress roots never foresaw
     One day they would stare at the sky,
     Nor the sands of the deep that oceans might
     Swirl their sediments to such a height.

80 Vasco da Gama, realizing that close
To his goal he was about to drown,
Watching the seas, now gaping to hell,
Now mounting in fury to the heavens,
Confused by fears, unsure of life
Where no human help could avail,
Cried out to Him, from the depths of despair,
To whom all things are possible, this prayer:

81 —'Divine guardian, merciful providence,
Who art Lord of earth, sea, and heaven;
You, who guided the children of Israel*
Through the waters of the Red Sea;
You, who delivered St Paul in safety
From the quicksands of Syrtes;
Who saved Noah with his sons, and bade him
Be to the drowned world a second Adam;

82 'Must I endure* another Scylla
And Charybdis like those we have passed,
More gulfs like Syrtes with its quicksands,
More rocks like the Acroceraunia?
At the climax of so many travails,
Why, O God, do you now forsake us?
Where is the offence? How are we to blame
For this service undertaken in Thy name?

83 'Blessed are those who met their death
At the point of an African lance,
Upholding the sacred law of Christ
In the deserts of Mauretania!
Whose illustrious deeds are exalted,
Whose memories are still fresh,
Who became immortal through the lives they gave,
For Death is sweet when Honour shares the grave.'

84 As he uttered this prayer the winds howled,
Butting like a herd of wild bulls,
Lashing the storm to greater fury,
And screaming through the shrouds;
The fork-lightning never paused;
Thunder hammered as if bent on
Demolishing the seven firmaments
As battle raged between the elements.

85 But now the amorous star,* morning's
    Messenger dawned on the horizon,
    Heralding the sun, and surveying
    Land and sea with her bright face.
    Venus, whose star it is, making
    Orion with his sword turn tail,
    Gazed below at the fleet she held so dear
    And was seized at once by anger mixed with fear.

86 —'This is, for certain, Bacchus' work,
    But it will do him no good,' she vowed,
    'Now, as will always happen,
    I know exactly what harm he intends.'
    So saying, she sped in an instant,
    Down from the sky to the broad ocean,
    Instructing her ardent nymphs to wear
    Chaplets of sweet rosebuds in their hair.

87 Chaplets, she advised, in varied colours
    Contending with their golden hair;
    Who could tell the flowers were not springing
    Naturally from the gold Love braided?
    Her plan was to appease through love
    The horrid regiment of the winds,
    By displaying her dear Nereids, who are
    Unmatched for radiance by any star.

88 So it proved, for as soon as the gales
    Glimpsed them, the virulence
    Of their combat dwindled, and they
    Surrendered like a beaten army;
    Their hands and feet seemed entangled
    By that hair which outshone the sun.
    The lovely Orithyia* played her part
    With Boreas, for whom she yearned at heart;

89 —'Do not assume, fierce Boreas, I am
    Seduced by your oaths of constancy;
    Tenderness is love's surest sign
    And fury does not rhyme with fidelity;
    If you cannot rein in your madness,
    From this day forward, do not expect
    To take me as your lover any longer
    For my fear of you will always be stronger.'

90 So, too, the beautiful Galatea
Admonished fierce Notus,* for she knew
How long he had been watching her
And that she could tempt him to anything.
The wild one could not believe his luck,
His heart thumping in his breast,
And keen to know what was the lady's game,
Cared not a scrap how pliable he became.

91 In the same manner, the other nymphs
Swiftly tamed the remaining lovers;
Soon they had surrendered to lovely Venus
All their anger and their tumult;
She promised, seeing them so fond,
Her eternal favour in their amours,
Receiving in her lovely hands their homage,
And their promise of a prosperous voyage.

92 At this, bright dawn broke in those heights
Where the River Ganges has its source,
As the sailors, aloft at the mast head,
Saw mountains glimmering before the prow.
Now, after the storm and the long,
Pioneer voyage, their fears subsided.
Then cheerfully said their Malindian pilot,
—'That land ahead is surely Calicut!*

93 'This is the land you have been seeking,
This is India rising before you;
Unless you desire yet more of the world,
Your long task is accomplished.'
Rejoicing to see he knew the country,
Da Gama contained himself no longer
But knelt on deck, arms raised towards the sky,
And gave his heartfelt thanks to God on high.

94 He gave thanks to God, as well he should,
Not only for guiding him to the coast
He had voyaged to with so many fears
And through such enduring travails,
But more that, in the face of death
Devised by the winds and the cruel
Waves, God had been so prompt to redeem
Them, like awakening from some dreadful dream.

95   For indeed, it is through such perils,
      Such wearisome and fearful labours,
      That those for whom fame is the spur
      Achieve honour and lasting esteem;
      Not by depending on an ancient name
      Or a long lineage of ancestors,
      Nor sprawling on gold beds made comfortable
      By furs of the finest Russian sable,

96   Nor with new and exquisite recipes,
      Nor relaxing, local excursions,
      Nor society's teeming pleasures
      Which emasculate noble hearts;
      Nor by surrendering to his appetites,
      Nor by allowing his sweet fortune
      So to pamper him that a man never
      Embarks upon some virtuous endeavour;

97   But by seeking out, with a strong arm,
      Honours he can make truly his own,
      Vigilant, clothed in forged steel,
      Exposed to gales and tempestuous seas,
      Conquering the numbing cold
      Of the deep, inhospitable south,
      Eating corrupt rations day after day,
      Seasoned only by the hardships of the way;

98   And by instructing the face, white with shock,
      To look resolute and cheerful
      As the hot cannon-ball whistles
      And takes the arm or leg of a comrade.
      So the heart develops a callous
      Honourable contempt for titles
      And wealth, rank, and money, which Destiny
      Counterfeits, but is never Virtue's way.

99   So one's judgement grows enlightened,
      And experience brings serenity,
      Studying, as from a great height
      Mankind's pettiness and confusion;
      Such a person, if order and justice
      Prevail, and not self-interest,
      Will rise (as he must) to great position,
      But reluctantly, and not through ambition.

Canto Seven

1   At long last, they were nearing the land
So many others before had longed for,
Spread out between the River Indus
And the Ganges which rises in Eden.
Courage, heroes! You have aspired
So long to bear the victor's palm,
You have arrived! The land of your pleasure
Extends before you, with all its treasure!

2   *To you, heirs of Lusus, I have this to say:*
Your share of the earth is a small one,
And small, too, your portion of Christ's
Fold,* shepherded from Heaven;
You, whom no forms of danger
Prevented from conquering the infidel,
Nor greed, nor reluctance in sacrifice
To the Holy Mother of God in paradise;

3   *You, Portuguese, as few as you are valiant,*
Make light of your slender forces;
Through martyrdom, in its manifold forms,
You spread the message of eternal life;
Heaven has made it your destiny
To do many and mighty deeds
For Christendom, despite being few and weak,
For thus, O Christ, do you exalt the meek!

4   *Consider the Germans,* haughty stock*
Who graze on such rich meadows,
In revolt against Peter's successor
Devising a new pastor, a new creed;
Look at the hideous wars they wage
(As if blind error were not enough!),
And not against the overbearing Turk
But against the Emperor in his holy work.

5   *Look at that rough Englishman,* self-styled*
     King of the ancient, most Holy City,
     Where the Muslims are now in control
     (What title was ever so fraudulent?),
     Disporting amid his northern snows
     With a new brand of the faith, as against
     Christ's people he directs his stratagem
     Instead of winning back Jerusalem.

6   *While an infidel monarch occupies*
     The earthly city of Jerusalem,
     He violates the most sacred law
     Of the Jerusalem in the heavens.
     And what of you, unworthy Gaul?*
     You took the name 'most Christian'
     Not to defend and cherish and enjoy it
     But to rise up against and destroy it!

7   *You lay claim to other Christian lands*
     As if your own were not enough,
     So why not to Barbary and Egypt
     Historic enemies of the sacred name?
     The sword's razor edge should be tested
     On whoever rejects earth's corner-stone.
     Are you Charles's heir? and Louis's? You degrade
     Their name and land, denying their crusade?

8   *And what of those who, in luxury*
     And the indolence which partners it,
     Waste their lives pursuing wealth,
     Forgetful of their ancestors' valour?
     Then tyranny gives birth to feuding
     As a brave people turns against itself.
     It is you I have in mind, Italy,
     Enslaved by vice, your own worst enemy!

9   *Wretched Christians! Are you sprung*
     From the dragon's teeth* sowed by Cadmus,
     That you deal murder one to the other
     When all are sprung from the same womb?
     Do you not see the Holy Sepulchre
     Occupied by dogs who now encroach
     With one accord against your own terrain,
     Their credit soaring with each new campaign?

10 *You see how, by practice and requirement*
  Which they follow to the last degree,
  They keep their restless army united
  By fighting the followers of Christ.
  But with you, the Furies never cease
  Sowing the hateful tares of discord.
  What safety lies in such a stratagem
  —To have two enemies, yourselves and them?

11 *If it is greed for vast dominions*
  Sends you conquering lands not your own,
  Have you forgotten the Pactolus and Hermus
  With their gold-bearing sands?
  In Lydia,* they weave with threads of gold;
  Africa buries it in shining seams;
  Perhaps dreams of such riches will spur you
  If the Holy Sepulchre cannot stir you.

12 *These dreadful new inventions, guns*
  And instruments of artillery,
  Why not deploy them in action against
  The strongholds of Byzantium and Turkey?
  Drive the Turkish multitudes back
  To the caves of the Caspian mountains
  And cold Scythia, before they conjure up
  Any more troubles for wealthy Europe.

13 *Greeks,* Thracians, Armenians, Georgians,*
  Cry out to you the brutal people
  Are levying children, dragooning them
  Into the teachings of the Koran.
  In punishing such vile acts,
  You would be praised for courage and vision
  Far greater than the arrogant renown
  Of victories secured against your own.

14 *But while in your blind, insane frenzy*
  You thirst for your brothers' blood in Christ,
  There will be no lack of Christian daring
  In this little house of Portugal.
  In Africa, they have coastal bases;
  In Asia, no one disputes their power;
  The New World already feels their ploughshare,
  And if fresh worlds are found, they will be there.

15   Let us see, meanwhile, what befell
      Those famous mariners, from the moment
      Gentle Venus assuaged the blustering
      Fury of the contending winds,
      And since the goal of all their
      Unremitting efforts rose before them,
      That great continent, to which they bring
      Faith in Christ, new customs and a new king.

16   As they neared the unfamiliar shore
      Small fishing-craft surrounded them,
      Pointing the course to Calicut*
      Where the fishermen had their homes.
      There at once they turned their prows,
      That city being known as the best
      Of the best in Malabar, and the port
      Where the country's ruler maintained his court.

17   Beyond the Indus,* as far as the Ganges,
      Lies an enormous, celebrated land,
      Extending to the sea in the far south
      And to the north the Himalayan caves.
      It is ruled by different kings,
      Of various faiths; some follow Mohammed,
      Some worship idols in their strange tongue,
      Some even the animals they live among.

18   There, in the great range which crosses
      The continent, for it divides Asia,
      Bearing different names in the different
      Nations which lie beneath its slopes,
      Spring the fountains, the twin sources
      Of the rivers whose powerful currents die
      In the Indian Ocean, giving the vast spur
      Of land the shape of a peninsula.

19   Enclosed by these two river systems
      Is a vast country ending in a cape,
      Shaped like a pyramid far to the south,
      Pointing at the island of Ceylon;
      Near the source of the mighty Ganges
      So rumour has it, from ancient times,
      The people there* have unexampled powers
      To subsist on the sweet scents of flowers.

20   Even today, the inhabitants have many
     Strange names and startling customs.
     Pathans and Delhis are the largest
     Both in numbers and their territory;
     Those of the Deccan and Orissa look
     To salvation in the murmuring waters
     Of the Ganges; and then there is Bengal,
     A land so fertile it transcends them all;

21   And then the warrior kingdom of Cambay
     (Once ruled, they say, by the great Porus*);
     And the powerful kingdom of Narsinga
     Richer in gems and gold than soldiers.
     But here, rising from the restless sea,
     A mountain range parallels the coast
     And serves Malabar as a barrier,
     Protecting it from neighbouring Kanara.

22   People who live there call it 'the Ghats',
     And at its foot, for a little distance,
     There runs a narrow strip, exposed
     To the sea's instinctive ferocity.
     Here, of all other towns, Calicut
     Is undisputed head, beautiful
     And prosperous, a city to glory in;
     Its ruler is known as the Samorin.

23   As the fleet anchored off this rich domain,
     One of the Portuguese was dispatched
     To make known to the Hindu king
     Their arrival from such distant shores.
     He left the estuary for the river,
     Where the like never having been witnessed,
     His pale skin, his garments, and strange air
     Brought crowds of people hurrying to stare.

24   Among those who came running to see him
     Was a Mohammedan* born in Barbary,
     That region where in ancient times
     The giant Antaeus held sway.
     Either he knew it as a neighbour,
     Or was already marked by its swords,
     But Portugal he knew at all events
     Though fate had exiled him a long way thence.

25 Catching sight of the envoy, he exclaimed
    In delight, and in fluent Castilian
    —'Who brought you to this other world
    So far from your native Portugal?'
    —'Exploring,' he replied, 'the vast ocean
    Where no human being ever sailed;
    We come in search of the River Indus;
    To spread the faith of Christ is our purpose.'

26 The Muslim, whose name was Monsayeed,
    Was astounded by the immense voyage,
    And the great sufferings undergone
    At sea, as the envoy recounted them.
    But discerning his main intelligence
    Was only for the Samorin's ears,
    He said the palace, where king held court,
    Lay beyond the town, but the road was short.

27 Meanwhile, as news of this unique arrival
    Was conveyed to the king, he was welcome
    To relax in his home, poor though it was,
    And sample the food of the country;
    Then, after the envoy had rested,
    He would return with him to the ships,
    For there were few delights so salutary
    As meeting neighbours in a foreign country.

28 The Portuguese complied readily
    With all the smiling Monsayeed proposed;
    He ate and drank and followed his lead
    As if their friendship was long-standing.
    Afterwards, both of them left the city
    For the fleet Monsayeed recognized,
    Visiting the flagship, where all on board
    Welcomed the Muslim with a friendly word.

29 The captain embraced him, overjoyed
    To hear clearly the accents of Castile;
    He sat, and calmly plied him with questions
    About India and all its ways.
    And as the trees in ancient Rhodope,*
    Charmed by the golden lute of Orpheus,
    Eurydice's lover, crowded to the fore,
    So the crew pressed to listen to the Moor.

30 —'You people,' he began, 'whom nature made
Neighbours of my own dear homeland,
What chance, what stroke of destiny
Led you to embark on such a passage?
Some deep, hidden purpose brings you
From the far Tagus and obscure Minho,
To voyage on dangerous and unsailed seas
To kingdoms so remote and strange as these.

31 'Surely, God brought you here, purposing
Some task of his own performed by you;
Why else would He guide you, and protect you
From enemies, the sea, and the angry winds?
You are now in India, with its various
Peoples who prosper and grow rich
From gold and sweet perfumes and peppercorns,
Cardamoms, hot chillies, and precious stones.

32 'This country, in which you have now
Made harbour is known as Malabar;
From time immemorial it worshipped idols,
A practice widespread in these parts;
Today, it has many different kings,
But in former times only one;
Their traditions claim the last imperial
Governor was one Sarama Perimal.*

33 'But then, when others invaded the land,
Descending from the Gulf of Arabia,
Bringing with them the faith of Mohammed
In which my own parents instructed me,
It happened that their wise and eloquent
Preachers converted Perimal,
Who adopted their faith with such fervour
He resolved he would die a holy mullah.

34 'He fitted out ships, carefully stowed
With offerings of rich merchandise,
And embarked to live a life of prayer
Where the Prophet rests in Medina.*
Before he sailed, he divided
His mighty kingdom, there being
No natural heir: he chose the most worthy,
So poor men became rich, and subjects free.

35   'To one he gave Cochin,* to another
      Cannanore, then Chale, and the Pepper Isle,
      And Quilon and to another Cranganore,
      According to their talents and service.
      But a young man, whom he much loved,
      Appeared at court after all was given:
      Calicut remained, so the youth was made,
      King of a noble city, enriched by trade.

36   'On him, too, he conferred the title
      Emperor, setting him above the rest.
      This done, he departed for Arabia
      To live and die in sanctity.
      And so the great name of Samorin,
      The most powerful in the land, passed
      From the youth and his descendants, down
      To the Samorin who now wears the crown.

37   'The people, rich and poor alike, share
      One religion, a tissue of fables.
      They go naked, with only a loincloth
      To cover what instinct makes us hide.
      There are two kinds of people, the Nairs
      Are the aristocrats, while all the rest
      Are Pariahs, and their type are classed
      Unfit to marry with the ancient caste.

38   'For those who practise a given craft
      May not take a wife from another skill;
      Nor may their sons follow any calling,
      But that of their fathers until death.
      For the Nairs, it is a defilement
      To be touched by them, and so much so,
      If a Pariah by chance brushes by him
      It takes a thousand rites to purify him.

39   'In the same way, the ancient Jews
      Would not touch the Samaritan people.
      But you will see stranger things than this
      In this land with its different customs.
      Only Nairs are allowed to venture
      Their lives for the king, bearing
      As the mark of their privilege to fight,
      A shield on their left arm, sword on the right.

40 'Their priests are known as Brahmins,
    An ancient and venerable title;
    They are disciples of Pythagoras,*
    Who gave philosophy its name;
    They will not kill any living creature
    And meticulously abstain from meats;
    Only in matters of love is their goal
    Greater indulgence and less self-control.

41 'They share their wives, but strictly
    Between those of their husband's line;
    Happy the circumstance, happy the people
    Untouched by the pangs of jealousy!
    These, and many different customs,
    Are practised by the Malabaris.
    The land is prospering, with mercantile
    Goods of all kinds from China to the Nile.'

42 So the Muslim spoke. By this time, rumours
    Were flying throughout the city
    About the coming of strangers, when
    The Samorin sought to learn the truth.
    So pacing the streets, and thronged
    By young and old of both sexes,
    Came courtiers, sent by the king to greet
    The captain of this newly anchored fleet.

43 Da Gama, who now had the king's licence
    To disembark, left for the shore
    Without delay, gorgeously robed
    And attended by knights of Portugal;
    The bright, contrasting colours
    Made the onlookers buzz with excitement;
    The oars stroked, in regular manœuvre,
    First the salt sea, then the fresh river.

44 On the beach was an official of the king
    Known in his own tongue as 'Catual',
    And surrounded by Nairs, who awaited
    The noble da Gama with rare excitement.
    As he landed, the Catual embraced him
    And conducted him to a palanquin,
    A richly cushioned chair which the holders
    Lift, and bear along upon their shoulders.

45   So the Malabari and the Lusitanian
     Set out to where the king was waiting;
     The other Portuguese went on foot,
     Like a fearsome group of infantry.
     The town people were bemused
     By the unfamiliar sight and would have
     Questioned them, had not the Tower of Babel
     In ancient times made that impossible.

46   As they went, da Gama and the Catual
     Conversed as opportunity provided,
     Monsayeed, between them, interpreting
     Those of their words which he understood.
     So, journeying across the city,
     They came to a richly furbished
     Temple, at which the palanquin made pause,
     And together they entered by the doors.

47   Inside were images of their gods
     Fashioned in wood and cold stone,
     The faces and colours as discordant
     As if the Devil had devised them.
     The carvings were repulsive, like
     The Chimera with its different members;
     The Christians, used to seeing God portrayed
     In human form, were baffled and dismayed.

48   One had horns* protruding from its head,
     Like Jupiter Ammon of Libya;
     Another had two faces on one trunk,
     As Janus was shown in Roman times;
     Another had so many different arms
     It seemed modelled on Briareus;
     Yet another had a dog's proboscis
     Like the idol of Anubis at Memphis.

49   Here, the Hindu idolater made
     His superstitious obsequies, then
     Without more diversion they continued
     To the king of those credulous people.
     As they passed, the crowds swelled,
     Pressing to see the strange captain;
     From every window and roof-top, there hung
     Men, women, married, single, old, and young.

50   Borne swiftly along, they soon drew near
The bright, sweet-smelling gardens
That hid the royal dwelling from view
For though sumptuous, it had no towers;
The noble palaces were spread
Among groves of delightful trees,
For the kings of that land contrive to dwell
In the city and countryside as well.

51   On the gates of the surrounding wall
Were carvings worthy of Daedalus,
Depicting the rulers of India
From her most remote antiquity.
The happenings of that ancient age
Were so strikingly presented
That anyone who studied them with care
Read truth in the shadows depicted there.

52   One showed a mighty army marching
East along the banks of the Hydaspes;*
A general led them, with a carefree face,
Who made war with fronds of thyrsus
(It was he built Nysa, on the bank
Of that same abundant river);
Were Semele near, so well was the work done,
She could not fail to recognize her son.

53   Further along, drinking the river dry,
Was a great host of Assyrians,
Subject to Semiramis,* a queen
As lovely as she was lewd;
For there, at her burning flank,
Was carved the great rutting stallion,
Whose place her son had afterwards to dispute:
So criminal her passion, so dissolute!

54   A little to the side, there fluttered
The banners of Alexander's Greece,
The world's third empire,* conquering
As far as the waters of the Ganges.
The youthful general was leading them,
The victor's palms circling his brow,
Already bragging he was son and heir
Not of Philip but almighty Jupiter.

55   As the Portuguese studied these records,
     The Catual remarked to the captain:
     —'Other conquests are fast approaching
     To eclipse these you are looking on;
     Fresh legends will be carved here
     By strange peoples yet to appear,
     For so the pattern of the coming years
     Has been deciphered by our wisest seers.

56   'And their mystic science declares
     Further, that no human resistance
     Can prevail against such forces,
     For man is powerless before destiny;
     But the newcomers' sheer excellence
     In war and peace will be such, they say,
     Even the vanquished will feel no disgrace,
     Having been overcome by such a race.'

57   So conversing, they passed into the room
     In which the mighty emperor lay
     Reclining on a couch, unsurpassed
     In its rich and delicate workmanship.
     In repose, his expression was that
     Of a venerable and prosperous lord;
     His robe was a cloth of gold, his diadem
     Studded with every kind of precious gem.

58   At his side, kneeling on the ground,
     An old man passed him, from time to time,
     A leaf of the peppery betel plant
     They make a custom of chewing.
     A Brahmin, one of their eminent men,
     Approached da Gama at a slow pace,
     And solemnly led him to be greeted
     By the king, who waved him to be seated.

59   Da Gama sat down near the royal couch,
     His men further off, and the Samorin
     Studied the dress and the bearing
     Of such people as he had never seen.
     Then, speaking from a wise heart
     In a voice whose grave authority
     Straightway impressed the king and all the court,
     The captain spoke the message he had brought:

60   —'A great king in the farthest west
     Where the sky, in its perpetual turning,
     Blocks the sun's light with the earth,
     Leaving half revolving in darkness,
     Having heard so far away the echo
     Of the echo of a tale, that on you
     All power throughout all India depends,
     Desires that you and he be bound as friends.

61   'By long, circuitous ways he sends you
     Tidings that in its sheer wealth,
     Whether traded by sea or land
     From the Tagus to the Nile,
     Or from the cold shores of the far north
     To Ethiopia, where the burning sun
     Times equally its setting and its rise,
     His kingdom overflows with merchandise.

62   'If you are willing, with sacred pacts
     And treaties of sincere friendship,
     To begin trade in the abundance
     Of goods between his land and yours,
     So that the wealth of your kingdom
     (For which men most struggle and sweat)
     May increase, this would beyond question be
     Profit for you, and for him greater glory.

63   'And to ensure this bond of friendship
     Between us is solid and enduring,
     He will be ready when any danger
     Of war should threaten your kingdom
     To support you with men, arms, and ships
     As if you were a friend and brother;
     Whatever your pleasure, you should proffer
     A straightforward answer to his offer.'

64   So the captain delivered his message,
     To which the Hindu king replied
     It was a great glory to receive
     Ambassadors from so remote a nation;
     But on a matter of such importance
     He must consult with his counsellors,
     To enquire into everything he claimed
     About the king, land, and people he had named;

65 Meanwhile, the captain should take rest
    After his labours; for very soon
    He would give his dispatch due reflection
    And a happy response to his king.
    By now, night was placing her daily
    Check on human weariness as,
    Luring tired limbs to sleep, she pressed
    On heavy eyes the blessings of sweet rest.

66 They were lodged together, da Gama
    And his countrymen, in a chamber
    Of the noble emperor's palace
    With feasting and general happiness.
    And now it became the Catual's task,
    In his diligent service of his master,
    To discover more about this strange breed,
    Their origins, their customs, and their creed.

67 As soon as he glimpsed young Apollo's
    Glorious chariot heralding day,
    He summoned Monsayeed, to discover
    What he could tell of these novel people.
    Eager and curious, he demanded
    A full account, and sure proof
    Of who they were, having come to understand
    Their home was very near his native land;

68 And he urged him, expressly in the king's
    Interest, to tell everything he knew,
    Holding back no detail which might
    Reveal how to act in this business.
    Monsayeed answered: 'Much as I wish,
    To say more, I know only this;
    They come from Iberia, where the sun descends
    Beyond my home and theirs, where the land ends.

69 'In religion, they follow a prophet
    Conceived of one who was yet a virgin,
    By the Holy Spirit, so favoured by God
    Who keeps order in the universe.
    Among old people, it is an old tale
    That in hand-to-hand warfare,
    Bloody with valour, they marked our history,
    As my ancestors found repeatedly.

70 'With superhuman might and exploits
Talked of to this day, they expelled us
From the fertile meadows of the rich
Tagus and the pleasant Guadiana;
And still not content, they crossed
The stormy seas to Africa, never
Leaving us in peace, unless as vassals,
Storming our cities, capturing our castles.

71 'They showed no less strength and strategy
In the other wars that engaged them
Whether against the fierce Castilians,
Or with armies descending the Pyrenees.
Never once against foreign lances
Are they known to have known defeat;
Nor, in short, can past or present tell us
Who to these Hannibals will prove Marcellus.

72 'But if this account is less complete
Than you would wish, question them
Yourself! They are a truth-loving people
Angered and insulted by falsehood.
Visit the ships! Examine the weapons,
The dreadful artillery! You will
Find it highly diverting to learn more
Of Portuguese conduct in peace and war.'

73 By now the Hindu burned to inspect
Everything the Muslim had told him;
He summoned boats, to go out and review
The ships in which da Gama sailed.
Both left for the beach, and the Nairs,
Following, choked the very seas;
They boarded the flagship with its armour
And were embraced by Paulo da Gama.

74 Purple were the awnings, purple the flags
In that rich fabric the silkworm spins;
On them were painted heroic exploits
Of warriors from times gone by;
Dangerous pitched battles, ferocious
Duels—they were fearful pictures;
But as the Hindu saw them, straight away
He feasted his eyes on the grim display.

75   His questions began, but da Gama first
Begged him to be seated, and sample
The pleasures of eating and drinking
Like a true-born Epicurean.
Wine, which was first made by Noah,*
Was poured for him from foaming jugs;
But our foods he was compelled to reject
As forbidden by the doctrines of his sect.

76   Trumpets, evoking even in peacetime
Warlike images, burst on the air;
The cannon's diabolical thunder
Shuddered from the depths of the sea.
The Catual took note; but his eyes
Were riveted on the unique
Deeds which, in that eloquent gallery,
Were depicted in such silent poetry.

77   He rose, and with da Gama to one side,
Coelho and the African to the other,
He examined the martial figure
Of a noble, white-haired veteran,
Whose name will never be extinct
While human society survives;
His costume was wholly Greek in manner;
In his right hand was a branch like a banner.

78   In his right hand was a branch . . . *But what
Blind folly is this that I embark,
On a voyage so hard, so long and varied
Without you, nymphs of Tagus and Mondego?
I implore your help, for I am sailing
The open sea with a wind so contrary
That, if you cease to inspire and maintain me,
My slight craft will no longer sustain me.*

79   *Consider the years I have spent, singing
Of your Tagus and your Lusitanians,
While Fortune kept me drifting
From one task and trial to the next,
Now tossed on the ocean, now suffering
The inhuman torments of war,
Like Cânace's* last letter to her brother,
Pen in one hand, a sword in the other.*

80 *Now banished, in hateful poverty,*
    To long exile under alien roofs;
    Now, just as prospects seemed mature,
    Dashed more than ever in my hopes;
    Now, my life on a thread, surviving
    Shipwreck* by no less a miracle
    Than the extra years given to Hezekiah,*
    As promised by the prophet Isaiah!

81 *And yet, my nymphs, it was not enough*
    To plague me with such sufferings,
    But that the very men whose deeds I praised
    Should reward my poetry as they did:
    Where I had hoped to exchange toil
    For honours and wreaths of laurel,
    Labours undreamed of they devised for me
    Encompassing my present misery!

82 *Observe, O nymphs, what perspicacity*
    Your Tagus nurtures in its worthies,
    That they deluge with such favours
    He who extols them in his song!
    What an incentive to future poets
    To quicken enquiry and skill,
    And keep before the nation's memory
    Those deeds which deserve eternal glory!

83 *So now, beset by such evils, your*
    Bounty must not fail me, especially
    Now I approach a canto where
    Further achievements must be praised.
    Give but yourselves. I return my oath
    I shall not waste it on the worthless,
    Nor spend flattery on today's favourite.
    No matter how spitefully they savour it.

84 *Have no qualms, nymphs, that I will squander*
    Metaphors on that man who places
    Self interest above king and commonwealth,
    Against divine and human law.
    Nor will I praise the ambitious
    Courtier who seeks exalted office,
    Only to place himself above complaint
    Indulging his every vice without constraint.

85   *Nor he who employs authority only*
     To attain his foul ambitions,
     Nor he who, to remain popular
     Is more adaptable than Proteus;
     Nor fear, my muses, I will praise
     Those who adopt grave, honest faces,
     To please their king and uphold the law
     Only to harass and despoil the poor;

86   *Nor he who thinks it just and politic*
     To enforce the king's decrees strictly,
     And does not consider it good and fair
     To reward the sweat of the workers;
     Nor that incompetent bureaucrat
     Who preens himself as prudent and thrifty,
     Taxing with his exorbitant demands
     Labours to which he never turned his hands.

87   *They alone shall fill my song who,*
     For God and king, ventured life itself,
     And when they lost it, won the honour
     And fame their achievements deserve.
     Apollo and the Muses, who have
     Travelled with me, will fire me anew,
     Having taken this brief interval of rest,
     To return to my task with redoubled zest.

Canto Eight

1   By the first of the paintings,* the Catual
Paused, to study the figure who bore
In his hand a green branch as an emblem,
His long beard white and spruce;
Who was he and what was declared
By that device he was carrying?
In a wise voice, Paulo annotated
And the wise Mauretanian translated.

2   —'All these figures depicted here,
In such magnificent, bold colours
Were yet more bold and magnificent
In their real lives and exploits;
They are ancient figures, but their names
Stand out among the greatest;
This is Lusus,* from whose legendary fame
Our kingdom Lusitania took its name.

3   'He was son and companion of Bacchus
Whose conquests took him to so many realms;
He wandered to his Iberian home
In his profession as a soldier;
The fertile lands between Douro and Guadiana,
Then named Elysium,* so pleased him,
He gave his weary bones eternal rest,
And our name as his perpetual bequest.

4   'The branch you see him bear as a token
Is the green thyrsus, symbol of Bacchus,
A reminder to our own times
He was his comrade and loved son.
See another figure,* by the Tagus,
Having for so long ploughed the seas;
He is raising time-defying walls,
And a shrine to Pallas memory recalls.

5   'This is Ulysses; the altar is sacred
    To the goddess who taught him eloquence;
    If there in Asia he burned great Troy,
    Here in Europe he founded fair Lisbon.'
    —'But who is this other, strewing
    The plain with corpses in his fury,
    Scattering battalions, bearing regal
    Standards inscribed with Jupiter's eagle?'

6   So the Hindu asked. Da Gama replied:
    —'The one you see was once a shepherd;
    We know him as Viriathus, and more
    Skilled with the lance than the crook;
    Ancient Rome's great reputation
    Was tarnished by his conquests.
    They could not afford to be so chivalrous
    As they managed long ago with King Pyrrhus.

7   'Not in battle, but with foul treachery
    They killed the man they most feared;
    In times of crisis, even men of honour
    Will break the laws of chivalry.
    Here is another angry with Rome,
    Who, in exile, joined us in revolt;
    He took our part in choosing to rebel,
    But eternity declares he chose well.

8   'Watch him at our head, overwhelming
    Standards marked with the Roman eagle;
    For even then, the most martial peoples
    Learned from us the art of defeat.
    Observe the subtlety and guile
    He used to gain the people's support,
    Consulting a hind gifted in prediction:
    He is Sertorius and she his scutcheon.

9   'Now regard this banner, and see displayed
    Our first king's great ancestor;
    We believe him Hungarian, but others
    Claim his birthplace was Lorraine;
    Having shamed Galicia and León,
    In fighting the Moors, saintly Henrique
    Went to the Holy Land on pilgrimage
    To bring God's blessing on his lineage.'

10   —'Tell me,' asked the astonished Malabari,
     'Who is this next prodigious figure
     Routing so many squadrons, devastating
     Such vast armies with so few men?
     Razing such rugged battlements,
     Never tiring of taking battle
     To so many countries, so many towns
     And cities, trampling such standards, such crowns!'

11   —'That is Afonso the First,' said da Gama,
     'Who seized all Portugal from the Moors,
     Of whom Fate herself swore by the Styx
     To forget her old favourites of Rome.
     He was the zealous one, loved by God,
     Who harried the Moors with his mighty arm
     Till all their strongholds yielded to defeat,
     Leaving nothing for his heirs to complete.

12   'Had Caesar, had Alexander commanded
     Such small resources, such tiny armies
     Against the multitudes put to flight
     By this most excellent warrior,
     Do you believe their glory would have
     Spread so far and endured so long?
     But enough of what defies explanation;
     His vassals also merit admiration.

13   'Such as this one gazing furiously
     At his beaten and truculent ward,
     Bidding him collect his scattered army
     And march back to the field just quit;
     The youth turns, with the old man,
     And the defeated become the victors:
     That fierce old man is Egas Moniz,
     The paragon of ancient fealties.

14   'Watch him surrender with his sons,
     A noose on his neck, his silks discarded,
     Because the young king would not submit
     To Castile, as the old man pledged.
     With prudence and foresight, he raised
     The siege, by then all but forfeit;
     His sons and his wife will pay the cost:
     To redeem his liege lord, he must be lost.

15   'Consul Postumius* did not match this,
      Caught by surprise in the Caudine Forks,
      And compelled to bow the head beneath
      The triumphal arch of the Samnites.
      With his army facing catastrophe,
      Steadfast and true, he surrendered himself;
      But Egas stood to forfeit more than life,
      Pledging himself, his sons, and his blameless wife.

16   'Do you see this one, sallying from ambush
      To fall on the king besieging the fort?
      He takes the king and the town is relieved:
      An exploit worthy of Mars!
      Here you see him again, this time at sea
      With the fleet, overwhelming the Moors,
      Capturing their galleys, claiming the glory
      Of Portugal's first naval victory:

17   'It is Dom Fuas Roupinho,* who on land
      And sea was equally resplendent,
      When, under the heights of Ceuta itself,
      Fires rose from the Moorish galleys.
      See how in so just and holy a war
      He is content to die fighting;
      And so his soul, dispatched by Muslim arms,
      Triumphs in heaven with a victor's palms.

18   'Do you see this band in foreign armour*
      Disembarking from a powerful fleet
      To support our first king in the battle
      For Lisbon, and so fulfil their crusade?
      Look at Heinrich, famous German knight,
      With the palm springing next to his tomb!
      So with a miracle, God determines
      The great faith of the martyred Germans.

19   'Now a priest, look, brandishing a sword
      Against Arronches, which he captures
      In revenge for Leiria, taken by those
      Who bloody their lances for Mohammed.
      He is Prior Teotónio.* Now study
      Santarém under siege, and observe
      The courage of the first to scale the wall
      Raising the five-shield flag of Portugal.

20 'See him again, in Sancho's campaign
    Against the Moors of Andalusia,
    Shattering the enemy, killing the ensign,
    And trampling the pennant of Seville:
    It is Mem Moniz,* whose valour copied
    That buried with his father's bones;
    He earned those standards, for he never failed
    Trampling the enemy's while his own prevailed.

21 'Watch this one, shinning down his lance
    Back to the ambush, with the heads
    Of the two watchmen, and so captures
    Évora with subterfuge and daring;
    That city has taken for its armorial
    That warrior with the two heads
    Cold in his hand (unique and chilling sight!):
    Gerald the Fearless* is that fearful knight.

22 'Do you see this Castilian?* He quarrelled
    With Afonso the Ninth over his feud
    With the house of Lara, and joined
    The Moors to become Portugal's enemy.
    Here, with the infidels in his train,
    He seizes the town of Abrantes,
    But observe! A Portuguese with a small
    Detachment, captures him and routs them all!

23 'Martim Lopes is that knight's name
    Who stole the Castilians' palm and laurel.
    Now watch this warrior Bishop* change
    His gold crosier for a steel lance:
    See him among the waverers, resolute
    In taking battle to the brave Moors;
    Behold God's sign, manifest overhead,
    Putting heart into the scant troops he led.

24 'See the kings of Córdoba and Seville
    Routed, and two others at a stroke.
    Routed? Killed rather: a miracle
    Wrought by God, not human hand!
    See also the town of Alcácer, humbled
    Despite its defences and walls of steel;
    Lisbon's Dom Mateus, is that fighter,
    Adding a crown of palms to his mitre.

25 'Here a Portuguese Master of the Order
Of Santiago,* returns from Castile
To conquer the land of the Algarves,
Finding no one to withstand him;
With guile, courage, and fortune's blessing,
See him capturing cities and castles.
See Tavira taken for the abuse
Of murdering Christians at a time of truce;

26 'See how cleverly he wins back Silves
Occupied by a host of Moors;
He is Dom Paio Correia, envied
By all for his skill and courage.
And do not miss these three knights,*
Perpetually famous for leaving behind
Trophies of their prowess with sword and lance
In jousts and tourneys throughout Spain and France.

27 'Observe them descending on Castile,
Preceded by reputation, and lifting
Every prize in the serious game
Of war, with great harm to some;
See lying dead the proud knights
Who challenged the chief of the three,
Gonçalo Ribeiro, a name that will live on,
Conquering Lethe's rule of oblivion.

28 'But now attend, for here is a man*
Fame prefers beyond all the ancients;
When the fatherland hung by a thread
He sustained it on his strong shoulders.
Do you see him, red with anger, rebuking
The people for their leaden distrust,
Goading them to accept the gentle rein
Of their true king, and not a king from Spain?

29 'Then observe how, with prudence and daring,
Guided in his destiny only by God,
Alone he did what seemed impossible:
He defeated the might of Castile.
Here you see fresh havoc, new victories
Won by toil, strength, and valour,
Against the countless people of Andalusia,
Between the Guadiana and Guadalquivir.

30 'Can you not see a Portuguese army
   On the verge of defeat, all because
   The devout captain has withdrawn in prayer
   To invoke the blessed Trinity?
   Look how his men pursue him in panic,
   Saying there is no resisting
   Such numbers, and pleading with him to act
   To restore them the fortitude they lacked.

31 'Watch how, with saintly assurance, he
   Answers: "It is not yet the moment",
   As one relying wholly on God
   For the victory He would shortly grant.
   So Pompilius,* learning with what forces
   The enemy were overrunning the land,
   Replied to those who brought such dire advice,
   "Now is the time for prayer and sacrifice."

32 'Should you wish to discover his name
   Who dares so much, with such faith in God,
   "Portugal's Scipio" he could be called,
   But Dom Nuno Álvares is the greater title.
   Happy the fatherland with such a son,
   Or better, father; for while there exist
   Land or sea to shed its warmth upon,
   The sun itself will yearn for such a son.

33 'Here in the same war, gathering booty
   Is another captain* with a small band;
   He defeats the commanders of two orders
   Retrieving the cattle they plundered;
   Witness his lance dipped yet again
   In Castilian blood, to liberate
   His captive friend, captive through being loyal;
   He is Pero Rodrigues do Landroal.

34 'Note Paio Rodrigues* and how he paid
   For his treachery and foul deceit;
   Gil Fernandes from Elvas defeated him
   And exacted the supreme penalty;
   The fields of Jerez were saturated
   With the blood of their Castilian lords;
   While Rui Pereira, there in the tide race,
   Held off the galleys with his very face.

35   'And here you see seventeen Portuguese*
       Holding this hill, and mounting defence
       Against four hundred Castilians
       Who encircle them, but cannot take them;
       Soon they find, to their cost, such men
       Can more than defend, they can attack:
       An action fit to be forever known
       As much in ancient times as in our own!

36   'We know in the past a mere three hundred
       Battled against a thousand Romans,
       In the days when the virile deeds
       Of Viriathus* were so much on display
       When, beyond gaining memorable
       Victories, they left us this injunction,
       That size and strength should never be equated,
       As has a thousand times been demonstrated.

37   'Now behold two princes,* Pedro
       And Henrique, the splendid sons of King João:
       Pedro in Germany won for himself
       The fame which eclipses death itself;
       Henrique, the renowned Navigator,
       Explored and charted oceans, starting
       At Ceuta, pricking the Moors' vanity,
       Being the first to penetrate that city.

38   'Here is Count Pedro,* defending Ceuta
       Twice against the might of Barbary;
       And here Duarte, his son, for strength
       And daring, a very Mars incarnate;
       It was not enough that he protected
       Alcácer-Ceguer from a mighty host,
       For he saved his king's life, which he cherished
       More than his own, shielding him, and perished.

39   'And there are many others the artist
       Might have elected to portray here,
       But brush and colours were lacking, I mean
       The rewards and favours which nourish art.
       It is the fault of their descendants
       Who have, beyond a doubt, abandoned
       Their forefathers' gallantry and lustre,
       As vain in their tastes as in their bluster.

40 'Those famous ancestors, from whom derive
The lineages which bear their names,
Founded by virtue of their virtues
The houses which descend from them.
How short-sighted they were! For though
Their own deeds and their fame endure,
They leave their descendants in obscurity,
Heirs to indifference and apathy.

41 'There are others among the rich and powerful
Undistinguished in their lineage:
Kings are to blame, rewarding favourites
Many times more than valour and wisdom.
Such do not wish their fathers painted
For the colours would not be flattering;
While nothing in nature so provokes their hate
As painting with words, the poet's fate.

42 'I do not deny there exist offspring
Of these noble lines and rich houses,
Whose worthy, blameless conduct
Sustains the name they have inherited;
And if the torch of their ancestors
Does not blaze as it did formerly,
It has, at least, not completely died away,
But the painter finds too few of them today.'

43 So da Gama expounded the great deeds
Rendered there in different colours
By the skilled hand of the painter,
With such rare and convincing artifice.
The Catual's eyes were spellbound
By history so well displayed:
He pressed hard upon our answers in his haste
To learn of battles so much to his taste.

44 But now in the divided light of dusk
As the sun's great beacon sank
Slowly beneath the horizon, to dawn
In the antipodes with another day,
The Catual and the noble company
Of Nairs took leave of the warship,
Seeking that rest which furnishes respite
To weary creatures in the peace of night.

45   Meanwhile, the king's soothsayers,
      Always venerated by the superstitious
      For reading in their false sacrifices
      Diabolical clues to the future,
      Were, at the king's command, zealously
      Practising their office and art
      About the arrival of these strange men
      From Iberia, a land not known till then.

46   The Devil, honest for once, revealed
      The newcomers would indeed impose
      A perpetual yoke, eternal bondage,
      Destroying the people and their power.
      Astonished, the augur rushed to the king,
      With his terrifying interpretation
      Of the dreadful portents he detected
      In all the victims' entrails inspected.

47   Allied to him was a priest, a devoted
      Follower of the law of Mohammed,
      Whose hatred for the supreme Faith
      Was as new-found as it was extreme;
      In the likeness of that false prophet,
      Descended from the line of Ishmael,
      To this priest, divine Bacchus, who kept
      His own hatred warm, appeared as he slept.

48   And told him: 'Be on your guard, my people,
      Against the designs of this enemy
      Who have travelled such watery highways
      Before danger looms any closer.'
      As he whispered, the Muslim
      Awoke suddenly, shocked by his vision;
      But then, thinking it but a dream, he went
      Quietly back to sleep, calm and content.

49   Bacchus returned: 'Do you not recognize
      The great lawgiver, Mohammed,
      Who revealed to your fathers the faith
      You obey, rather than be baptized?
      I watch over you, peasant, yet you sleep on!
      Understand that, through these upstarts,
      The laws I gave to ignorant mankind
      Will soon be desecrated and maligned.

50 'While they are still weak in number,
Oppose them in every way you can;
When the sun first rises, it is easy
To stare directly at its beams;
But when it is dazzling and incandescent,
The eyes are forced to turn aside
To avoid blindness: such will be the fruit
Of this business if not attacked at root.'

51 With these words, he and the vision vanished;
The Ishmaelite was aghast. Leaping
From bed, he called his servants for a lamp,
With the poison coursing through his veins.
As soon as dawn's earliest light
Unveiled her serene, angelic face,
He summoned the priests of the unredeemed
And gave a strict account of all he dreamed.

52 Many conflicting opinions were voiced
As each proposed what he thought;
Various plots, ingenious tactics,
And treacheries were elaborated;
But rejecting the more headstrong
Methods of destroying the Portuguese,
They took the option subtlety prescribes,
Suborning the king's counsellors with bribes.

53 With bribes, of gold and other seductions,
They co-opted the country's rulers,
And with sophistry persuaded them
Of the ruin the Portuguese would bring,
Declaring they were restless people
Who, spilling from the seas of the west,
Lived lawlessly by piracy and rapine,
Without king or country, human or divine.

54 To govern well, how much a monarch
Must guard that his counsellors and friends
Are men of rectitude and genuine
Honour and absolute devotion!
For placed as he is, elevated
On his throne of state, he knows
Little more of his kingdom or his court
Than what his ministers choose to report.

55   This is not to say he should take on trust
       That all-too-apparent rectitude
       Which wraps itself in a humble cloak,
       Disguising, perhaps, ambition.
       Even the truly righteous and saintly.
       Give poor advice on worldly matters;
       Such men, fixed wholly on what is holy,
       Have little wit for human vice and folly.

56   And so these self-seeking Catuals
       The Hindu peoples' governors,
       Were induced by those infernal priests
       To prevaricate with the Portuguese.
       But while the Muslims were conspiring,
       Da Gama, having fulfilled his
       Voyage, was preoccupied by one thing:
       To carry the sure proof back to his king.

57   He worked only for this, well aware
       That as soon evidence reached his hands,
       Arms, ships, and people would be sent
       By King Manuel, as supreme commander,
       To reduce to his yoke and to Christ's faith
       The whole expanse of lands and ocean;
       He, meanwhile, being merely a diligent
       Explorer of the distant Orient.

58   He resolved to speak with the Samorin
       And finish his business and go home,
       For already he sensed a disposition
       To oppose him in whatever he wished.
       As for the king, from the lies and slurs,
       One could guess why he was aghast,
       For his trust in what his augurs had read
       Was reinforced by all the Muslims said.

59   This fear chilled his ignoble heart;
       Countering it was the power of greed
       Which controlled his very nature,
       A burning greed which raged insatiably;
       He could envisage all the profit
       If, with truth and honour, he concluded
       The long-term treaty, just and mutual,
       Offered him by the King of Portugal.

60 But taking counsel on this matter,
   He found many opposing opinions,
   For on those from whom he sought advice,
   Money was exerting its power.
   He summoned da Gama and pronounced
   As he arrived: 'If here and now,
   In my presence, hiding nothing, you confess,
   You will be pardoned for your wickedness.

61 'My informers tell me the document
   You presented from your king is forged,
   For you have no king, nor loved homeland,
   But live the life of a vagabond;
   What king or lord so far away,
   In the utmost west would commit such folly
   As to venture not just a ship but a fleet
   On a voyage so distant, so indiscreet?

62 'Suppose there exists some great king
   Holding sway over mighty realms,
   What precious gifts* do you bring me
   As proof of your improbable claim?
   Sumptuous fabrics, magnificent gifts
   Are what seal the friendship of rulers;
   So far, every proposal we have heard
   Hangs on a wandering mariner's word.

63 'If, by chance, you come here as exiles
   Having once been men of high fortune,
   You will be guests in my kingdom,
   For to the brave all the world is home;
   Or if you are pirates on the high seas,
   Admit it, without fearing blame or death,
   Because all men, in every age, contrive
   To act as best equips them to survive.'

64 As he finished, da Gama, who had quickly
   Guessed that only Muslim intrigue
   Could be the source of the insinuations
   To which the king had given voice,
   With the confidence the case demanded,
   Advancing his credit, was inspired
   By Venus of Acidalia* to impart
   These words of wisdom from a steadfast heart:

65   —'Had not the crimes which sinful Man
     Committed in the earliest age
     Caused that vessel of iniquity,
     That cruel scourge of Christendom,
     To sow with his lies perpetual hatred
     Among Adam's sons, then you, O king,
     Would never have descended to suspect
     The things alleged by this dangerous sect.

66   'Because no venture is carried forward
     Without vexations, and in every quest
     Fear follows in hope's footsteps
     And only sweat keeps hope alive,
     You allow yourself scant confidence
     In my good faith, without considering
     The counter-arguments which would seem just
     Had you not trusted men you should not trust.

67   'For to be frank, were I a buccaneer.
     Roaming the seas in perpetual exile,
     Why do you think I should voyage so far
     Seeking so unknown and remote a port?
     From what ambition, or for what motive,
     Would I come risking turbulent seas,
     Antarctic blizzards, or the sultry rays
     Endured beneath the sign of Aries?*

68   'If you ask for gifts of great worth
     As the warrant for what I report,
     I come as simply as explorer, to find
     Where nature placed your ancient kingdom;
     But if Fortune should so reward me
     That I behold my dear king and country,
     You will see then what merchandise you earn
     As the sure evidence of my return.

69   'If it seems beyond belief that a king
     In the Hesperides sends me to you,
     That noble heart, that royal breast
     Rejects what is merely possible.
     Indeed, it appears the exalted aims
     Of the Lusitanian spirit require
     Larger ambitions, faith of a higher state,
     Before crediting a feat as truly great.

70 'Learn, then, it is many decades since
Our former kings first determined
To surmount the toils and dangers
That attend all great achievements;
And, exploring the ocean, that enemy
Of repose, they took as their goal
To locate the seas' frontiers, to behold
The uttermost beaches where breakers rolled.

71 'It was a task worthy of the brilliant
Son of our most favoured King João,
Who first crossed the sea to drive
From their homes the people of Ceuta.
Then Henrique, by industry and genius,
Built and dispatched ship after ship
To investigate the southern hemisphere*
Of Argo, Hydra, Ara, and the Hare.

72 'Fired by their first successes to take
Still greater risks, voyage by voyage
They discovered new seaways which,
Ship after ship, they explored;
In the far south where the Pleiades
Never dawn, we saw the remotest peoples
Of Africa, leaving astern legions
Of the sun-scorched in the tropic regions.

73 'And so, with steadfast hearts and great
Ends in view, we conquered Fortune
And reached your distant country
To plant the last of our stone columns;
Conquering the power of dead calms,
Of sudden and awesome tempests,
We have voyaged to your court. I have spoken.
What remains is to take my king some token.

74 'This, king, is the truth; were it
Otherwise, I would not spin so long
And so fanciful a yarn, for such
Uncertain benefit, so feeble a reward.
It would, indeed, profit me more
To spend my days as a pirate
On the never-resting bosom of the sea,
Amassing wealth from others' industry.

75   'And so, O king, if you accept my story
     For what it is, free of deceit,
     Grant me your reply, and soon,
     To speed my pleasure in returning home;
     Or if it still appears falsehood,
     Judge by reason, by what can be proved,
     Which an open mind will always recognize
     For truth declares itself without disguise.'

76   The Samorin was struck by the confidence
     Which reinforced all da Gama said;
     And began to give complete credit
     To everything he had asserted.
     He pondered the sufficiency of his words
     Sensing their great authority;
     And judged his Catuals wrong in what they warned,
     Not comprehending they had been suborned.

77   That, with his greed for the profits
     Expected from the Portuguese treaty,
     Led him to trust and respect the captain
     And not the Muslim conspiracy.
     At length, he bade da Gama return
     Directly to the ships, secure from harm,
     And send ashore whatever merchandise
     He wished to sell, or to exchange for spice.

78   He begged especially for textiles
     Not found in the kingdoms of the Ganges,
     If he had brought anything fine from there
     Where the land ends and the sea begins.
     Then, taking leave of the royal presence,
     The captain returned to the Catual,
     His custodian, but had to implore
     A boat to convey him, his being offshore.

79   A boat he requested, to re-embark;
     But the churlish governor, planning
     Fresh obstacles, interposed problems
     And delays, conceding him nothing.
     He escorted him as far as the quay,
     Well beyond earshot of the king,
     Where he could risk exposing his malice
     Without tidings returning to the palace.

80 There, at a safe distance, he promised
A boat suitable for da Gama's purpose,
But not today; till tomorrow's light
He should postpone his departure.
By now, the captain was well aware
From such tardiness, the Hindu made one
With the stratagems the Muslims had devised,
Something he had not fully realized.

81 For this Catual was another of those
Bought over by the Muslim leaders,
Being the chief of those governing
The cities of the powerful Samorin;
From him principally the Muslims hoped
For success in their wicked plans;
He was committed to their machinations
And did not fail them in their expectations.

82 Urgently, da Gama pressed his need
To return to the ships, but uselessly;
Despite this being the express order
Of Perimal's noble descendant.
Why was he prevented and delayed
From bringing the Portuguese goods ashore?
No subject had the right to countermand
Orders issued under the king's own hand.

83 The corrupted Catual paid scant heed
To such complaints, spinning instead
Elaborate day-dreams, subtle,
Ingenious, and diabolical, such
As bathing his sword in the blood
He detested, standing there before him,
Or burning the fleet down to the waterline
So no one would return to hearth and shrine.

84 That none should return home was the sole
Purpose of the Muslims' strategy,
So Portugal's king should never know
Where the lands of the east lay.
There da Gama remained, in the custody
Of those uncivil people's governor;
To leave without permission was denied him,
Canoe men forbidden to provide him.

85   To the captain's arguments and complaints,
The Catual replied he should instruct
The ships to anchor in shore
So he could come and go more freely.
—'It is a hostile act,' he said,
For the fleet to stand so far off;
'A sure and faithful friend would soon forget
He had been under any kind of threat.'

86   At these words, wary da Gama discerned
The Catual wanted the ships nearer
To storm them with fire and sword,
Venting his hatred in open attack.
He fell to weighing his various options,
Planning in advance with what
Feint to react whatever might befall;
So fearing all, he was prepared for all.

87   As the reflected light* from a mirror
Of burnished steel or lovely crystal,
A ray of sunlight, perhaps, glancing
Sideways to focus somewhere else,
Is directed by the idle hand
Of a curious youngster, up
Walls and across roof-tiles like a will-
o-the-wisp, ever-quivering, never still:

88   So da Gama, held captive, let his mind
Wander, and remembered Coelho*
Still, by chance, waiting on the beach
With boats as he had been ordered.
At once, he mandated him to leave
Secretly to return to the fleet,
And not to be caught napping by the plans
He foresaw of the fierce Mohammedans.

89   So must the captain be, who wishes
To copy or equal the great in war:
Flying in thought to every part,
Scenting dangers and averting them,
Knowing the enemy, and outwitting him
With strategy and subtle design;
Considering all, in sum: for he who says
'I failed to foresee that,' forfeits any praise.

90   The Malabari continued to imprison him
     Till he ordered the ships inshore;
     But da Gama was fired with noble anger
     And was in no way cowed by his threats;
     Rather, he sought to take on himself
     Whatever malice or dishonour
     Was mounting, than to put in jeopardy
     The king's fleet, riding beyond harm at sea.

91   All that night he was detained there
     And part of the day, when he resolved
     To return to the king; but his guard
     Was large enough to prevent him.
     The Hindu then tried another tactic,
     By now fearing to be punished
     For his plots, of which the Samorin would know
     Unless very soon he let da Gama go.

92   He insisted all the commodities
     We had on board should be landed
     To be traded or bartered at leisure,
     For to deny commerce was to declare war.
     Though he saw clearly the evil motive
     Concealed in this, da Gama agreed,
     For he recognized at once that a handsome
     Show of merchandise could be his ransom.

93   They agreed the Catual should provide
     Boats suitable for conveying the goods,
     For he did not wish to risk his own
     Where the enemy might detain them.
     So canoes set out accordingly
     To ferry the Iberian wares,
     And he told his brother* to be sure to send
     Means to bring his entrapment to an end.

94   The goods were brought ashore and at once
     The corrupt Catual took them in charge;
     Álvaro and Diogo* accompanied them
     To sell them for what they were worth:
     But that profit mattered to him far more
     Than honour, orders, or obligation,
     The Catual showed to any who had eyes,
     Releasing da Gama for the merchandise.

95   He freed him, convinced he had in hand
     Sufficient stake to guarantee him
     Greater gain than would accrue
     By detaining the captain longer.
     Da Gama accepted it would be foolish
     To return ashore and risk being
     Re-imprisoned, so having boarded ship.
     He rested and reflected on his trip.

96   He stayed with the fleet, relaxing
     Until the future should declare itself,
     For he put no trust in the avaricious,
     Corrupt, and ignoble governor.
     Here discerning judges may consider
     How, with the rich as with the poor,
     Vile self-interest and the sordid thirst
     For gold compels us to our very worst.

97   The king of Thrace* murdered Polydorus
     Solely to command his great treasure;
     Jupiter breached the walls protecting
     Acrisius' daughter as a shower of gold;
     Avarice worked on Tarpeia so grimly
     That, for payment in gold bracelets,
     She betrayed to the Sabines Rome's guard
     And perished under the weight of her reward.

98   Gold conquers the strongest citadels,
     Turns friends into traitors and liars;
     Persuades the noblest to acts of infamy,
     Betraying their leaders to the enemy;
     It corrupts maidens, who ignore
     The threat to honour or reputation;
     Even scholarship at times has been bought,
     Blinding discernment and impartial thought.

99   It glosses and glozes authorities
     Subtly making and unmaking laws;
     It leads people to perjure themselves
     And makes tyrants of a thousand kings;
     Even of those sworn only to God
     Countless more times you will hear
     How this enchanter can corrupt and tarnish,
     But all the while preserving virtue's varnish!

Canto Nine

1   The two factors remained in the city
    Many days without trading the goods,
    For the Muslims, mixing guile and falsehood,
    Ensured no merchant would buy them:
    Their whole purpose and intention
    Was to detain the discoverers, until
    The annual fleet from Mecca should descend
    Bringing Portuguese endeavours to an end.

2   Far off in the Red Sea, where Ptolemy*
    The Egyptian once founded Arsinoe
    —Naming it after his sister, though
    It was afterwards better known as Suez—
    Nearby is the port of the famous
    City of Mecca, which came to greatness
    Because its well of Zemzem was rumoured
    Wholly belonging, and holy to Mohammed.

3   Jidda is that port's name, centre
    Of the Red Sea's flourishing trade,
    A large source of agreeable
    Profit to the Sultan of that realm.
    From Jidda to the Indian Ocean
    Under contract to the Malabaris,
    A great fleet, sailing on the monsoons, made
    Its annual voyage* in the spice trade.

4   These ships, the Muslims hoped, given
    Their great size and number, would oust
    The interlopers seizing the commerce
    In sheets of crackling flames.
    So much they trusted in this recourse,
    They sought nothing more than to delay
    The navigators, letting them survive
    Until the fleet from Mecca could arrive.

5   But the Ruler of Heaven and of mankind
    Who, in whatever He has ordained,
    Finds in advance some suitable means
    To accomplish what is determined,
    Made certain impulses work in the mind
    Of Monsayeed, who became His instrument,
    Alerting da Gama (for which advice
    The Moor deserves to enter Paradise).

6   Being a Muslim, and one from whom
    His fellow Muslims had no reserves
    (Having been party to former intrigues),
    He knew what mischief they were plotting.
    Many times he had visited the ships
    Offshore, and was distressed
    And saddened by the unfair stratagem
    The malign Saracens had in store for them.

7   So he told wary da Gama of the ships
    Which sailed each year from Arabian Mecca,
    And which his own people now awaited
    As the agents of their planned assault;
    He said the Arabs came heavily manned
    And armed with Vulcan's thunderbolts;
    There was no knowing how the fleet would fare
    If they attacked before he could prepare.

8   Da Gama had already begun to sense
    Time and the elements beckoned departure,
    And not now expecting any proposals
    From a king governed by the Muslims,
    He gave strict orders to the factors
    To return at once to the ships,
    But advised, lest they should be forbidden,
    To keep their plans and preparations hidden.

9   Even so, it was not long before rumours
    Did take wing, and with substance,
    That the factors had been captured
    As they were seen quitting the city.
    When news reached the captain's ears
    He seized as hostages those merchants
    Who regularly to the ships would throng
    To trade the precious stones they brought along.

10   These merchants were long established,
      Wealthy, and well known in Calicut;
      Being missed among the men of substance
      News spread they were detained at sea.
      Meanwhile in the ships, the crew
      Were turning the winch, dividing
      Their tasks, some at the capstan taking strain,
      Others hauling the heavy anchor chain,

11   While yet others hung from the yardarm,
      Unfurling the mainsail like a thunderclap
      When, amid greater uproar, the king
      Was told the ships had weighed anchor.
      Panicking, the wives and children,
      Of the hostages stormed the palace
      Besieging the Samorin, as they yelled
      About husbands and fathers that were held.

12   At once, he set the Portuguese factors
      Free with all their merchandise,
      Overruling the hostile Muslims
      To get his own imprisoned people back,
      And apologized for his treachery;
      Da Gama welcomed the factors more
      Than the apologies, then, having put
      Some men ashore, he sailed from Calicut.

13   He sailed by the south coast, reflecting
      He had laboured in vain* for a treaty
      Of friendship with the Hindu king,
      To guarantee peace and commerce;
      But at least those lands stretching
      To the dawn were now known to the world,
      And at long last his men were homeward bound
      With proofs on board of the India he had found.

14   For he had some Malabaris, seized
      From those dispatched by the Samorin
      When he returned the imprisoned factors;
      He had hot peppers he had purchased;
      There was mace from the Banda Islands;
      Then nutmeg and black cloves, pride
      Of the new-found Moluccas, and cinnamon,
      The wealth, the fame, the beauty of Ceylon.

15 He obtained these through the diligence
    Of Monsayeed, who was also on board,
    Desiring, through heaven's influence,
    To be written in the book of Christ.
    O happy African, whom divine
    Mercy rescued from his ignorance,
    And, so far from his homeland, was blessed
    With the means of gaining eternal rest.

16 So there sailed away from the torrid coast
    Those happy ships, turning their prows
    To where nature ordained her southern
    Outpost at the Cape of Good Hope,
    Bearing to Lisbon the joyous news
    And the response of the Orient,
    Fearful, facing a second time the sea's
    Hardships, but hopeful and with minds at ease.

17 The joy of reaching their dear homeland,
    Their cherished hearths and families,
    To reminisce about their far-flung
    Voyage, the various climes and peoples;
    Grasping at last the prize attained
    Through such travail and such dangers,
    For each man the delight was so complete
    His brimming heart had scarcely room to beat.

18 Venus the Cyprian, meanwhile, ordained
    By Jupiter to guard the Portuguese
    And serve as their presiding genius,
    Having many years been their guide,
    Wished now, as reward for their exploits,
    And to compensate their sufferings,
    To provide with every power in her employ
    On the dreary seas an interval of joy.*

19 And after turning a little in her mind
    What vast oceans they had navigated,
    What obstacles, what extra toils,
    Had been caused by Theban-born Bacchus,
    She resolved to indulge an old scheme
    To crown their efforts by creating
    Some haven of enchantment and repose
    In that crystal element from which she rose;

20 Some restful harbour where her sailors
    Could restore their spent humanity,
    Some recompense for exertions such as
    Snip the brief span of our lives.
    It seemed right to involve her son
    Cupid, for through his great powers
    Even deities are dragged through the mire
    While humans soar on pinions of desire.

21 Considering this, she resolved further
    To make ready for them, in the midst
    Of the sea, some divine, enchanted
    Isle adorned with greenery and flowers.
    For she owned many* in the various
    Oceans washing the earth's shores,
    As well as those subject to her decrees
    Enclosed within the gates of Hercules.

22 There she intended the sea nymphs
    Should wait upon the mighty heroes
    —All of them lovely beyond compare,
    The eyes' delight, the heart's longing—
    With dances and singing, secretly
    Working on the nymphs' affections
    So with redoubled zeal, each would endeavour
    To please her beloved mariner, whoever . . .

23 Such a device* she had once invoked
    To greet Anchises' son, Aeneas,
    In that meadow where Dido's subtlety
    Bought Carthage with a bull's hide.
    She sought out Cupid, whose powers alone
    Availed her in these matters and who,
    Having often in the past done much the same,
    Was eager to comply and join her game.

24 She yoked to her chariot white swans
    Whose lives are spent lamenting their death;
    And doves, like that to which Peristera*
    Was transformed as she gathered daisies;
    Around the goddess in her aerial
    Journey, kisses were exchanged;
    Wherever she passed, her gentle influence
    Calmed the restless winds and left a silence.

25   Soon she was over the hills of Cyprus
      Where her archer son was even then
      Marshalling a force of lesser cupids
      For an expedition against mankind
      To punish the heresy, still prevalent
      In these present days, of expending
      All their passion (for so they were accused)
      On things intended merely to be used.

26   He saw Actaeon,* so austere in the chase,
      So blind in his brutish pleasures,
      That, to pursue ugly, ferocious beasts
      He shunned the lovely female form;
      As harsh, sweet punishment, he planned
      To unveil to him Diana's beauty;
      Take care, Actaeon you are not supper for
      The very dogs you now so much adore!

27   He saw, throughout the world, not one
      Ruler anxious for the public good;
      Whatever love they felt was for
      Themselves and for others like them;
      He saw that instead of honest truth
      The hangers-on at palaces peddle
      Flattery, which serves no prince's need
      To separate the growing wheat from weed.

28   He saw those whose duty was to show
      God's love to the poor and charity to all,
      Fawning instead on power and wealth,
      In a parody of truth and justice;
      They call foul tyranny order,
      And false severity firmness,
      Passing laws in the interest of the king,
      While the rights of the people are decreasing.

29   He saw, in short, none loving what they should
      But all led astray by perverse desires;
      And was no longer willing to postpone
      Their harsh but fitting punishment;
      He summoned reinforcements, to take
      To battle sufficient levies
      To establish a proper sense of awe
      In all those disobedient to his law.

30   Many of these diminutive flyers
Were engaged in various preparations
Some grinding the points on iron darts,
Some whittling the shafts of arrows.
Working, they sang harmoniously
Of love's curious workings;
Smooth are the verses, heavenly the tune,
When measured lines and tempered parts commune.

31   In the immortal smithy they forge
The piercing barbs for the arrows;
For fuel, they use burning hearts,
Still palpitating with ardour;
The waters in which the iron is tempered
Are the tears of unhappy lovers;
The living flame, the undiminished fire
Which burns without consuming, is desire.

32   To try their hand, some experiment
On the stony hearts of peasants;
The air hums with the repeated sighs
Of those wounded by the arrows;
Lovely nymphs are at hand to cure
Wounds so received, for their succour
Not only reinvigorates the lovelorn,
But stimulates to life the yet-unborn.

33   Some are beautiful, and others ugly
According to the nature of the wound,
For the poison spreading through the veins
Demands at times drastic treatment;
Some of the victims lie bound in chains,
Through the subtle spells of magicians.
This especially baffles and disturbs
When the arrows are tipped with certain herbs.

34   From shafts so careless and haphazard
Fired by such inexpert cherubs,
Were born among their wounded victims
A thousand ill-assorted passions.
And even among the noblest were seen
Countless cases of profligate love,
Such as happened* to Byblis and Myrrha,
Assyrian Ninyas, and Amnon of Judaea.

35   How often have the hearts of potentates
Been smitten by various shepherdesses,
Or ladies, with rough, common lovers,
Been ensnared in Vulcan's net?*
Some spend their lives waiting for darkness;
Others scale walls and parapets;
But I believe that lovers so beguiled
Are more so by the mother than the child!

36   But now the white swans were bringing
Her chariot to rest in the lush meadow
And Venus, her countenance radiant
With roses among the snows, stepped down;
The archer, impudent to the heavens,
Welcomed her with a joyful smile;
All around him, his diminutive band
Saluted Love's goddess and kissed her hand.

37   Not wishing to waste time on courtesies,
She embraced her son, and addressed him
Freely: 'Beloved son, from whose hand
Now as always, all my powers derive;
You who proved fearless even against
The thunderbolts that killed Typhoeus,*
I come here of necessity to ask
Your expert help in a particular task.

38   'You see what hardships the Portuguese
Endure, whom I have so protected
Knowing from my friends, the Fates,
How they worshipped and esteemed me;
And because they copy so uncannily
The deeds of my old Romans, I propose
To show them every kindness, be benign
To the limits of our powers, yours and mine.

39   'And because Bacchus, so molested them
In India, with all his treacheries,
And because the heaving ocean alone
May leave them less exhausted than dead,
On those same seas which were always
A threat, I wish them to find repose,
And, for these labours, which can never perish,
Such a reward as memory will cherish.

40 'My request is this, that the daughters
    Of Nereus, in their watery depths,
    Should burn with love for the Portuguese
    Who came to discover the new world,
    And should assemble and await them
    On an island I am preparing
    In the midst of the ocean—one supplied
    With all Zephyr and Flora* can provide.

41 'There with every kind of food and drink,
    With fragrant wines, and sweet roses,
    In palaces of marvellous crystal,
    On lovely couches, themselves more lovely,
    In short, with countless special delights,
    The amorous nymphs should await them,
    Wounded by love, prepared to be tender
    To those who desire them, and surrender.

42 'I wish to populate* Neptune's realm
    Where I was born, with the strong and beautiful,
    And let the base and wicked world
    Which challenges your powers, take note,
    That neither walls of adamantine
    Nor hypocrisy can avail against it;
    For who will find on land any quarter
    If your fires rage unquenched in the water?'

43 So Venus proposed, and mischievous
    Cupid prepared at once to obey her;
    He called for his ivory-coloured bow
    And steeped the arrowheads in gold.
    With a happy, wanton air, the Cyprian
    Took her son into her chariot;
    Giving rein to the lovely birds* whose long
    Requiem for Phaethon is their swan-song.

44 But Cupid said he would need the help
    Of a certain, notorious go-between
    Who had countless times opposed him
    And as often been his companion:
    This was the giant goddess Fame,*
    Hot-blooded, boasting, lying, truthful,
    Who sees, as she goes, with a hundred eyes,
    Bringing a thousand mouths to propagandize.

45   They sought her out and sent her ahead
      To broadcast from her blaring trumpet
      Her acclamation of the mariners,
      More than any she had extolled before.
      Re-echoing, Fame penetrated
      To the deepest caverns of the ocean;
      She spoke the truth, and so it was received,
      Credulity helping her to be believed.

46   Such praises and the marvellous story
      Touched the hearts even of those gods
      Bacchus had incensed against the heroes,
      And inclined them in their favour;
      The goddesses, feminine and fickle
      About any opinion they had taken up,
      Now condemned it as cruel knavery
      To have wished evil on such bravery.

47   Now cruel Cupid fired one by one
      His shafts: the sea hummed with the arrows.
      Some went straight through the turbulent
      Waves, others curved to their mark;
      The nymphs capitulated, ardent sighs
      Issuing from their innermost hearts;
      Each was conquered before she saw her man
      For fame can do as much as seeing can.

48   Then bending his bow's ivory horns
      Ruthlessly, the indomitable boy,
      Struck Tethys most severely of all
      For she of all was the most disdainful.
      By now, his quiver was empty, nor
      Had one nymph survived in the seas,
      For if any of the wounded still bloomed,
      It was only to know that they were doomed.

49   But make way, you steep, cerulean waves,
      For look, Venus brings the remedy,
      In those white, billowing sails
      Scudding swiftly over Neptune's waters;
      Now ardent loving can assuage
      Female passion, which though constrained
      By what modest reluctance may require,
      Will do everything Venus could desire.

50   By now, the lovely troop of Nereids
Had arrayed themselves and voyaged
To the island, guided by Venus,
With choric dances in the old style.
There the goddess counselled them
In what she had done a thousand times;
Enslaved by love, and eager to entice,
They drank in every word of her advice.

51   The ships were ploughing their way over
The vast ocean to their dear homeland,
On the look-out for fresh water
For the prolonged voyage ahead,
When with sudden rapture, all at once,
Caught sight of the Isle of Love,
Just as Memnon's* radiant mother, the dawn
Was heralding a calm and delightful morn.

52   The lovely, verdant island hovered
As Venus wafted it over the waves
(As the wind will convey a white sail)
To where the ships were to be seen;
For to prevent their sailing past
Without making port, as she desired,
Wherever they went, she kept it full in view,
Shifting it, as she had the power to do.

53   But she anchored it on the instant
She saw the mariners speeding towards it,
As Delos* paused when Latona gave birth
To Apollo and Diana, the huntress.
The prows parted the waves to a bay
With a curving, tranquil beach,
Whose white sand, by another of her spells,
The goddess had bestrewn with rosy shells.

54   Three towering peaks came into sight
Thrusting upwards with a noble grace,
And draped with grassy enamel
On that lovely, happy, delightful island;
Clear streams, festooned with creepers,
Cascaded from the summits,
Until with soft gurgles and little moans
They bubbled gently over pearl-white stones.

55   Between the hills, in a pleasant valley,
     The translucent rivers came together
     To form a lagoon which stretched and brimmed
     With a beauty beyond imagining;
     A charming grove leaned over it
     As if sprucing up its appearance,
     Staring at its crystal-bright reflection,
     Which captured every detail to perfection.

56   Trees beyond number climbed to the sky
     With luscious, sweet-smelling fruits;
     The orange with its bright lanterns,
     The colour of Daphne's hair;
     Citron-trees, brushing the ground
     With the weight of their yellow burden;
     And fragrant, moulded lemons which, when pressed,
     Are curved and nippled like a maiden's breast.

57   Gracing the hills with their leafy crowns
     Were the various trees* of the forest:
     Hercules' sacred poplars, laurels
     Once loved and pursued by Apollo,
     Venus' myrtles, with Cybele's
     Pines, once her celibate lover,
     And tapering to the heavens, the cypress
     A signpost to perpetual happiness.

58   Nature, prodigal with her goods
     In all Pomona's* various guises,
     Careless of husbandry produced,
     Without it, more abundant harvests;
     Cherries, as purple as *amoras*,
     (Or mulberries, with their name of love);
     The peach, that apple found in Persian fields,
     But grown in exile gives much better yields.

59   Pomegranates gaped, exposing jewels
     Richer, redder than any rubies;
     Vines threaded the boughs of the elm
     With hanging clusters, purple and green;
     And pear trees were so heavily laden
     They took the shape of pyramids,
     Yielding to a myriad of birds, deft
     With their ravenous beaks, intent on theft.

60 As for the bright, flowery meadow
  Carpeting the untended ground,
  It exceeded Persia's finest
  As it graced the valley shade.
  Here Narcissus* drooped his head,
  Above his fated, flawless pool;
  And springing from Adonis'* wound, the flower
  The goddess sighs for, to this very hour.

61 It was hard to know, seeing in the earth
  And the heavens the self-same colours,
  Whether Dawn had given the flowers
  Their livery, or they her lovely pigments.
  Zephyr and Flora had painted there
  Violets in white, the lovers' colour;
  Lilies in scarlet, and the new-blown rose,
  Pink as the soft cheeks where it also grows;

62 There, too, the madonna lily, bedewed
  With dawn's tears, and marjoram,
  And hyacinths,* the flowers inscribed
  With the very letters of Apollo's grief.
  Such fruits and flowers made it plain
  Flora was rivalling Pomona.
  If birds were singing as they flew around,
  Joyful animals colonized the ground.

63 The snowy swan sang from the lake;
  From the bough, the nightingale replied;
  The sight of his horns did not alarm
  Actaeon staring in the crystal water;
  Here a swift hare, or timid gazelle,
  Broke suddenly from the thicket;
  There, with a laden beak, the linnet pressed
  Back with her gift of food to her dear nest.

64 Amidst all this fresh luxuriance,
  The second Argonauts disembarked,
  Where the lovely nymphs were strolling
  In the forests as if all unaware;
  Some were playing on sweet zithers;
  Some on harps or harmonious flutes;
  Others with gold bows feigned they pursued
  Creatures quite otherwise from those they wooed.

65   So their expert mistress had advised them;
They should scatter, roaming in the meadows,
So the glimpse of uncertain quarry
Should rouse desire first in the heroes.
Some, trusting to the unadorned
Beauty of a glorious body,
Laid to one side all artifice and fake,
To languish naked in the crystal lake.

66   But the sturdy youths, racing up the beach
In the sheer joy of being on dry land,
—For no one failed to come ashore—
And hoping to find woodland game,
Hardly expected among those hills,
Without nets or snares, to stumble on prey
So gentle, so compliant and benign
As the goddess had drilled in her design.

67   Some, armed with muskets and crossbows,
And hoping to get a shot at deer,
Flung themselves without hesitation
Into the woodlands and shady thickets.
Others strolled in cool glades,
Sheltered from the noon sun,
Along that tranquil, barely moving reach
Flowing between the pebbles to the beach.

68   Suddenly, they began to discern
Colours between the green boughs,
Colours which sight and sense judged
Were too vivid to be flowers,
But fine wool and variegated silks
To incite the ardour of lovers,
As those breathing, human roses veiled part,
Making themselves more beautiful by art.

69   Astonished, Veloso gave a great shout:
—'Men,' he said, 'this is rare hunting!
If ancient pagan rites survive,
These woods are sacred to the nymphs.
We have found more than the human spirit
Could ever desire: plainly,
Wonders exist, and marvels are apparent,
Though the world hides this from the ignorant.

70   'Let us follow these goddesses and see
      If they are fantasies, or flesh!'
      At this, swifter than any stags
      They galloped by the river-banks.
      The nymphs fled between the branches
      But, more contriving than nimble-footed,
      One by one with smiles and little sighs
      They let the greyhounds overtake their prize.

71   As they were running, their golden tresses
      And flimsy silks were blown aside;
      Desire was redoubled by the glimpse
      Of naked skin, suddenly revealed;
      One tripped on purpose, making it clear
      By signs more tender than indignant,
      Her breathless pursuer along the strand
      Should fall and lie beside her on the sand.

72   Others, elsewhere, stumbled upon
      The unclothed nymphs who were bathing;
      These began to utter little screams
      As if surprised by such an invasion;
      Some pretending to be troubled less
      By shame than by action, scampered
      Naked into the bush, letting them see
      Just where their itching hands would like to be.

73   One, resorting faster to the famed
      Modesty of Diana the Huntress
      Hid herself in the lake, as another
      Dashed for her tunic on the bank.
      But at this, a sailor flung himself
      Fully clothed and shod as he was (not
      Bothering to undress for hurry's sake)
      To quench his ardour right there in the lake.

74   As a crafty hunter's dog, practised
      In retrieving shot birds from the water,
      When he sees the barrel raised to the cheek
      For the usual heron or wild duck,
      Does not wait for the report but sure
      Of the prize, plunges in the lake
      Paddling and yelping: so climbing upon her
      The youth discovered she was no Diana.

75   Leonard, an accomplished soldier,
     Resourceful, and an amorous knight,
     Whom love had dealt not just one rebuff
     But constant mishaps and reversals,
     Until he was convinced his stars
     Doomed him to frustration, though
     Not quite bereft of hope, nor desperate
     Nothing could be done to change his fate,

76   Now tried his luck again, pursuing
     Ephyre, beauty's paragon, who sought
     To bestow more dearly than the others
     What nature gave us to be given.
     Tired already of the chase, he cried
     —'O beauty, too lovely to be cruel,
     The victory is yours in what you stole,
     But take my body now you have my soul!

77   'The rest, pure nymph, are weary of running,
     And are surrendering willingly;
     Why do you alone fly through the forest?
     Who told you it was I pursuing you?
     If my fortune it was informed you,
     That dogs me everywhere I go,
     Do not believe it, it always deceived
     Immeasurably whenever I believed.

78   'You are tireless, yet tire me! Why run
     To avoid me, when my luck is such
     That even if you halted in my path
     It would prevent my attaining you!
     So halt, if you will! I want to see
     What subtle way it will free you;
     It always happens; no need to press so;
     *Tra la spica e la man, qual muro è messo.**

79   'Oh, fly not from me! So may
     Your bloom of beauty never fly!
     You have only to check your furious pace
     To conquer the force of destiny.
     What emperor, what army has the power
     To curb the fury of my fate
     Which makes every ambition turn out ill?
     You can change it, merely by standing still.

80 'Do you make an ally of my misfortune?
It is weak to give succour to the strong.
Why kidnap a heart that belongs to you?
Release me, and run with more ease.
Why burden yourself with a soul so
Paltry as this one you have wrapped
In these threads of gold? Or will you confess
My luck has altered, so it now weighs less?

81 'In pursuing you, this is my hope;
Either its burden will prove too much,
Or by virtue of your lovely face
My misfortune will change forever.
If change is coming, flee no longer,
For love must wound you, gentle maiden,
And you will stay if you feel love's fire;
And if you stay, what more could I desire?'

82 By now the lovely nymph was fleeing
Less fast, and was glancing behind her
To attend the better to his sweet lament
In his tale of amorous griefs.
Then, turning her face, benign and tender,
Wreathed in happiness and smiles,
She fell in rapture at her victor's feet
Who melted utterly in passion's heat.

83 What ravenous kisses filled the wood!
What little moans and tender weeping!
What sweet caresses! What virtuous anger,
Yielding to happy, compliant laughter!
What further happened that morn and noon
As Venus fanned the flames of love,
Better to relish than disparage it;
Let those begrudge who cannot manage it.

84 And so now the lovely nymphs, in perfect
Consort with their beloved mariners,
Bedecked them with delightful garlands
Of gold and laurel and countless flowers.
Then offering their milk-white hands,
With formal vows and covenants,
Promised with joy and honour to be bound
Companions through life and for life beyond.

85   Tethys herself, the greatest among them,
      Whom all the nymphs obey, and said
      To be daughter of Coelus and Vesta
      As her lovely face plainly attests,
      Filling land and sea with wonder,
      Took, as he deserved, the captain
      In a manner both regal and sincere,
      Proving herself a lady without peer.

86   Then having revealed to him her name,
      She explained, in noble, gracious words,
      Her task, at Fate's immutable
      Bidding, was to reveal through prophecy
      The still-unmapped continents,
      The oceans as yet unsailed,
      All bound together on this earthly sphere,
      Which Portugal alone deserved to hear.

87   Taking his hand, she guided him
      To the summit of a holy mountain,
      The setting of a magnificent palace
      Of clear crystal and finest gold.
      There they passed the long day
      In sweet games and continuous pleasure;
      She in her palace loved away the hours,
      Her sisters in the shade among the flowers.

88   So the brave men and their lovely brides
      Lingered the best portion of the day,
      With a sweet joy they had never known,
      As quittance for their labours;
      Thus the world bestows on great deeds,
      Of special courage and distinction,
      The recompense of long-maturing fame
      And the high glory of an exalted name.

89   For the ocean nymphs in all their beauty,
      Tethys, and the magic painted island,
      Are nothing more than those delightful
      Honours which make our lives sublime.
      Those glorious moments of pre-eminence,
      The triumphs, the forehead crowned
      With palm and laurel—these are what is meant
      And what this island's pleasures represent.

90   Those immortals whom men of antiquity.
      In their love of great deeds, imagined
      Living there on starry Olympus,
      Soaring on fame's happy pinions
      Through brave acts, or through
      Mighty labours which were thought
      Virtue's path, rocky and precipitous,
      But ending in delight and happiness,

91   Were enjoying only those rewards
      The world bestows for the superb,
      Deathless achievements of heroes
      Who, though human, became divine;
      Jupiter, Mercury, Phoebus, and Mars,
      Aeneas, Romulus, and the two Thebans,*
      Ceres, Pallas, Diana, Juno, they
      Were all composed of feeble human clay;

92   But fame, trumpeting their exploits
      Everywhere added strange titles
      Such as gods, demigods, immortals,
      Deities, heroes, and the like.
      So let all men who covet glory,
      Who value the world's esteem, rise
      From sloth which exacts its degrading toll,
      Binding in slavery the free-born soul;

93   Keep Avarice under the strictest curb,
      And Ambition too, with its thousand
      Temptations, and vicious, sombre
      Tyranny, obscene in its exactions;
      Such empty honours, even pure gold,
      Confer no genuine distinction;
      Better to merit them and do without
      Than own what true worth will always doubt.

94   Maintain peace with equitable laws,
      Shielding the poor from levies of the rich,
      Or gird yourself in shining armour
      Against the enemy Saracens;
      You will make your kingdom rich and mighty,
      And all will have more, and none suffer;
      Yours will be deserved wealth, such as thrives,
      And those honours which shed lustre on our lives.

95   You will bring fame to your beloved king,
Now with your well-considered counsels,
Now with your swords which will make you
Immortal, as your ancestors are today.
Count nothing impossible! He who will,
Always can, and will come to be
Numbered with the great in the arenas,
And revered in this sanctuary of Venus.

Canto Ten

1   By now bright Apollo, once the lover
    Of adulterous Coronis,* was plunging
    His team in the seas which lap
    Mexico, there in the Aztec west;
    Gentle zephyrs tempered his rays
    As he sank in those far lagoons,
    Rippling the waters and reviving sweet
    Lilies and jasmine wilting in the heat;

2   When the beautiful nymphs with their lovers,
    Hand in hand and in happy accord,
    Approached the radiant palace which dazzled
    With the sheen of glittering metals,
    For Tethys had summoned them and tables
    Laden with exquisite dishes
    Were spread there, all selected to refresh
    And stiffen the sinews of exhausted flesh.

3   There, two by two, lover by lady,
    They sat on couches of finest crystal;
    And on others at the head, of pure gold,
    Were the goddess and famous da Gama.
    Not Cleopatra's Egypt could rival
    Those divine, delicious relishes,
    Nor the tawny plates heaped with savouries
    From the rich garden of the Hesperides.

4   The smoky wines* surpassed in fragrance
    Not only the Falernian of ancient Rome
    But ambrosia, so favoured by Jove
    And all the assembly of the immortals.
    In cups, hard and flawless as diamond,
    The beaded bubbles leaped and frothed
    As ice-cold water was added, to bless
    Every heart there with instant happiness.

5   Gaily they talked, on a thousand topics,
    With sweet smiles and subtle words,
    Re-awakening their merry appetites
    As various courses came and went;
    Music's instruments were at hand
    (Which, even in Hell's eternal suffering
    Persuade tormented spirits to rejoice),
    And the siren sound of an angelic voice.

6   The lovely nymph sang, and at a pitch
    Which soared through the lofty halls,
    While the instruments, in harmony,
    Conformed smoothly to the measure.
    Sudden silence restrained the winds
    And made a sweet murmuring
    In the waters, while savage beasts, deep
    In their natural lairs, were lulled to sleep.

7   Her ravishing voice was telling the heavens
    The names of heroes* yet to be born,
    Whose luminous souls Proteus had glimpsed
    In that revolving, transparent globe
    Sent him by Jupiter in a dream
    So that afterwards, in Neptune's kingdom,
    He prophesied, and now from memory
    The nymph rehearsed the glorious history.

8   What she learned there in the ocean depths
    Was in the tragic not the comic mode,
    And not known to Iopas of Carthage
    Nor to Demodocus* among the Phaeacians.
    Here, my Calliope, in my final labour,
    I implore you, as my just reward,
    To reinstate in this extremity
    My joy in writing which is failing me.*

9   *My years decline, and of my summer days
    Few remain as Autumn fast closes;
    Ill fortune has starved the genius
    I no longer vaunt, nor can vouch for;
    Sorrows are carrying me off to the river
    Of dark oblivion and endless sleep;
    Queen of the muses, grant that what I will
    For my nation, I have strength to fulfil!*

10   The goddess sang that from the Tagus,
      Over the seas da Gama had opened,
      Would come fleets to conquer all the coast
      Where the Indian Ocean sighs;
      Those Hindu kings who did not bow
      Their necks to the yoke would incite
      The wrath of an implacable enemy,
      Their choice to yield or, on the instant, die.

11   She sang of one among the Malabaris,
      King of Cochin* and a high priest
      Who, rather than sever the bonds
      He had forged with the mighty heroes,
      Would suffer his cities and farms laid
      Waste by the Samorin's iron and fire,
      In his cruel rage and abiding hate
      Of the Portuguese encroaching on his state.

12   She sang of one who would embark*
      In Belém destined to repair this wrong,
      The great Pacheco, Portugal's Achilles,
      Not knowing what future he takes to sea.
      As he embarks above the seething
      Ocean, the great ship's timbers
      Will groan and uncharacteristically
      Wallow a little deeper in the sea.

13   Arriving at length in the far east
      He will hurry with his tiny crew
      To succour the King of Cochin,
      And there in the Strait of Cambalon,
      In the salt delta of the winding river,
      Will rout the infernal Nairs,
      Chilling the sultry Orient that such
      A small company could achieve so much.

14   The Samorin will summon reinforcements;
      The kings of Beypore and Tanur* will come
      From the hills of Narsinga, swearing
      Firm allegiance to their lord;
      From Calicut to Cannanore, every
      Nair will be summoned in support,
      As both the hostile faiths prepare for war,
      Muslims by sea and Hindus on the shore.

15   So a second time, dauntless Pacheco,
     Will destroy them by land and by sea,
     And all Malabar will be astounded
     At the multitudes of those killed.
     Again, impetuously, the Samorin
     Will rush back into battle,
     Insulting his men, howling incantations
     To his deaf gods in their wooden stations.

16   Pacheco will not only hold the fords,
     But burn towns, houses, and temples;
     Inflamed with anger, watching his cities
     One by one laid low, that dog
     Will force his men, reckless of life,
     To attack both passages at once,
     But Pacheco will have wings, and his complete
     Command of them both will seal their defeat.

17   The Samorin will be spied in person
     Observing the battle, inciting his men,
     Until one whistling cannon-shot
     Bespatters with blood the royal palanquin.
     Then, discovering neither strategy
     Nor force can impress Pacheco,
     He will try poison, treachery, and finesse,
     But always (so Heaven wills) without success.

18   'A seventh time,' she sang, 'he will return
     To attack the invincible Portuguese
     Whom nothing will daunt or dismay
     As they continue wreaking confusion:
     The Samorin will take into battle,
     New, terrible wooden engines,
     To grapple with the caravels, till then
     Beyond attack, even by the bravest men.

19   'He will launch towering fireships
     To burn as much of the fleet as he can;
     But the soldier's skill and ingenuity
     Will make all such onslaughts futile.
     No one in the annals of warfare,
     Who has soared on the wings of fame,
     Can match this man whose triumphs never cease
     —Allow me this, Rome and illustrious Greece.

20   'That he bore the brunt of so many battles
     With barely one hundred soldiers,
     Routing so many accomplished foes
     With such stratagem and resource,
     Must seem nothing more than fantasy,
     Or that the heavenly choirs came down,
     Summoned to assist him and to impart
     Zeal, courage, skill, and a steadfast heart.

21   'Not even Miltiades* at Marathon
     When he destroyed the might of Darius,
     Nor Leonidas defending Thermopylae
     With four thousand Lacedaemonians,
     Nor young Horatius, who held the bridge
     Against all the forces of the Etruscans,
     Nor Quintus Fabius—none of them showed more
     Wisdom and strength than this paragon of war.'

22   But at this, the nymph dropped her pitch
     To a throaty dirge, heavy with tears,
     As she sang of the deep ingratitude
     With which bravery was rewarded:
     'Belisarius,'* she sang, 'whom the nine
     Muses never cease to celebrate,
     If your feats went unrecognized, behold
     One by whose destiny to be consoled.

23   'Here is a comrade, alike in deeds
     As in his harsh, thankless end:
     In both you and him, we see noble hearts
     Brought to wretchedness and obliquity.
     To die in the beds of a hospice
     Who were bulwarks to their king and faith!
     So kings behave, it being their royal way
     To subject truth and justice to their sway.

24   'So kings behave when, besotted
     By what is smooth and plausible,
     They award the prize Ajax deserves*
     To the fraudulent tongue of Ulysses.
     Yet revenge follows, for where gifts
     Are showered on the sycophant
     Instead of on some worthy knight-companion,
     They vanish among greedy hangers-on.

25   'As for you, O king, who so badly repaid
     Such a servant, this is your one blot:
     You denied him a fair estate
     When he won for you a rich realm.
     So long as Apollo's rays circle
     The earth, I give you my poet's word*
     He will be among the great and glorious,
     And you reprobated for your avarice.

26   'But here', she resumed, 'comes another,
     Francisco de Almeida,* the viceroy,
     And his son, destined to win on the seas
     Fame as great as any Roman of old.
     Together, by the power of arms,
     They will castigate fertile Kilwa,*
     Driving out its perfidious princeling
     To impose a loyal and humane king.

27   'Mombasa,* too, furnished with such
     Palaces and sumptuous houses,
     Will be laid waste with iron and fire
     In payment for its former treachery.
     Along the Indian coast, swarming
     With enemy ships plotting Portugal's
     Downfall, Lourenço with sail and with oar
     Will give his uttermost, and then give more.

28   'Though the powerful Samorin's giant ships*
     Choke the entire sea, his cannon-shot
     Thundering from hot brass
     Will pulverize rudder, mast, and sail;
     Then, daring to grapple the enemy
     Flagship, watch him leap
     On deck, armed only with lance and sword,
     To drive four hundred Muslims overboard.

29   'But God's inscrutable wisdom (He knows
     Best what is best for his servants)
     Will place him where neither strength nor wisdom
     Can avail in preserving his life.
     In Chaul,* the very seas will churn
     With blood, fire, and iron resistance,
     As the combined fleets of Egypt and Cambay
     Confront him with his destiny that day.

30   'The united power of many enemies
(Might was defeated only by might),
Faltering winds and a swelling sea
Will all be ranged against him.
Here, let ancient heroes rise
To learn from this scion of courage
This second Scaeva* who, however maimed,
Knows no surrender and will not be tamed.

31   'With one thighbone completely shattered
By a wayward cannon-ball, still
He battles on with his forearms alone
And a heart not to be daunted,
Until another ball snaps the ties
Binding flesh and spirit together:
The leaping soul slips its body's prison
To claim the greater prize of the arisen.

32   'Go in peace, O soul! After war's
Turbulence, you have earned supreme peace!
As for that scattered, broken body,
He who fathered it plans vengeance.
Already, I hear their hot perdition
Looming in a thunderous barrage
On Mameluke and cruel Cambayan*
From catapult, from ordnance and cannon.

33   'Here comes the father, magnified
By his anger and grief, his heart
On fire, his eyes swimming, his soul
Transfixed by paternal love.
He has taken an oath his noble rage
Will make blood run knee-high
In the enemy ships; the Nile will mourn,
The Indus witness, the Ganges be forlorn.

34   'As an impassioned bull, rehearsing
For terrible combat, tests his horns
On the trunk of an oak or tall beech,
Attacking air in a trial of strength,
So Francisco, before descending
In wrath on the coast of Cambay,
Plunges his sword in opulent Dabhol,
All its pretensions made contemptible.

35   'Then sailing into the bay of Diu,*
      Scene of famous battles and sieges,
      He will scatter the vast but feeble fleet
      Of Calicut that is powered by oars;
      While the ships of wary Melik-el-Hissa,
      Caught in a hail of cannon-fire,
      Will be relegated to their cold, dread
      Burial places on the ocean bed.

36   'But it is Emir Hussein's grappled fleet
      Bears the brunt of the avenger's anger,
      As arms and legs swim in the bay
      Without the bodies they belonged to;
      Bolts of fire will make manifest
      The passionate victors' blind fury,
      And nothing will penetrate ears and eyes
      But smoke, iron, flames, and battle-cries.

37   'But sadly, after this great triumph
      As he sets sail for his native Tagus,
      His glory is all but stolen away
      In the dark and mournful outcome!*
      The Cape of Storms, which keeps his memory
      Along with his bones, will be unashamed
      In dispatching from the world such a soul
      Not Egypt nor all India could control.

38   'For there, brute savages will achieve
      What eluded more skilled enemies,
      And fire-hardened knobkerries do
      What bows and cannon-balls could not;
      God's judgements are inscrutable;
      Pagans, unable to comprehend,
      Attribute to ill fortune or mischance
      What providence ordains and heaven grants.

39   'But what great light* do I see breaking,'
      Sang the nymph and in a higher strain,
      'Where the seas of Malindi flow crimson
      With the blood of Lamu, Oja, and Brava?
      This is Cunha's doing, to be remembered
      In seas which wash remote islands,
      And on those beaches which once bore the name
      St Lawrence—the whole south will know his fame!

40   'That light, too,* is from Persian Ormuz
        From the fires and the gleaming arms
        Of Albuquerque as he rebukes them
        For scorning his light, honourable yoke.
        There they will see their hissing arrows*
        Turn miraculously in the air
        Against the archers—so God ever fights
        For His Church and for those who spread its rites.

41   'Not all that land's mountains of salt
        Can preserve from corruption the corpses
        Littering the beaches, choking the seas
        Of Gerum,* Muscat, and Al Quraiyat,
        Till, by the strength of his arm, they learn
        To bow the neck as he compels
        That grim realm to yield, without dispute,
        Pearls from Bahrain as their annual tribute.

42   'What glorious palms I see, plaited
        By Victory to crown his forehead
        When, without fear or indecision,
        He seizes the famous island of Goa.
        Then, yielding to hard circumstance,
        He abandons it, and waits the occasion
        To return and hold it, for so strength and skill
        Can bend both Mars and fortune to their will.

43   'Watch him as he renews the attack, despite
        Ramparts, fire, lances, and cannon,
        Breaking with his sword the packed, bristling
        Squadrons of Hindus and Muslims;
        His noble warriors will match in fury
        Famished lions or raging bulls
        On that morning sacred to St Catherine,*
        Born in Egypt and now Goa's patron.

44   'Nor will you evade him, for all your
        Vast treasures and your location
        There in Dawn's very emporium,
        Renowned, opulent Malacca!
        For all your arrows tipped with poison,
        The curved daggers you bear as arms,
        Amorous Malays and valiant Javanese
        All will be subject to the Portuguese.'

45 This siren would have sung more stanzas
    In praise of illustrious Albuquerque,
    But recalled that act which damned him
    Even as his fame circled the earth.
    The great captain, fated to earn
    Glory for his deeds, should have been
    A comrade to his fellows in distress,
    Not a judge, absolute and merciless.

46 Yet at a time of hunger and hardships,
    Sickness, arrows, and constant bombardment,
    When season and place dealt harshly
    With men rigid in their discipline,
    It seems the brutal, savage act*
    Of an arrogant and inhuman heart
    To execute a comrade who had known
    What love and human weakness must condone.

47 This was not the crime of incest
    Nor the violent abuse of a virgin,
    Still less of hidden adultery
    For this was a slave, anyone's woman.
    Whether from jealousy, or shame
    Or too habituated to cruelty,
    He gave unremitting rein to his fury,
    And left an ugly stain on his memory.

48 Alexander, seeing Apelles* enamoured
    Of Campaspe, released her willingly
    Though he was not one of his veterans
    Not sharing the rigours of a siege.
    Cyrus knew how Araspas smouldered
    Like hot charcoal for Panthea
    Whom he held captive, though he had promised
    His love for her would never be dishonest;

49 The great Persian, seeing him conquered
    By love, which no defence keeps out,
    Readily pardoned him, and was served
    In a weighty matter in recompense.
    Through kidnap and rape, Judith
    Became wife of the iron Baldwin.
    But Charles her father raised him to be great,
    And be the founder of the Flemish state.

50   But resuming her song, the nymph
Sang now of Soares de Albergaria,*
Whose standards will strike terror
Along the whole coast of the Red Sea:
'Medina's abomination will fear him,
And Mecca and Jiddah, to the farthest shores
Of Abyssinia, while Berbera will await
The market town of Zeila's dreadful fate;

51   'Even the noble isle of Taprobana,
As famous under its ancient name
As today when its fragrant groves
Of hot cinnamon make it supreme,
She, too, will be taxed by the flag
Of Portugal, hoisted mighty and proud
In Colombo, high on the great tower
Where all the people recognize its power.

52   'Then Lopes de Sequeira,* parting
The Red Sea, will open a passage
To you, Abyssinia, mighty empire,
Home of Candace and the Queen of Sheba;
He will see Massawa with its cisterns
And the port of Arkiko close by,
Discovering to the world further marvels
As remote islands glimpse his caravels.

53   'After will come Duarte de Meneses,*
Showing much of his metal in Africa;
He will punish proud Ormuz for revolt
By making it pay double tribute.
You, too, da Gama, as prize for this
And your future exile, will return
With a count's title, honoured overlord
To govern the great region you explored.

54   'But Death, that dire necessity
No human being can avoid,
Will remove you, amid royal dignity,
From this world and all its deceit.
Then a second Meneses,* a youth
Far wiser than his years, will rule
And the fortunate Henrique will perform
Such deeds as will keep his memory warm.

55   'Defeating not just the Malabaris,
      Destroying Ponnani along with Coulete,
      Spiking guns whose volleys could target
      Only the bodies which stormed them;
      Rarer still, he will overcome
      The seven enemies of the human soul;
      He will conquer greed and concupiscence,
      In one so young the sum of excellence.

56   'He, too, will be summoned to the heavens,
      And you, brave Mascarenhas,* will succeed,
      And though enemies oust you from power
      I vouch your fame will be eternal.
      For even they are forced to confess
      Your immense courage, as Fortune
      Reinstates you in command, but made great
      More by your victories than a just fate.

57   'On the island of Bintan, for so long
      The scourge of Malacca, your valiant
      Company will avenge in a single day
      The injuries of a thousand years.
      Superhuman toils and dangers,
      Iron caltrops, narrow tracks,
      Will be overcome and mastered, as all
      Ramparts will be scaled, all stockades fall.

58   'But in India, envy and ambition
      Boldly setting their faces against God
      And all justice, will cause you—
      No, not shame, no—but sorrow!
      He who abuses his powers to commit
      A vile and irrational crime
      Will not win—for victory's truly won
      When full, transparent justice is seen done.

59   'But I do not deny Sampaio,* the usurper's,
      Valour and distinction, as he drops
      Like lightning on an ocean packed
      With a thousand enemy ships.
      In Bacanore he will strike such a blow
      Against Malabar that ever afterwards
      Kutti Ali, for all his enormous fleet,
      Will sail in terror of a fresh defeat.

60 'Likewise, Diu's ferocious armada,
   Whose size and daring daunts Chaul,
   The mere sight of Heitor de Silveira,
   Will be enough to rout and destroy it:
   —That Portuguese, they prophesy,
   Raiding along the Cambay coast, will
   Be to the Gujeratis such a spectre
   As haunted the Greeks in mighty Hector.

61 'To fierce Sampaio there will succeed
   Da Cunha,* at the helm for many years;
   He will build the fortress of Chale
   Making famous Diu quake at his name;
   Strong Bassein will surrender to him
   Though not without much blood,
   Its governor grieving, as with swords alone
   His mighty palisade is overthrown.

62 'After will come Noronha,* destined
   To repulse from Diu the Turkish siege
   —Diu, defended by the strategy
   And courage of Antonio da Silveira.
   When death in turn claims Noronha,
   Your son,* da Gama, will try his hand
   At ruling the empire, when at his sight
   The Red Sea will turn yellow in sheer fright.

63 'From your Estêvão the reins will pass
   To one already honoured in Brazil,
   Martim Afonso de Sousa,* scourge
   Of French pirates infesting the seas;
   As captain-general of the Indian Ocean,
   He will scale the ramparts of Daman
   And, breaching the gate, be furthest forward
   Though a thousand bowmen have it covered.

64 'The King of Cambay, for all his pride,
   Will surrender rich Diu's citadel,
   In return for protecting his kingdom
   From the all-conquering Mogul;
   Later, in a tactic of great daring,
   He will block the Samorin in Calicut,
   Despite the multitudes he brings that day,
   Driving him back in bloody disarray.

65   'He will destroy the city of Etapilly
     Routing the king with his many followers,
     Then afterwards, off Cape Comorin,
     Performs his most famous exploit;
     The Samorin's first fleet, cocksure
     It would sweep the world's oceans,
     Is vanquished in a hail of fire and iron,
     And Beadala city, too will burn.

66   'Having cleared India of enemies
     He will take up the viceroy's sceptre
     With no opposition, nor any danger,
     For all fear him and none complain,
     Except Bhatkal, which brings on itself
     The pains Beadala already suffered;
     Corpses will strew the streets, and shells burst
     As fire and thundering cannon do their worst.

67   'So Martinho, his mighty name deriving
     From deeds themselves derived from Mars,
     As famed, throughout the empire, for arms
     As for wise and thoughtful counsel.
     João de Castro* will follow him
     Hoisting Portugal's banner high;
     The inheritor will match the inherited;
     One building Diu, the other saving it.

68   'Ferocious Persians, Abyssinians, and Turks
     (*Rumes*, they are called, after ancient Rome),
     Varied in faces, varied in dress
     (A thousand nations will join the siege),
     Will curse the heavens that a mere handful
     Down on earth withstands them,
     Vowing in Portuguese blood and ashes
     To baptize their scimitar moustaches.

69   'Outfacing ordnance and cannon,
     Fierce catapults and buried mines,
     Mascarenhas and the heroes
     Delight in their certain death,
     Until, where the crisis is greatest,
     Castro the liberator will sacrifice
     His dear sons, asking of each the same
     —To give their lives to God and eternal fame.

70 'Fernando, the elder, true to his lineage,
There where a land-mine blasts the rampart
To fragments in a ball of fire,
Will be snatched away and ascend to heaven;
Álvaro, his brother, despite winter's
Waves blocking the ocean roads
Will force them open, subduing the sea
With its gales to confront the enemy.

71 'And here in his wake, their father comes
Ploughing the waves with reinforcements,
And with power and skill, which counts for more,
Prospers and prevails in battle.
Some leap the walls, dodging the gate;
Others, hacking savagely, breach it.
Their deeds that day will live in memory,
Greater than verse records, or history.

72 'Afterwards, he will battle again,*
Intrepid conqueror of the all-powerful
King of Cambay, striking panic
Into his squadrons of elephants;
Not even Hidel Khan will secure
His kingdom from that triumphant arm,
Which sacks both Dabhol on its coastal sand,
And Ponda too, despite being far inland.

73 'All these heroes, and others worthy
In different ways of fame and esteem,
Performing great feats in war
Will taste this island's pleasures,
Their sharp keels cutting the waves
Under triumphant banners, to find
These lovely nymphs, these tables richly furnished
The glorious rewards for tasks accomplished.'

74 So sang the nymph: and all the others
Gave voice in sonorous applause,
Rejoicing in the happy vows
Pledged with such mutual delight:
'For longer than Fortune's wheel revolves'
(All sang, blending their voices)
'Most noble people, just will be your claim
To honour, esteem, and everlasting fame.'

75   When all had feasted to the full
      From the noble dishes set before them,
      And from the nymph's harmonious strains
      Had glimpsed those noble deeds to come,
      Then, radiant in her serious grace
      And eager to redouble the glory
      And pleasures of that bright and joyful day,
      Tethys addressed da Gama in this way:

76   —'God in supreme wisdom* favours you,
      O hero, to behold with bodily eyes
      What is beyond the shallow knowledge
      Of erring and wretched mortals.
      Follow me, with courage and wisdom,
      You and your men, by this mountain path':
      And saying this, she led him through a wood
      Too dark and dense for humans to intrude.

77   Soon they found themselves on a summit
      And in a meadow so thickly sown
      With emeralds and rubies, they perceived
      They were treading on holy ground.
      Here, in the air, they saw suspended
      A lustrous and translucent globe,
      Its brilliant centre shining just as clear
      As the bright surface of the outer sphere.

78   Its substance they could not discern,
      But saw plainly it was composed
      Of different spheres the divine rod
      Had shaped with one fixed centre.
      As each revolved, falling or rising,
      The whole neither rose nor fell,
      But looked the same all round, while every part
      Revealed a handiwork of sacred art,

79   Uniform, perfect, and self-sustained
      As the very Creator who fashioned it.
      Da Gama, seeing it, stood transfixed,
      Torn between fear and eagerness.
      Then the goddess spoke: 'This sphere
      I set before you, represents
      The whole created world, so you may see
      Where you have been, and are, and wish to be.

80   'This is the great machine of the universe
      Ethereal and elemental, as made
      By the deepest and highest Wisdom,
      Who is without beginning and end.
      He who with his very essence
      Hedges this polished and perfect globe
      Is God; but who God is none comprehends
      For human wit cannot attain such ends.

81   'The first sphere which circles round
      The lesser orbs which it contains
      And which radiates with such brightness
      It dazzles mortal sight and mind,
      Is named the Empyrean, where pure souls
      Dwell and enjoy that infinite Good
      Whose essence is entirely self-defined;
      Nothing resembles it among mankind.

82   'Here dwell in glory only the genuine
      Gods, because I, Saturn and Janus,
      Jupiter and Juno, are mere fables
      Dreamed by mankind in his blindness.
      We serve only* to fashion delightful
      Verses, and if human usage offers
      Us more, it is your imagination
      Awards us each in heaven a constellation.

83   'Given, however, that Sacred Providence
      —Represented here by Jupiter—
      Governs the whole world it sustains
      By means of a thousand prescient angels
      (Prophetic knowledge speaks of them
      With many examples, showing how
      The good are favoured in the sacred plan;
      The bad they try to hinder if they can);

84   'The painter with words, in his varied aims,
      At times to delight, at times instruct,
      Applies to them names the ancient poets
      Once gave their imagined gods;
      Even the Bible describes as "gods"
      The angels of the sacred company,
      Though this pre-eminent name is misapplied
      To fallen angels, wrongly deified.

85   'Ultimately, one all-powerful God
     Works in the world through His agents.
     Now, turning to speak of the profound
     Handiwork of the mysterious Creator,
     Inside this first, motionless sphere
     Where the pure souls live in their bliss,
     Another, too swift and volatile to see,
     Spins round: it is the Primum Mobile.

86   'Each of the spheres that lie within
     Is impelled by this rapturous movement:
     The sun, obeying a course not its own.
     Meticulously creates day and night;
     Within this, another rotates
     Measuredly, on so tight a rein*
     That, ever generous with its light, the sun
     Circles two hundred times while this makes one.

87   'Look further inside at the next sphere,
     Enamelled with radiant, polished bodies,
     Moving on its predestined course
     As it turns on its shining poles.
     See how it dazzles and is adorned
     With the starry belt of the Zodiac.
     Twelve beasts are represented, and their signs
     Are the twelve stages from which Phoebus shines.

88   'Look in these other parts at the pictures
     The glistening stars are fashioning;
     Behold the Great and Little Bears,
     Andromeda, and Cepheus the Dragon;
     See Cassiopeia in all her beauty,
     And the wild countenance of Orion;
     See Cygnus sighing, before she must expire,
     The Hare, the Dogs, the Argo, and sweet Lyre.

89   'Beneath this spacious firmament
     Is the heaven of the old god Saturn;
     Jupiter is revolving close by,
     Above Mars, his belligerent enemy;
     Fourth is the heaven of the sun's brilliance,
     Then Venus with all her loves in tow;
     Sweet-tongued Mercury is next in line,
     Then Diana (huntress, moon, and Proserpine).

90 'Each of these planets moves in a different
    Course, some ponderous, others swift,
    Wandering far off from the centre
    Or just a short distance from earth,
    Following the almighty Father's plan,
    Who made fire, air, wind, and snow,
    Which can be seen located right within
    At the centre where sea and land begin.

91 'This is the hostel of humanity,*
    Who, too ambitious to be content
    With the afflictions of solid land,
    Have launched out on the restless oceans.
    Look at the various regions, divided
    By turbulent seas, where there are lodged
    Nations and tribes with various kings and chiefs,
    Contrasting customs, various beliefs.

92 'Here is Christian Europe, advanced and envied
    For its might and for its governance;
    Here is Africa, desperate to share
    The world's goods, and racked by violence,
    With the Cape which till now has barred
    All passage, nature's southern home;
    Look at this huge, inhabited region
    Without boundaries, without religion;

93 'Look at the empire of Monomotapa*
    With its forest peoples, black and naked,
    Where Gonçalo da Silveira* will undergo
    Insult and death for the holy Church.
    This unknown hemisphere abounds
    With the metal for which men most sweat;
    Behold the lake which is the Nile's source
    And the green Zambesi, too, begins its course.

94 'See how the Negroes' houses are like nests,
    Without doors, entirely confident
    Of royal justice and protection
    And the honesty of their neighbours;
    Then see this brutal multitude,
    Like a thick black cloud of starlings,
    Besieging the fortress at Sofala,*
    Well built, and well defended by Anhaia.

95   'Yonder are the great lakes, unknown
     To the ancients, where the Nile springs;
     Watch it watering, with its crocodiles,
     The Christian peoples of Abyssinia;
     Look how their defence takes the novel form
     Of living without any defences;
     And see Meroé,* that island of such fame
     Which now has Nubia as its local name.

96   'In that remote land, your unborn child*
     Will win great victories over the Turks
     (Dom Cristovão will be his name),
     But his death will be the price.
     Note here on the coast, rich Malindi
     That received you with such kindness;
     And give the river Rapto, too, your glance,
     Also called Obi; its bar is at Quilmance.

97   'Now see Cape Guardafui, once known
     By its inhabitants as Aromata,
     Guarding the entrance to the famous
     Red Sea, so named for its coloured sands.
     Its waters mark the frontier
     Where Africa ends, and the best towns
     Just where Asia is about to begin,
     Are Massawa, Arkiko, and Suakin.

98   'Far to the left is Suez, known of old
     (Some maintain) as Heroopolis
     (Arsinoe, say others), and which today
     Harbours the mighty Egyptian fleet.
     Behold waters where in olden times
     Great Moses opened a causeway.
     Here Asia starts, the famous Orient
     With its many kingdoms, vast and opulent.

99   'See Mount Sinai,* further ennobled
     By the sepulchre of St Catherine.
     See Tur and Jiddah, a town starved
     Of refreshing, crystal fountains,
     And the portals of that strait which ends
     In Aden's desert kingdom, bordering
     The mountains known as Asir, living stone
     Where heaven's refreshing rains are never known.

100   'See the three Arabias, so bountiful
      With land for their dark nomads;
      From there come the noble steeds prized
      By warriors for their fire and pace;
      Look how the coast barricades
      The Straits of Ormuz, and marks out
      The promontory of Ras Fartak, so named
      From its city which is equally famed.

101   'Notice Dhofar,* source of the loveliest,
      Most aromatic of all altar-incense;
      But now attend; for there opposite
      Ras el Hadd with its barren beaches,
      Begins the coast of the kingdom
      Of Ormuz, shores destined to be known
      When a fleet of galleys, with Turks aboard,
      Confronts Castelo-Branco's naked sword.

102   'This Cape nearby is Asaborus, now
      Known to sailors as Ras Mussendum;
      It marks the entrance to that gulf enclosed
      By Arabia and opulent Persia;
      See Bahrain Island where the ocean bed
      Is bedecked with pearls, matching the dawn,
      And watch the Tigris and Euphrates merge,
      Sharing one delta in their seaward surge.

103   'See mighty Persia,* that noble empire,
      Its warriors for ever in the saddle,
      Scorning the use of smelted bronze,
      Or to have hands uncalloused by weapons.
      Note Gerum, the island which reveals
      What the passage of time can do;
      While old Ormuz was green in memory,
      It stole the name and with it all the glory.

104   'Here Dom Filipe de Meneses, the governor,
      Will show his aptitude for battle
      When, with a handful of Portuguese,
      He routs a Persian host at Lar;
      They will know further blows and reverses
      From Dom Pedro de Sousa, who showed
      His powers at Ampaza, brought to heel
      By soldiers armed with nothing more than steel.

105   'But we leave the Straits of Ormuz
      And Cape Ras Jaskah, formerly Carpela,
      And the land nearby, so ill-favoured
      By nature and her customary gifts
      (Carmania this desert was once called);
      Instead, gaze now on the beautiful
      Indus,* its source high amid yonder snows
      While, from the nearby crest, the Ganges flows.

106   'See the most fertile land of Sind
      And the deep-seated Gulf of Cutch
      Where the flood tide is like a torrent
      And the ebb retreats as impetuously;
      See the treasure-laden land of Cambay
      Where the sea bites deeply into the coast;
      I pass by a thousand other cities
      Awaiting you with their amenities.

107   'See how the famous Indian coast runs
      All the way south to Cape Comorin,
      Once called Cape Cori, with Taprobana
      (Afterwards Ceylon) lying offshore;
      These are the coasts where Portuguese
      Who come in your wake will levy war,
      Conquering cities and kingdoms in their prime,
      And holding them in partnership with time.

108   'The realms between the two rivers
      Are beyond count and thronged with peoples,
      Some kingdoms Muslim, others Hindu,
      The devil himself writing their laws.
      Now behold the land of Narsinga
      Where lie the most blessed remains
      Of St Thomas,* whom our risen Christ defied
      To thrust his hand into His very side.

109   'Here was an elegant city named
      Mylapore,* vast and prosperous,
      Worshipping its ancient idols;
      As the pagans do to this day.
      It was far inland in those days,
      And the religion of the risen Christ
      Was newly broadcast, when St Thomas trod
      A thousand regions with the word of God.

110 'As he came here, preaching, and dispensing
    Health to the sick, life to the dead,
    One day the sea threw up on shore
    A tree-trunk of enormous girth.
    The king, who was building, sought
    To use it as timber, never doubting
    To drag it ashore through the contrivance
    Of strong men with machines and elephants.

111 'So heavy was the trunk that nothing
    The king devised could shift it;
    But the ambassador of the true Christ
    Made little work of the matter:
    He simply tied his girdle to the log,
    Raised it, and carried it for use
    As the corner-post of a splendid shrine
    Which would serve to the future as a sign.

112 'He understood that, if perfect faith
    Could move even a deaf mountain,
    It would respond at once to Christ's
    Injunction, and so it came to pass.
    Excitement spread among the people;
    The Brahmins took it as a miracle;
    But eyeing such wonders and such sanctity,
    They feared to forfeit their authority.

113 'These are the priests among the Hindus
    And them envy had pierced the most;
    They cast around for a thousand means
    To silence Thomas, or to kill him.
    Their leader, who wore their threads of office,*
    Did a fearful thing—showing the world
    There is nothing false virtue will eschew
    When it fights without scruple with the true.

114 'He killed his own son and laid the crime
    At the innocent hands of Thomas;
    They called false witnesses, as could be done;
    They condemned him promptly to death.
    The saint, who could see his only recourse
    Lay in his all-powerful father,
    Before the king and lords in the packed hall
    Prayed for the greatest miracle of all.

115 'He ordered the corpse brought before him
     And restored it to life, and enquired
     Who was his killer, as the one witness
     Whose testimony would be credited.
     All saw the youth alive, raised up
     In the name of the crucified Christ;
     He thanked Thomas as his true deliverer
     And denounced his father as the murderer.

116 'This miracle so astounded everyone
     The king submitted at once to baptism,
     And many more; some kissed his gown,
     Others sang hymns to Thomas's God.
     But the Brahmins were hostile, and envy
     So poisoned their thinking, they resolved
     To use the rabble to enforce their will
     Inciting mayhem with the aim to kill.

117 'One day as St Thomas was preaching
     They feigned a disturbance among the people
     —Now Christ had, in that hour, ordained
     His martyr should join him in glory—
     As the multitude of stones descended
     The saint was a willing sacrifice;
     One of the villains, to fulfil his part
     With a cruel lance stabbed the apostle's heart.

118 'The Ganges and Indus mourn you, Thomas;
     Every land weeps where you trod;
     But those souls lament the most who remain
     Clothed in the holy faith you taught them!
     God's angels, with joy and singing,
     Welcomed you to your glorious reward;
     And with God we pray you will intercede
     To help your Lusitanians in their need.

119 'As for you others, who usurp the name
     Envoy of God, as was Thomas, tell me:
     If you are missionaries, why do you not
     Go forth to preach the holy faith?
     If, being earth's salt,* you lose savour
     At home, where no man is a prophet,
     Wherewith will you salt, in times like these
     (Forget the infidel), such heresies?

120 'But I pass over such perilous matters
    To return to the coast* passing below:
    For with this famous city of Mylapore
    The Bay of Bengal begins its curve;
    Pass by rich and mighty Narsinga,
    Pass by Orissa, with its busy looms;
    At its head, the famous and (to some) occult
    River Ganges joins the domain of salt;

121 'The Ganges, in which when people die
    They are baptized, it being their creed
    That, even having been great sinners,
    That sacred water will cleanse them.
    Behold Chittagong, the finest city
    Of Bengal, a province which boasts
    Of its wealth, just beyond the Ganges's mouth,
    Where the coastline turns sharply to the south.

122 'See the Arakan kingdom and the throne
    Of Pegu, once peopled by monsters
    —Children of the horrible coupling
    Of a solitary woman and a dog:
    Today, men wear on their genitals
    Tiny tinkling bells, a custom
    Invented very subtly by their queen
    To put pay to behaviour so obscene.

123 'See the city of Tavoy, on the border
    Of the long, broad empire of Siam;
    Then Tenasserim, and Kedah, where
    The region's pepper is harvested.
    But you must go further on to view
    Malacca, that vast sea's emporium,
    Where every kingdom of whatever size,
    Dispatches all its richest merchandise.

124 'There is a saying that in ancient times
    The noble isle of Sumatra was joined
    To the main, until mountainous seas
    Eroded its base and cut it off.
    It was known as "The Chersonese"
    And, from its seams of the precious metal,
    The epithet "Golden" came to adhere
    (Some think it was the biblical Ophir).

125   'The peninsula's tip is Singapore
       Where the straits are at their narrowest;
       Then, curving to face the Lesser Bear,
       The coast points east* towards the dawn.
       See Pahang and Patani, and the shores
       Of Siam to which these are subject;
       And behold the Menam River flowing by
       From a lake in Siam named Chieng-Mai.

126   'In this vast land are a thousand nations
       Of which even the names are unknown:
       The Laos, mighty in extent and numbers;
       The Avas and Burmese, high in their hills.
       And the Karens, rumoured to be savages,
       Remoter still in the mountains beyond:
       They eat human flesh (inhuman!) and they char
       Their own flesh with iron brands (bizarre!).

127   'Look: dividing Cambodia is the great
       River Mekong,* the "prince of waters";
       Its tributaries are such, it floods
       The wide plains even in summer;
       Its inundations resemble the Nile's;
       Its people believe, in their ignorance,
       That at death, even animals are consigned
       To be punished or rewarded, like mankind.'

128   *Gently, compassionately, he will receive
       On his broad bosom these Cantos, snatched
       Soaking from sad, wretched shipwreck,
       Surviving treacherous shoals, and hunger
       And countless other dangers, when
       An unjust mandate is imposed on him
       Whose lyre, played with such sweet dexterity
       Will bring him fame, but not prosperity.*

129   'The coast beyond is called Tsian Pa;
       In its forests grow fragrant aloes;
       See Cochin-China, still scarcely known,
       And Hainan in its undiscovered gulf.
       Here begins the mighty, famous empire
       Of China, its lands and riches
       Unimaginable, its dominion felt
       From the Arctic Circle to the tropic belt.

130   'See the Great Wall, incredible structure,
       Dividing one empire from another,
       Most certain and obvious proof
       Of sovereign power in its pride and wealth.
       Yet their emperors are not born princes,
       Nor do sons succeed their fathers,
       But they elect one already famous,
       Accomplished, discerning, and virtuous.

131   'There are lands beyond, veiled from you
       Until the time is ripe to reveal them;
       But do not omit the oceans' islands
       Where nature seems most inventive;
       This one, half hidden, facing the coast
       Of China, from whence it may be reached,
       Is Japan, with its reefs of silver ore,
       And soon to be illumined by God's law.

132   'Look there, how the seas of the Orient,
       Are scattered with islands beyond number;*
       See Tidore, then Ternate with its burning
       Summit,* leaping with volcanic flames.
       Observe the orchards of hot cloves
       Portuguese will buy with their blood;
       And birds of paradise, which never alight,*
       But fall to earth the day they end their flight.

133   'Behold the Banda Islands, enamelled
       With the changing colours of the nutmeg;
       And the various birds which leap about
       Exacting their own tribute in nuts.
       See Borneo where will be found
       Tear-drops of a liquor that sets,
       Oozing from the bark of the camphor tree,
       Which gives the island its celebrity.

134   'And here is Timor, with its forests
       Of scented, invigorating sandalwood.
       Look at Java, so vast its southern
       Mountains to this day are unexplored.
       The forest people who travel the land
       Talk of a magic river, in whose
       Uppermost reaches, where it flows alone,
       The twigs that fall in it are turned to stone.

135   'And again, Sumatra, made an island
       By time, with its tremulous crest of fire;
       Here is a spring which issues oil,
       And the marvel of the aromatic tears,
       Wept by a tree, which surpass
       In fragrance all Arabia's myrrh;
       And matching what the other have, behold
       It yields as well soft silks and finest gold.

136   'Observe in Ceylon, a mountain so high
       It tops the clouds and eludes sight;
       It is believed sacred, for there
       On a rock is the footprint of a man.
       In the Maldive Islands, the coconut palm
       Springs from the sea-bed, its milk
       For the most atrocious poison, take note,
       Being said to be the perfect antidote.

137   'Further on, facing the Red Sea strait,
       Is Socotra, with its bitter aloes;
       And other islands, subject to you
       Along the desert coast of Africa,
       Are the source of ambergris, most secret
       And precious perfume known to man.
       And here is Madagascar, better famed
       When it honoured St Lawrence and was so named.

138   'Such are the new regions of the East
       You Portuguese are adding to the world,
       Opening the gates to that vast ocean
       Which you navigate with such courage.
       But it is fitting you glance westwards*
       To observe the exploit of a Portuguese
       Who, believing himself snubbed by his king,
       Made another voyage beyond imagining.

139   'Behold a vast continent which stretches
       From the Great Bear to the opposite pole,
       Soon to be famous for its mines
       Of metal gleaming like Apollo's hair;
       Castile, your friend, will have the honour
       Of bringing these rough lands under her sway;
       Various peoples in the various regions,
       All differ in their customs and religions.

140 'Here where it bulges, you will colonize
Brazil, named for its red brazil-wood,
Though first christened Santa Cruz
When your fleet is the first to find it.
Along this coast, which you will own,
Will sail, exploring the remotest parts,
Magellan—in all his actions Portuguese
If not completely in his loyalties.

141 'After crossing more than half-way
From the equator to the Antarctic pole
He will come upon men, in the lands
Of that latitude, giants in their stature.
Further still, in the straits now bearing
His own name, his voyage will lead
To another sea, and to those dominions
The South hides under her frozen pinions.

142 'Thus far, Portuguese, you are permitted
To see into the future, learning
Of the deeds heroes will accomplish
On oceans no longer unmapped.
Now, having glimpsed the scale
Of your exploits, so admired
By your inseparable and loving wives
Who weave the coronets that crown your lives,

143 'Now you may embark, with following winds
And a tranquil sea, for your homeland.'
So she spoke: and at once they made ready
To set sail from that happy lovers' isle.
They took cool water and the finest food;
They took the delectable company
Of the nymphs, bound to them eternally
Longer than sunlight warms the earth and sea.

144 So behold them ploughing the calm seas,
With friendly winds, not a hint of a storm,
Until their homeland, the country long
Yearned for, rose before their sight.
They entered the pleasant Tagus, and gave
Their country and their honoured king
The prize for which they sailed at his command,
Placing still greater titles in his hand.

145   *No more, Muse, no more,* my lyre*
      Is out of tune and my throat hoarse,
      Not from singing but from wasting song
      On a deaf and coarsened people.
      Those rewards which encourage genius
      My country ignores, being given over
      To avarice and philistinism,
      Heartlessness and degrading pessimism.

146   *I do not know by what twist of fate*
      It has lost that pride, that zest for life,
      Which lifts the spirits unfailingly
      And welcomes duty with a smiling face.
      In this regard, my King, whom Divine
      Will has set on the royal throne,
      Take note of other nations, and applaud
      The excellence of those who call you lord.

147   *See how cheerfully they venture forth*
      Like rampant lions or wild bulls,
      Yielding their flesh to hunger and vigils,
      To iron and fire, arrow and cannon-ball,
      To burning tropic and Antarctic cold,
      The blows of idolaters and of Muslims,
      To Nature's every hazard and caprice,
      Shipwreck, Leviathan, even to the abyss!

148   *Ready for anything in your service;*
      Obedient, no matter how far flung,
      To your every order, however rigorous,
      Willingly and without question.
      Only because they know you are watching
      They will, without demur, attack
      Infernal demons, burning in their heat
      To bring you victory, never defeat.

149   *Rain favour on them and gladden them*
      With your humane and gracious presence;
      Ease their burden of harsh laws
      And so lay open the road to virtue;
      Promote only men of experience,
      As your counsellors, who join shrewdness
      With benevolence, for such men best know
      The how, the why, the where affairs will go.

150   *Show favour in their professions to all*
       As they bring their talents to bear:
       And let holy men make observances
       Of fasting and due penance, bringing
       Blessings on your reign, checking vice,
       And treating ambition as the wind,
       For the truly religious man is empty
       Of all desire for estates and glory.

151   *Hold your knights in high esteem*
       For their bloody and intrepid fervour
       Extends not only the Holy Faith,
       But the boundaries of your great empire;
       For those who venture in your service
       Gladly to the earth's uttermost ends
       Must overcome two enemies: the living
       And (much harder) the pain of persevering.

152   *So rule, my lord, that no wondering*
       German, French, Italian, or Englishman
       Can boast Portugal is more commanded
       Than given to exercise command.
       Take counsel only of those with many
       Months and years of experience;
       For all the knowledge studying bestows,
       In particulars it is the expert knows.

153   *Phormio,* that elegant metaphysician,*
       Was ridiculed by Hannibal when,
       In his presence, he philosophized
       At length about war and its conduct.
       The useful discipline of war
       Is not learned, my lord, in the mind
       Through dreams or books or visionary lore,
       But watching, rehearsing, and waging war.

154   *But whose is this rough, unworthy voice*
       Unknown, even undreamed of by you?
       Yet from out of the mouths of babes,
       Praise may at times be perfected;
       I am not without honest study,
       Conjoined with long experience,
       Nor genius, here amply demonstrated,
       Qualities almost never found conflated.

155   *In your service, an arm inured to battle;*
       In your praise, a mind given to the Muses;
       All I lack is due approval where
       Merit should meet with esteem.
       If heaven grants me this, and your heart
       Embarks on an enterprise worthy of song
       —As my prescient mind can readily divine
       Seeing which way your heavenly thoughts incline—

156   *Whether to petrify Mount Atlas**
       More profoundly than old Medusa,
       Or to destroy by way of Cape Espartel
       The ramparts of Morocco or Taroudant,
       My triumphant, happy Muse will extol
       Your exploits throughout the world;
       Alexander will share with you his bays,
       No longer coveting Achilles' praise.

EXPLANATORY NOTES

Canto One

3 *Arms are my theme*: the opening imitates Virgil's *Aeneid* ('Arma virumque cano') but with the difference that Camões's subject is the achievements not of one man but of 'the Portuguese'. The challenge to the ancients, both in matter and style, is explicit in stanzas 1–3.

Taprobana: the Greek name for the eastern limit of the known world. In canto 10. 51, Camões identifies it with Ceylon.

4 *my boy King*: the dedication is to King Sebastião who came to the throne in 1568, aged 14. The only grandson of João III, and the sole means of preventing the Portuguese crown passing to Philip II of Spain, his wildness, fanaticism, and lack of interest in women are reflected in Camões's eulogy, which is a masterpiece of controlled anxiety—praising the young king for what he is yet to accomplish, urging him to 'anticipate his maturity', and setting him the example of his illustrious ancestors. Even his duty to marry is hinted at in the reference to Tethys who is preparing the 'world's green oceans' as a dowry (st. 16).

Ourique: a small town south of the River Tagus, said to be where Afonso Henriques defeated the Almoravids (the 'Moors') in 1139. The battle was of little strategic significance but, as Afonso's first victory, became invested with the legend that Christ appeared on the battlefield promising the complete liberation of Portugal. The following year, Afonso (1140–85) became Portugal's first king. The vision is commemorated in the arms of Portugal where five shields are said to represent Christ's wounds on the cross. For Camões's account of the battle, see canto 3. 42–54.

5 *counterfeit exploits*: in dismissing Boiardo's *Orlando innamorato* (1486–1506) and Ariosto's *Orlando furioso* (1532), Camões is again insisting on the primacy of historical truth.

Instead I give you . . . : references follow to Afonso I and his many victories; to Egas Moniz and Fuas Roupinho, his counsellors and allies; to João I (1385–1433), who defeated the Spanish at Aljubarrota in 1385, and Nuno Álvares Pereira, hero of that battle; and to the other kings who secured Portugal's modern frontiers, João II (1481–95) and Afonso III (1248–79), IV (1325–57), and V (1438–81). Camões fulfils his promise to describe these figures in cantos 3. 28–84, 4. 2–50 and 8. 16–17 and 28–32. The story of Magriço and the twelve of England is told in canto 6. 42–70.

Those who in the lands of the Dawn: references are to soldiers and viceroys in Portuguese India. Duarte Pacheco Pereira conquered the Malabar coast; Francisco de Almeida, viceroy (1505–9) with his son Lourenço as deputy, established a chain of fortresses from Sofala to Cochin; Afonso de Albuquerque (1509–15) conquered Goa and Malacca; João de Castro was governor (1545–8) and briefly viceroy shortly before Camões arrived in India. The careers of these and others are celebrated in canto 10. 12–47 and 67–72.

6 *Your two grandsires*: Sebastião's grandfathers were João III (1521–57), known as 'the pious' (he brought the Inquisition to Portugal) and the Emperor Charles V (1519–56).

Portuguese Argonauts: the first of many references to the legend of man-kind's first voyage with Jason and the Argonauts in search of the Golden Fleece. The legend is associated with human daring and with the end of the Golden Age (see canto 4. 102).

cattle of Proteus: seals and other sea-mammals were under the protection of the sea-god Proteus.

7 *When the gods . . .* : for Camões's use of the Roman deities, see Introduc-tion, pp. xiv–xviii. Venus, the patron of Virgil's Aeneas, supports the Portuguese as the inheritors of Roman virtues. She is backed by Mars, who admires their conquests, and opposed by Bacchus, cast in his role as an eastern god about to be displaced by the navigators. The whole pas-sage is redolent of the divine council in Ovid, *Metamorphoses*, i. 168–85.

the seven Spheres: Tethys explains the Ptolemaic system in canto 10. 79–91.

8 *Ourique . . . Aljubarrota*: see notes to pp. 4 and 5.

Viriathus: led a successful revolt against Roman occupation of Iberia until his dishonorable murder in 139 BC.

Sertorius: a rebel Roman captain who ruled Hispania (83–72 BC). Plutarch describes his use of a milk-white hind for divination (see cantos 3. 22 and 8. 6–8).

9 *It was Bacchus who dissented*: the passage imitates Virgil's description of Juno's anxieties in *Aeneid*, i. 12–33.

Ceuta: in Morocco, captured by the Portuguese in 1415 as their first foothold in Africa.

the Cytherean: Venus was venerated in a number of islands, including Cythera.

10 *beaver*: the lower face-guard of a helmet.

Lusus: companion of Bacchus and legendary founder of Portugal—hence its Roman name Lusitania and Camões's title *The Lusíads*. See canto 7. 77 and 8. 2–4 for descriptions.

11 *between Madagascar and Mozambique*: we meet the navigators off the East African coast in the Mozambique Channel. Camões picks up his story *in medias res* not simply in imitation of Virgil but because Vasco da Gama had by now passed the Great Fish River where Bartolomeu Dias was forced to turn back in 1488 and was genuinely in uncharted waters.

Taking refuge as dolphins: Venus and Cupid changed into fish to escape the Titan Typhoeus.

Cape Corrientes: see Introduction, p. xviii.

11 *Vasco da Gama*: the first clear mention of the fleet's captain, praised only for his unshakeable endurance and his genius for success.

12 *From the island nearest the main*: the fleet reached Mozambique Island in January 1498 and found a city state occupied by Swahili (i.e. Africanized Arab) traders, with fine houses, one of the best harbours of the whole coast, and ample supplies from the mainland close by. It was prospering from the trade in gold from the Zambesi escarpment, and was a centre of boat-building. Camões knew the island well (being stranded there, 1567–9), and much of this detail features in his description, as does the evident surprise of the navigators in encountering such a place.

Phaethon: Apollo's son, who borrowed his father's sun-chariot but, frightened by the signs of the Zodiac, steered too near the earth, creating drought and desert and scorching black the people of Ethiopia. Jupiter intervened with a thunderbolt, hurling him into the River Po.

13 *Acheron*: one of the four rivers of the underworld.

the one Lord: i.e. Mohammed, assumed to be descended from Abraham both through his Jewish mother and his Arab father.

14 *Hyperion's son*: Apollo, steering the Sun's chariot.

16 *Vulcan's sons*: the bombardiers. Vulcan manufactured Jupiter's thunderbolts.

17 *born from Jove's thigh*: when Semele, princess of Thebes, was pregnant with Bacchus, she asked to see Jupiter, the father, in all his radiance, and was scorched to death. Bacchus was rescued and hidden in Jupiter's thigh. Hence, the joke 'the twice born' (see canto 2. 10).

Fate has already settled: Juno's speech in *Aeneid*, i. 37–49 is again being imitated.

18 *Philip's precocious boy . . .* : references follow to Alexander the Great, son of Philip of Macedonia, and to the the Emperor Trajan (see canto 1. 3).

With these words: the lines are based on *Aeneid*, i. 50–2.

Cape Corrientes: note to p. 11.

22 *Amphitrite's*: one of Neptune's wives (see canto 6. 22); the nereids, sea-nymphs, are daughters of the god Nereus.

lost Christian tribe: the enduring belief that somewhere in Africa was a lost Christian kingdom gained force when emissaries from Ethiopia reached Europe in the early fifteenth century, including one who visited Lisbon in 1452. Among Vasco da Gama's commissions was a letter from King Manuel to Prester John. Sinon was the Greek who persuaded the Trojans to take in the wooden horse.

23 *Mombasa*: another of the Swahili city states, reached in April 1498. Seeing it, the Portuguese were reminded of the cities of southern Spain.

24 *O great and grave dangers*: each canto of *The Lusiads* ends at a point of some suspense and with some moral reflections appropriate to the situation.

Canto Two

27 *twice-born*: see canto 1. 73.

   Pentecost: see Acts 2. 1–4.

28 *Ericina*: one of Venus' temples was on Mt Eryx in Sicily.

29 *Blocking the way*: the Portuguese fleet was indeed unable to cross the dangerous bar at Mombasa. Vasco da Gama attributes this to Divine Providence (st. 30–2), Venus assumes she and the Nereids are responsible, while the Muslims mistake the sailors' chants and oaths for war cries (st. 25).

   As ants: the simile is a mock-heroic version of *Aeneid*, iv. 401–7.

30 *As in a pond*: in *Metamorphoses*, vi. 339–81, the goddess Leto, in a display of anger, murders Niobe's children before turning the peasants of Lycia into frogs for refusing to let her drink at their lake. By contrast, Camões's simile is obviously comic.

31 *sixth sphere*: in the Ptolemaic system, Venus is in the third and Jupiter in the sixth sphere (see cantos 1. 21 and 10. 89).

32 *She displayed herself*: the scene is a greatly enhanced version of Venus' appeal to Jupiter in *Aeneid*, i. 223–304.

   Paris: in the beauty competition on Mt Ida between Venus, Juno, and Minerva, Paris awarded the prize to Venus and was rewarded with Helen.

   Diana: Actaeon, out hunting, stumbled upon Diana bathing and was turned into a stag and torn to pieces by his hounds.

   Mars' rekindled passion: Venus was Vulcan's wife and Mars' mistress.

33 *Another Cupid*: Camões takes Cupid to be the son of Jupiter and Venus.

34 *Though Ulysses . . .*: references follow to Ulysses on the island of Calypso (Ogygia); to Antenor who after the fall of Troy discovered the Adriatic Sea and the River Timavus; and to Aeneas and the rocks and whirlpools of the Straits of Messina.

   a miracle: Vasco da Gama described a sea-tremor off the coast of Cambaya on his second voyage, recording his comment: 'The sea is afraid of us.'

   the island: Mozambique.

   You will see . . .: all these events are described in canto 10. 12–25, 36, 40–2, 50–2, and 60–1.

35 *Actium*: the naval battle where Octavius defeated Anthony on his triumphal return from conquests in Asia and Egypt. The images echo *Aeneid*, viii. 675–88.

   Golden Chersonese: the Malay Peninsula. Its capital, Malacca, was captured in 1511.

36 *Magellan*: Fernão de Magalhães, who set out in 1519 to circumnavigate the globe and discovered the Straits of Magellan, but in the service of Spain (cf. canto 10. 138–41).

   Cyllene: a mountain in Arcadia where Mercury was born.

36 *Malindi*: the third of the Swahili city states visited by da Gama. Despite sharing a common origin and links of kinship with Mombasa, commercial rivalry led the Sultan into an alliance with the Portuguese which endured, somewhat precariously, until the end of the seventeenth century.

37 *Diomedes*: king of Thrace (one of Hercules' labours was to feed him to his carnivorous horses).

Busiris: king of Egypt, who sacrificed all foreigners to Jupiter.

Night and day equal: Malindi is 3° south of the equator.

39 *Taurus*: it was April (with the sun in Taurus) and Easter Sunday. References are to Jupiter's rape of Europa, disguised as a bull, and to the goat-nymph Amalthea who suckled the infant Jupiter and whose horn became the famous Cornucopia.

Malindi: see note to p. 36.

40 *Minerva*: or Pallas Athene, goddess of eloquence.

41 *Ulysses*: welcomed as a castaway by king Alcinous of the Phaeacians, to whom much of the *Odyssey* is narrated, just as the Sultan of Malindi is to hear Vasco da Gama's account.

43 *Cyclops*: Vulcan's blacksmiths (cf. canto 1. 68).

Memnon's: son of Aurora the goddess of dawn, and king of Ethiopia.

44 *Tyrian*: from the Phoenician city of Tyre.

Iris: the rainbow.

45 *the long wars*: largely the subject of cantos 3 and 4.

Hesperides: Hesperus, the evening star, sets in the far west. The term 'Hesperian' was applied by the Greeks to Italy and by the Romans to Spain and the Atlantic Islands. Camões uses the term Hespéria to refer at different times to Portugal or to Iberia as a whole (see st. 108, and cantos 4. 54 and 8. 61 and 69); the term Hespério for the Cape Verde islands (canto 5. 8); and the term Hespérides as here, for Morocco. The reference is to the daughters of the giant Hesperus whose golden apples were guarded by a dragon, eventually slain by Hercules.

O generous king: the passage imitates Aeneas' address to Dido, *Aeneid*, i. 597–610.

46 *Aeolus*: the god who kept the winds in a bag.

47 *The proud Titans* . . . : references follow to the Titans who made war against the gods on Olympus (see canto 5. 51), and to Pirithous and Theseus who tried to kidnap Proserpina, wife of Pluto, king of the Underworld. Pirithous was eaten by the dog Cerberus and Theseus made prisoner until released by Hercules. For Nereus, see canto 2. 19.

Ctesiphon: the architect of Diana's temple at Ephesus, one of the seven wonders of the ancient world. Herostratus is said to have burned it with the sole aim of being remembered.

Canto Three

48 *Calliope*: the epic muse, invoked in *Aeneid*, ix. 525.

Apollo: god of medicine, and Orpheus' father by Calliope, though compulsively unfaithful to her.

49 *Hyperborean*: literally 'beyond the north', here the back of beyond of Russia.

Scythians: Russians, in legend rivalling Egyptians in antiquity. Damascus is said to have been founded by Adam.

50 *Helle*: escaped with her brother on the ram with the Golden Fleece, and fell into the strait which bears her name while on the way to Colchis.

Constantine the Great: the Turks took Constantinople (Byzantium) in 1453 (cf. canto 1. 60).

Antenor: see canto 2. 45.

51 *the Keeper of the Keys*: St Peter's descendants as popes.

Pyrene: a nymph who fled from her angry father after yielding to Hercules and was eaten by animals in these mountains.

last labour: Hercules' last labour was to open the Straits of Gibraltar, sealing them with the pillars of Calpe and Abyla (supposedly the origins of the name Gibraltar, but see also note on p. 53 below).

Naples: conquered in 1442 by Alfonso V of Aragon.

all restored: the conquest of Spain was completed with the capture of Granada in 1492.

52 *Lusus*: see canto 1. 24.

Viriatus: see canto 1. 26 (Camões is punning on the Latin *virtus*, manliness, strength).

Alfonso: Alfonso VI (1065–1109) of Castile who captured Toledo, ancient capital of the Visigoth kings, in 1085.

53 *Henrique*: Henry of Burgundy (not Hungary), who married Teresa, illegitimate daughter of Alfonso VI, and fathered the first king of Portugal, Afonso I (1143–85).

Ishmaelites: Camões makes a curious distinction between Saracens, meaning descendants of Sarah, Abraham's legitimate wife, and Ishmaelites, descendants of Hagar, Abraham's 'mistress'. Visigoth Spain was invaded in 711 by a Berber army from Morocco, said to have been led by Tariq who gave his name to the rock (*jebel*) where he landed (Jebel Tariq: Gibraltar), and by 715 most of what became Spain and Portugal was under Arab rule. Initially, Muslim Iberia was ruled by governors based in Córdoba appointed by the Umayyad caliphs in Damascus, but after the overthrow of the Umayyad dynasty by the Abbasids in 750, it became a semi-independent outpost of Islam, racked by internal divisions between the Arab rulers and the Berber majority, and eventually, after the decline of Córdoba *c*.1000, split into separate states or *taifas*. It was these *taifas* which began to be attacked by the kings of Spain and Portugal in the eleventh and twelfth centuries, beginning effectively with the capture of Toledo (see st. 23) in 1085. Meanwhile, Iberia was invaded from Morocco by successive revivalist groups which had come to power there and which brought some unity to the Muslim states. These were the Almoravids, orthodox and puritan, who began to intervene in 1086, and the Almohads, equally orthodox but stressing spiritual renewal, who succeeded them from the mid-twelfth century. It was against Almoravid- and Almohad-led armies that Portugal was captured piecemeal between the Battle of Ourique 1139 and the conquest of the Algarve, completed by 1249.

53 *the Holy City*: references are to the First Crusade (1096–9) and its leader, Godfrey of Boulogne. It is disputed whether Henry was present.

his mother: Queen Teresa. She is said to have been mistress, not wife, of Fernando Peres, Count of Trava.

54 *So at Guimarães*: the Battle of Guimarães (1128) is taken to mark the beginning of Portuguese independence from Castile.

cruel Procne . . . Medea: references follow to Procne, who avenged her husband's rape of her sister Philomena by killing her son Itys and feeding him to Tereus, his father; to Medea who, abandoned by her husband Jason, murdered their two sons; and to Scylla, who killed her father, king of Megara, in order to deliver his head to King Minos of Crete whom she loved and who was besieging the city.

55 *Faithful Egas*: the legend of Egas Moniz, Afonso's tutor, provides one model of personal fealty. There are other models as Camões's history proceeds. Even here, no reflection is intended on Afonso's honour.

Sinis . . . : references are to Sinis, a thief slain by Theseus, who bent branches to the ground and tied his victims to them, tearing them to pieces; and to Perillus, who invented for his master Phalaris of Agrigentum a brazen bull in which to roast his enemies.

56 *Zophyrus*: one of Darius I's generals who, when besieging Babylon, mutilated himself to deceive the defenders into believing he had changed sides and so captured the city.

the plain of Ourique: for the Battle of Ourique 1139, see canto 1. 7.

Penthesilea: Queen of the Amazons, of the River Thermodon in Asia Minor.

58 *the proud white buckler*: this explanation of the shields on Portugal's escutcheon supplements canto 1. 7.

59 *Leiria . . . Arronches*: captured 1140.

Santarém: captured 1147.

Mafra: taken 1146.

Sintra: taken 1147. The Promontory of the Moon was named by Ptolemy. Camões seems to be indicating Cabo da Roca.

most noble Lisbon: the legend is that Lisbon, named 'Ulysippo' in Latin, was founded by Ulysses. The city fell in 1147 after a five-month siege with the aid of knights *en route* to the Second Crusade.

60 *Vandals*: Visigoth invaders, including 'Vandals' after whom, Camões claims wrongly, the Spanish province of Andalusia is named.

Estremadura: the province bordering Lisbon to the north, containing Óbidos, Torres Vedras, and Alenquer, captured 1147–8.

lands of the Alentejo: the strongholds listed in this stanza, beyond the Tagus, were taken 1166. Ceres was the goddess of agriculture, with whom even the conquering Portuguese admitted the 'Moors' were on good terms.

even Évora yielded: once Sertorius' capital (see canto 1. 26), captured 1165 by Gerald the Fearless after the bloody exploit described in canto 8. 21. The famous aqueduct was built by João III.

Beja: captured 1162.

Trancoso: far to the north, in Beira Alta province, had been destroyed in 1140.

61 *Sesimbra*: captured 1165. Afonso's defeat of the Almoravid ruler of Badajoz was followed by the fall of Palmela in 1166.

laid siege to Badajoz: Afonso captured Badajoz from the Almohads in 1169. He was then himself besieged by his son-in-law Ferdinand II of León and taken prisoner after breaking his leg.

62 *grieve no longer*: Pompey was defeated by Julius Caesar, his father-in-law, at Pharsalia in Thessaly, 48 BC. The following stanzas refer to the various lands conquered by Pompey, from Asia to the Atlas Mountains.

engines of God's ire: see st. 33.

Santarém: besieged 1173; the presumed remains of St Vincent, Lisbon's patron, were translated in 1175.

63 *Sancho*: later Sancho I (1185–1211), conducted these southern campaigns in 1179.

They came together: Camões has conflated several invasions, beginning with the capture of Granada in 1154, by the Almohads under their spiritual leader Amir 'Abd al-mu'nin (see note to p. 53 below). The Amir died in 1163. It was his successor, Yusuf I, who died at the siege of Santarém in 1184.

Atlas Mountains: the giant Atlas was petrified by sight of the head of the gorgon Medusa.

Antaeus: the giant Antaeus, killed by Hercules and buried near Tangier.

64 *Afonso*: the Great, d. 1185.

65 *Silves*: ancient capital of the Algarve, taken 1189 with the help of English (not German) knights sailing to join Emperor Frederick (Barbarossa) I on the Third Crusade. Guy de Lusignan was defeated by Saladin in the waterless plain of Tiberias (1187) where he had encamped.

the splendid frontier city: Sancho I campaigned against Alfonso IX, capturing the frontier town of Tuy in 1197.

66 *second Afonso*: Afonso II (1211–23), retook Alcácer do Sal finally in 1217.

66 *Sancho the second*: (1223–47). References in the following stanzas are to Roman emperors Nero (AD 54–68) and Heliogabalus (AD 218–22); to Sardanapalus, the last Assyrian king of Nineveh (9th century BC); and to Phalaris, the Sicilian tyrant (d. 552 BC), for whom Perillus devised the brazen bull (cf. st. 39).

his brother: Sancho II was deposed 1245 by the Count of Boulogne, who became Afonso III (1248–79) on Sancho's death.

67 *The land assigned by fate to Portugal*: the conquest of the Algarve was completed in Afonso III's reign.

King Dinis: Dinis I (1279–1325), was known as *O Lavrador* (the worker). He founded Portugal's first university, created the great state forest of Leiria, reformed local government, rebuilt much of Portugal, and was Portugal's first patron of the arts. He was also a fine poet, no less than 137 of his *cantigas* being preserved in the song-books.

army of Moors: though by *c*.1300 all of Portugal and most of Spain was under Christian rule, Grenada remained an amirate. In 1340 the Amir summoned reinforcements from Morocco in a last attempt to recapture Spain. They were defeated at the Battle of the River Salado, near Tarifa, by the combined forces of Afonso IV and his son-in-law Alfonso XI of Castile (1312–50). Camões highlights it as one of the three major battles of *The Lusíads*, partly because of Portugal's central role but principally because it marked the last serious threat from North Africa.

68 *Semiramis*: legendary Queen of Assyria.

Attila: (433–53), leader of the Huns (not Goths, as suggested here).

70 *Ishmaelites*: see note to p. 53.

robust and brutal giant: for David and Goliath, see 1 Samuel 17. 20–54.

Santiago: St James, patron saint of Castile.

71 *home of Tethys*: one of Neptune's wives, hence, the ocean.

Roman Marius . . . : references follow to the victory of Marius over the Teutons (101 BC); of Hannibal over the Romans at Cannae (216 BC); and to the destruction of Jerusalem by Emperor Titus (AD 70), prophesied in the Old Testament and by Christ (Luke 21. 20–4).

But now the tragic history: in the tragedy of Inês de Castro, all the actors existed historically. Yet the story sounds like myth, being capable of different interpretations. She came from a noble Galician family and her two brothers were ambitious for thrones. Her long-standing affair with Pedro, the crown prince, began when she was lady-in-waiting to Princess Constança, Pedro's wife. When she bore him four children and when, after Constança's death, Pedro refused to marry, she became a danger to the succession and national fervour demanded her removal. Was Inês, in all this, the hapless victim of statecraft? This is the version Camões presents. Or was she a manipulator, dangerously ambitious for her sons and for Spain? And what was the role of Pedro? Was it her death that turned him into Pedro the Cruel? The story (see st. 118) that he had her body exhumed at his succession and crowned queen speaks of some derangement. Yet his decree that they should be buried feet to feet in the great monastery at Alcobaça, so that hers will be the first face he sees at the resurrection, seems the action of a lover.

73 *little children*: the legendary rearing of Semiramis by doves (cf. st. 100), and of Romulus and Remus by the she-wolf.

74 *Polyxena*: daughter of Priam of Troy, sacrificed by Pyrrhus in the presence of her mother Hecuba to appease the ghost of Achilles.

Atreus: king of Mycenae, who took this terrible revenge against Thyestes, his adulterous brother.

75 *Pedro was avenged*: Pedro I (1357–67) persuaded his contemporary, Pedro the Cruel of Castile (1350–69) to hand back Inês's killers for execution. The two 'Peters' are compared to the triumvirate of Octavius, Mark Antony, and Lepidus who likewise disposed of their enemies.

harsher penalties: Hercules and Theseus were known for killing outlaws.

Gentle Fernando: Fernando (1367–83) was dominated by his mistress, Leonor Teles, and left Portugal exposed to the Castilean invasion of 1373—events to be settled by the Battle of Aljubarrota (see canto 4. 7–45).

76 *Lust always has the consequences*: the canto concludes with reflections on the power of love to destroy and to transform. Paris stole Helen; Appius Claudius raped Virginia, following the example of Sextus Tarquinius, violator of Lucretia, and afterwards committed suicide; King David stole Bathsheba from her husband; the tribe of Benjamin was massacred after its members raped a woman of the tribe of Levi; Pharaoh's passion for Sarah, Abraham's wife passing herself off as his sister, resulted in the plagues afflicting Egypt; Shechem raped Dinah, Jacob's daughter and was killed; Hercules, infatuated with Omphale of Lydia, swapped clothing and weapons with her; Anthony lost an empire for Cleopatra; and Hannibal, after the Battle of Cannae (see st. 116) all but threw his victory away for a woman from Apulia.

Canto Four

77 *longed for a hero*: King Fernando's death in 1383 bequeathed a succession crisis, presided over by his former mistress, the hated Leonor Teles, and her lover, the Count of Ourém. The principal claimant was Juan of Castile, husband of Fernando's daughter Beatrice, whose accession would have meant subjugation to Spain. The Portuguese pretender was the popular João of Avis, a bastard son of King Pedro. Camões (see st. 7) doubts Beatrice's legitimacy but that question aside, Juan of Castile had the better claim while João of Avis seemed likely to make the better king. At this point in *The Lusíads* loyalty to country and the 'common will' supersedes feudal fealty of the kind demonstrated by Egas Moniz (canto 3. 35–41).

77 *an infant girl*: Burton points out the 'Delphian adroitness' of the 'loyal and loquacious child' in uttering a name which fitted both contenders.

outright cruelties: in the civil disorders, the Count of Ourém was stabbed to death by João of Avis, and the Castilian Bishop of Lisbon, Martinho, suffered the fate of Astyanax, hurled by the Greeks from the walls of Troy.

78 *cruel Marius . . .* : references follow to Marius (157–86 BC) and Sulla (138–78 BC), political rivals in Rome's civil war.

Assembled his troops: the Battle of Aljubarrota (1385), one of the great set-pieces of *The Lusíads*, sealed Portugal's independence from Spain. Camões describes the massing of an immense Spanish army (st. 8–11), the rallying of Portugal's weak forces (st. 12–22), the departure from Abrantes (st. 23–7), and finally the battle itself, more than matching Ourique and Salado (canto 3. 44–53 and 109–16) in ferocity.

Derives its name . . . : references follow to Brigus, legendary founder of Burgos, to Fernán González (930?–70), first count of Castile, and to El Cid, Rodrigo Díaz de Bivar (*c.*1043–99).

Vandals: see canto 3. 60.

pillars of Hercules: see canto 3. 18.

79 *Dom Nuno Álvares*: Dom Nuno Álvares Pereira (1360?–1431), constable of the Kingdom, was military leader of this revolution and is one of Portugal's most revered heroes. His brothers, Diogo and Pedro, like the majority of Portugal's noblemen (together with Camões's own ancestor Vasco Lopes de Camões), fought with Castile.

80 *ferocious Henrique*: the victory of Afonso I at Arcos de Valdevez (cf. canto 3. 34).

81 *young Scipio*: Scipio Africanus and his rallying speech at Canosa, after Rome's defeat by Hannibal at Cannae (see canto 3. 116).

Abrantes: on the River Tagus where it curves west above Santarém. The Tagus marshes being then impassable, all battles for Lisbon were won or lost in the northern approaches (cf. Wellington's lines at Torres Vedras in the Peninsular War, some 40 km. from Aljubarrota).

Xerxes: king of Persia who crossed the Hellespont to attack Greece (480 BC) with an army supposedly of two million men.

Attila: see canto 3. 100. There is an untranslatable pun on Dom Nuno and *o fero Huno* (the fierce Hun).

82 *Antão Vasques de Almada*: one of Camões's rare historical errors. It was Antão's nephew, Alvaro, who fought at Aljubarrota and was later made count of Avranches (in Normandy) by Henry VI of England (see also canto 6. 69).

Cape Ortegal . . . : references follow to Cape Ortegal in north Galicia, to the Guadiana and Douro rivers in southern Spain and northern Portugal respectively, and to the Alentejo.

83 *O Sertorius* . . . : references follow to the revolts of Sertorius (see canto 3. 63), and Coriolanus (d. 488 BC), and to the conspiracy of Catiline (d. 62 BC), attacked in Cicero's speeches.

84 *Massylia*: in North Africa.

the Seven Brothers: an unspecified range in northern Morocco, known by that name to the geographers Camões follows.

85 *Many they dispatched*: the dead included masters of the military orders of St James and Calatrava (founded in the twelfth century), together with Nuno Pereira's two brothers (see st. 32). Souls of the dead entered the underworld by crossing the River Styx.

Cerberus: the three-headed dog who guarded the crossing of the Styx.

86 *His fortune favoured him*: Nuno won a second victory over Castile in 1385 at Valverde, near Mérida (cf. canto 8. 30–1).

English princesses: in 1387 João I of Portugal and Prince Henry (later Henry III) of Castile married Philippa and Catherine, daughters of John of Gaunt, duke of Lancaster (who later claimed the throne of Castile: see canto 6. 47).

Ceuta: captured in 1415, the first of Portugal's overseas possessions. For Hercules' Pillars, see note to p. 51. Count Julian, in legend, conspired with the Moors at the time of the first invasion of 711.

87 *a progeny*: João's gifted sons were Duarte, his heir (1433–8), Pedro, a notably enlightened regent during Afonso V's minority, Henry the so-called Navigator, João, and Fernando, the 'constant prince' (see st. 52).

Fernando: captured in Tangier in 1437 and died in captivity rather than surrender Ceuta. Accounts differ on whether Duarte gave him any choice.

Codrus . . . : references follow to Codrus, King of Athens (eleventh century BC), who sacrificed his life because the oracle had foretold that only so could the city be saved; to consul Regulus, captured by the Carthaginians, sent by them to Rome to negotiate peace, and executed on his return (251 BC) for having recommended war in Rome; to Curtius who leaped into a chasm in the Forum (300 BC), which the oracle declared could only be closed with Rome's greatest treasure; and to the Deciians, grandfather, father, and son, who died fighting for Rome in 338, 296, and 280 BC respectively.

Afonso the Fifth: (1438–81) won victories in North Africa, capturing Alcácer-Ceguer in 1458 and Arzilla and Tangier in 1471.

88 *Hesperides*: see note to canto 2. 108.

throne of Castile: on the death of Henry IV of Castile, Afonso V, who was married to his daughter Joana, claimed the throne. The result was an Aljubarrota in reverse as the Spaniards prefered the claim of Isabella, Henry IV's sister, and her husband Ferdinand of Aragon. At the Battle of Toro (1476), Afonso V was saved from defeat only by the intervention of his son João, later João II (1481–95). Isabella and Ferdinand became the famous 'Catholic Monarchs', conquerers of Granada and sponsors of Columbus.

88 *Philippi*: the two battles of Philippi in 42 BC, when Brutus and Cassius, Caesar's assassins, were defeated.

89 *He appointed envoys*: the most famous of João's agents were Pero de Covilhã and Afonso de Paiva, dispatched in 1487 in search of the African Christian emperor Prester John (see canto 1. 98). They followed roughly the route indicated by Camões as far as Aden, where they divided, Afonso de Paiva continuing to Ethiopia where he disappears from history, Pero de Covilhã travelling to the Persian Gulf and India (including Cannanore, Calicut, and Goa). He also visited the Swahili city states of East Africa, probably reaching as far south as Sofala. Returning in late 1490, he was intercepted in Egypt by an emissary from King João ordering him to proceed to Ethiopia. This he did, after compiling a full report on his travels. He was hospitably received by the negus or emperor and given a wife and land, but was never permitted to leave and died there over thirty years later. One of the mysteries of Portuguese history is whether his report of 1490 ever reached the king. If it did, it would explain why Vasco da Gama had orders to proceed to Calicut, the most important entrepôt of the spice trade. If it didn't, it would explain why the Portuguese were so surprised at the sophistication of the Swahili states, and took with them such unsuitable goods for trading in India.

Parthenope: a nymph who drowned herself for love of Ulysses and was cast up on the shore where Naples was founded.

the river banks: Pompey died in 48 BC at Pelusium (now Tineh) in the Nile Delta.

Nabathean hills: see Genesis 25. 13.

Myrrha: committed incest with her father Cinyras, fled to Arabia and was turned into the fragrant shrub after giving birth to Adonis.

Tower of Babel: supposedly built beside the River Euphrates (Genesis 11).

ended all his victories: the Persian Gulf was the limit of Trajan's conquests.

90 *Manuel*: Manuel I (1495–1521), 'the Fortunate', inherited the results of King João II's efforts.

Morpheus: god of sleep.

first sphere: in the Ptolemaic system, the circle described by the moon.

91 *flowing . . . underground*: the river god Alpheus pursued Arethusa under the sea to Syracuse, mixing his waters with hers when she turned into a fountain.

accept the tribute: by contrast with João II's fascination with Prester John, Manuel's vision is of taxing India.

I am the famous Ganges: the Tiber gives similar advice to Aeneas (*Aeneid*, viii. 36).

93 *vast labours*: da Gama refers to five of the twelve labours of Hercules, imposed by the king of Mycenae, Eurystheus.

There offered to sail with me: the fleet consisted of the flagship *São Gabriel*, commanded by Vasco da Gama, the warship *São Rafael*, under his elder brother Paulo da Gama, the caravel *Bérrio*, under Nicolau Coelho, and a supply ship under Gonçalo Nunes. On board were Pero de Alenquer, who had been Bartolomeu Dias's pilot in 1487–8; Fernão Martins, who spoke Arabic, and Martim Afonso, who had lived in the Congo; a certain Álvaro Velho, who kept a diary of the whole voyage as far as Guinea on the return journey; together with four masters, three ships' clerks, and an unknown number of priests, mariners, caulkers, soldiers, and condemned prisoners (see canto 2. 7), in total somewhere between 150 and 200 men. Also mentioned in *The Lusíads* are Fernão Veloso (cantos 5. 31, 6. 41–69, and 9. 69), Lionardo Ribeiro (cantos 6. 40 and 9. 75–82), Álvaro Vaz de Almada (cantos 4. 25 and 6. 69), and Álvaro de Braga, the clerk, and Diogo Dias, the overseer (canto 8. 94). Paulo da Gama was apparently offered the command and turned it down in his younger brother's favour. He died at the Azores on the return journey in 1499. Nicolau Coelho died in a shipwreck in 1504.

93 *Ulysses' . . . harbour*: see note to p. 59.

94 *the night sky*: the Argonauts' ship, the *Argo*, became a constellation.

The holy chapel: built at Belém (Bethlehem), by Henry the Navigator.

95 *But an old man*: the deeply moving episode of the Old Man of Belém, denouncing the whole enterprise, reflects opposition in Portugal to King Manuel's overseas policy. But the words Camões has given his invented character far transcend politics. They invoke a pre-lapsarian, golden age before men first 'put dry wood on the waves with a sail' to voyage in search of wealth and power. It is a vision which mocks the whole imperial thrust of *The Lusíads* with all its religious, philosophical, and adventurous trappings, and which haunts us throughout the epic in its recurring episodes of elegy or pastoral.

96 *heirs of that madcap Adam*: having first addressed 'Pride' (st. 95), the Old Man addresses the ships' company, now on board, mentioning the expulsion from Eden (Genesis 3. 22–4) and the four ages of the world, gold, silver, bronze, and iron (Ovid, *Metamorphoses*, i. 125–35, among many others).

afraid to die: see Matthew 26. 38–42.

97 *Ishmaelite*: see note to p. 53.

Seigneurs: Manuel did indeed assume the title 'Lord of Guinea and of the Conquest, Navigation and Commerce of Ethiopia, Arabia, Persia, and India'. Camões's satire could hardly be more pointed.

nor eloquent poet: the denunciation includes, by implication, Camões himself.

Prometheus: created mankind by breathing life into clay figures, and afterwards stole fire from heaven to make man's circumstances more tolerable.

Daedalus: the architect and sculptor made wings of feathers and wax for himself and his son Icarus, but Icarus soared too near the sun and fell into the (Icarian) sea.

Canto Five

98 *The sun was in Leo*: the fleet sailed on 8 July 1497. The sun enters Leo on 14 July (for Hercules' labours, see note to canto 4. 80), the discrepancy being caused by Pope Gregory XIII's reform of the calendar in 1582.

Henry: later termed the Navigator. Recent research denies his pre-eminent role and stresses the initiatives of his brother Pedro, the regent.

Antaeus: see note to p. 63.

99 *Madeira*: the word means 'wood'.

Barbary: Mauretania.

Asinarius: the name is Ptolemy's, but probably for Cape Blanco in Mauretania rather than Cape Verde in Senegal, Africa's furthest point west.

Canary Islands: known to Roman geographers as the Fortunate Isles. Less plausible is Camões's identification of Cape Verde archipelago with the Hesperides (cf. canto 2. 103).

Santiago: the largest of the Cape Verde islands, and the fleet's only landfall before South Africa.

100 *We crossed the broad gulf*: heading south into the Gulf of Guinea, the fleet bypasses Senegal and the Gambia, with their Jalof and Mandingo peoples, and the Bissagos Islands off Guinea-Bissau, which Camões takes to be the islands of the Gorgons. One of these was Medusa, loved for her hair by Neptune, and cursed by Athene in revenge with ugliness and a head of writhing snakes. When Perseus beheaded her and flew back with the evidence, it shed adders across the Sahara, and the sight petrified the giant Atlas (see canto 3. 77).

Our prows pointing ever south: the fleet passes (with no further classical identifications) Sierra Leone with its lion-like mountain, Cape Palmas on the southern tip of Liberia, and the vast delta of the River Niger, before reaching São Tomé (St Thomas) island, off Gabon (for St Thomas, see John 20. 19–29 and also canto 10. 108–19).

kingdom of the Congo: not the modern territory but the old Congo kingdom of northern Angola, extending south of the River Zaire. It was not converted to Christianity until the reign of the remarkable Nzinga Nvemba (1506–43), a detail which confirms that from here until stanza 23, Camões is blending Vasco da Gama's voyage with his own voyage fifty-six years later.

the burning line: the equator.

the Southern Cross: Camões's knowledge of constellations was exact and detailed, and alien skies caused him far more unease than alien lands or peoples.

101 *both tropics*: Cancer and Capricorn, the limits of the sun's course north and south of the equator.

both Bears: the Great and Little Bear, constellations near the North Pole. Callisto, one of Jupiter's innumerable loves, and her son Arcas were changed to bears by Juno and then to constellations by Jupiter, to which Juno riposted that they should never bathe in the ocean (see *Metamorphoses*, ii. 171 and xiii. 293 and 726).

101 *St Elmo's Fire*: the electrical discharge seen on mastheads. St Elmo was a patron of sailors.

103 *the astrolabe*: a forerunner of the sextant, invented by the Arabs and indispensable for the Portuguese voyages. It enabled positions to be taken by reading the height of the sun. The Portuguese were skilled navigators, incapable of the inspired blunders of Columbus.

We went ashore: the landing, five months into the voyage, was at Saint Helena Bay, north of Cape Town.

Polyphemus: the one-eyed giant Ulysses blinds to free his companions in *Odyssey*, ix. 180 ff.

104 *Fernão Veloso*: see also cantos 6. 41–69 and 9. 69.

Coelho: see canto 4. 82.

Ethiopian: the conventional term, from Herodotus and Pliny, for all Africans south of the Sahara (see Introduction, p. xvii).

105 *an immense shape*: for Adamastor, see Introduction, p. xvi.

106 *Colossus of Rhodes*: the statue raised to Apollo at the harbour entrance at Rhodes, one of the seven wonders of the ancient world.

the next fleet: Pedro Alvares Cabral was driven back from the Cape in 1500, with the loss of four ships, to become inadvertently the discoverer of Brazil.

Dias: Bartolomeu Dias, who first rounded the Cape in 1488, was aboard one of the ships which foundered in 1500.

107 *first viceroy*: Francisco de Almeida, who captured Kilwa and Mombasa in 1505 and defeated a combined Egyptian–Gujarati (not Turkish) fleet in 1509, was killed at the Cape in 1510 on his way home (cf. cantos 1. 14 and 10. 26–37).

another will come: references follow to the deaths of Manuel de Sousa de Sepulveda and his wife and children after being shipwrecked in 1552.

108 *Cape of Storms*: Dias's original name for the Cape is said to have been overruled by João II. Ptolemy, Pomponius Mela, Strabo, and Pliny the Elder were the best known geographers of the first and second centuries AD.

I was one of those rugged Titans: references follow to the ancient myth of the war between the Titans and Jupiter (the shaker of Vulcan's thunderbolts), when mountain was hurled on mountain and the Titans were buried.

Peleus' immortal wife: Peleus, a man, was permitted to marry Thetis, the daughter of the sea-gods Nereus and Doris, so she could give birth to Achilles. Camões takes Thetis and Tethys to be identical.

110 *The people who owned the country*: for this episode, see Introduction, pp. xii–xiii. The landing is taken to have been at São Braz, near Mossel Bay.

111 *Santa Cruz*: Bartolomeu Dias reached the Great Fish River, reporting that the southern African coast continued endlessly eastwards. He erected a memorial cross on the island still named Santa Cruz.

three kings from the Orient: this landfall on the Feast of the Epiphany, 1498, is given variously as the mouth of the Limpopo, Inharrime, or Save rivers. The close proximity of Sofala in stanza 73 suggests the River Save.

112 *Sofala*: south of the modern port of Beira, a trading post for gold from the Manica highlands. Camões does not explain how Vasco da Gama knew of it, but see canto 4. 61.

St Nicholas: a patron of sailors.

113 *a river flowing to the open sea*: the River Kwakwa, on which Quelimane is situated, was then a mouth of the River Zambesi. Some maps still label it the 'Bons Sinais' ('Good Signs').

Ethiopians: see note to p. 104.

some Arabic words: Vasco da Gama's (and apparently Fernão Martins's) first encounter with the Swahili language.

naming it for St Rafael: the archangel who was Tobias's guide in the apocryphal Book of Tobit (5. 5–21).

114 *a disease more cruel*: the symptons are those of scurvy.

115 *the Aonian spring*: Mt Helicon (see cantos 1. 4 and 3. 97) was in Aonia. Rhodes, etc. all claimed the honour of being Homer's birthplace (as Lisbon, Coimbra, Santarém, and others compete to be Camões's). Virgil was born in Mantua, through which runs the River Mincius.

Let them sing on: Vasco da Gama's dismissive summary of the *Odyssey* and *Aeneid* matches Camões's introduction (see canto 1. 3), but note also st. 94–9 and cantos 7. 81 and 10. 145.

117 *as Fulvia found*: Martial (*Epigrams*, xi. 20) describes the verses Augustus wrote about Fulvia's reactions to Antony's affair with Glaphyra.

Scipio: the myth that Scipio the Younger wrote comedies seems to derive from his role as the Roman playwright Terence's patron.

Canto Six

119 *illustrious pillars*: see note to p. 51.

120 *his new pilot*: Da Gama's pilot was long reputed to have been Ahmed Ibn Majid, the greatest Arab navigator of his day and author of numerous treatises on the Indian Ocean. He is now thought to have retired in 1465.

wicked Bacchus: the second half of *The Lusíads* begins with a further assembly of the gods, this time in Neptune's underwater palace. Only the sea-gods are present and there is no debate, just a harangue from Bacchus.

the underwater god: Neptune.

121 *primeval chaos*: the shapeless mass out of which the four elements (fire, air, earth, and water), the basic components of all creation, were separated.

Typhoeus: one of the Titans, imprisoned after the war beneath Mount Etna (see canto 5. 58, where Enceladus has suffered the same fate).

Smiting the earth: the legend is that Neptune's gift of the first warhorse was countered by Minerva's gift of the first olive tree (see Ovid, *Metamorphoses*, vi. 80).

122 *Triton*: the description imitates *Metamorphoses*, i. 330–42.

123 *Father Ocean came*: the various sea-gods who assemble include Father Ocean, god of the oceans surrounding the ancient world as opposed to the Mediterranean which was enclosed by it; Nereus his son with his wife Doris, parents of the Nereids or sea-nymphs (see cantos 1. 96 and 2. 18–33); Proteus, custodian of seals and other sea animals (see canto 1. 19) and a prophet; Tethys, Neptune's wife, who appears regularly in *The Lusiads*; Amphitrite, Neptune's second wife, accompanied by the dolphin which persuaded her to accept his love; Ino and her son Melicertes, who fled from her infanticidal husband and became, with the help of the nymph Panopea, a sea-god jointly with her son; and Glaucus, who accidentally became a sea-god by eating a herb, spurned Circe for love of Scylla, and saw her changed into a sea-monster (afterwards, she became the rocks of the Messina Straits).

125 *one of my former vassals*: Lusus (see canto 1. 39).

Boreas, and his friend Aquilo: the names of north winds.

126 *Aeolus*: see note to p. 46.

The bells of the first watch: watches at this time were changed at midnight.

127 *Leonard*: Lionardo Ribeiro (cf. cantos 4. 81–2 and 9. 75–82).

Veloso: see cantos 4. 81–2 and 5. 31. William Mickle (Camões's eighteenth-century translator) comments: 'All but the second watch are asleep in their warm pavilions: the second watch sit by the mast sheltered from the chilly gale by a broad sail cloth; sleep begins to overpower them, and they tell stories to entertain one another. For beautiful, picturesque simplicity there is no sea-scene equal to this in the Odyssey or Aeneid.'

The Twelve of England: most of the figures mentioned in this story are historical, the context (chivalry with its blood-sports) is entirely plausible, and Camões insists the tale itself is true. No Portuguese football team sets out for England without the press invoking the name of Magriço and wishing them equal success.

129 *Magriço*: the 'skinny one', was Álvaro Gonçalves Coutinho, son of the Marshal of Portugal and chamberlain to the Duke of Burgundy.

131 *the Tagus to the Bactrus*: the River Bactrus, a tributary of a tributary of the Aral Sea in Uzbekistan, standing here for the East as the Tagus does for the West.

132 *Corvinus and Torquatus*: Marcus Valerius Corvinus and Titus Manlius, both victors in single combat in Rome's fourth-century wars against the Gauls.

132 *Another of the twelve*: said to be Álvaro Vaz de Almada (see canto 4. 25).

133 *A sudden, almighty tempest*: the description of the storm is partly modelled on *Metamorphoses*, xi. 475–543.

134 *The Halcyon birds*: Alcyone, daughter of Aeolus, threw herself into the sea when her husband Ceyx was drowned, and both were changed into kingfishers. It was believed they built floating nests, and that their nesting time brought calm weather.

sooty blacksmith . . . : references follow to Vulcan (who forged Aeneas' armour to please his wife, Venus); to the weapons hurled at the Titans (cf. cantos 1. 20 and 5. 51); and to the Greek version of the biblical flood, when Deucalion and Pyrrha cast stones which changed into people to repopulate the world (*Metamorphoses*, i. 381 ff).

135 *the children of Israel* . . . : references follow to Moses and the Red Sea crossing (Exodus 14. 19–31); to St Paul's voyage past the sandbanks of North Africa known as Syrtes (Acts 27. 14–44); and to Noah and his ark (Genesis 6–9).

Must I endure . . . : references follow to Scylla and Charybdis in the Straits of Messina (cf. canto 2. 45); to Syrtes (see st. 81); and to Acroceraunia, a rocky cape on the coast of Epirus, excoriated by Horace (*Odes* i. 3).

136 *the amorous star*: Venus (cast as the Morning Star) sees the fleet which has survived without her, but still believes her intervention necessary (cf. canto 2. 18–33). Orion, with his sword, sets as Venus rises.

Orithyia: daughter of the Athenian king Erechtheus, and wife of Boreas.

137 *Galatea* . . . *Notus*: Galatea was a sea-nymph; Notus, a south wind.

Calicut: their destination on India's south-west coast, described in detail in canto 7.

Canto Seven

139 *Christ's fold*: the Catholic Church. *The Lusíads* was composed when the Reformation was splitting Christendom, as stanzas 2–14 reflect.

Consider the Germans: Luther's home and the heart of the Reformation, in revolt against Emperor Charles V.

140 *rough Englishman*: Henry VIII (1509–47), attacking the English Reformation, and his claim to the title 'King of Jerusalem', then under Turkish control. It has been urged that this stanza must have been composed before Henry's death. But in this survey of Christendom's divisions, the English break with Rome comes appropriately after Germany's revolt.

unworthy Gaul: Francis I of France, also d. 1547, criticizing his claims to Naples and Navarre, and his alliance with Suleiman II of Turkey against Charles V. Charles and Louis are Charlemagne and Louis IX (St Louis).

dragon's teeth: Cadmus, after slaying the dragon which killed his companions, took Minerva's advice and sowed the dragon's teeth, which sprang up as armed men and fought each other until five survivors helped him build Thebes.

141 *Lydia*: home of King Croesus, containing the gold-bearing rivers Pactolus and Hermus.

Greeks . . . : after capturing Constantinople (Byzantium) in 1453, Turkey occupied Athens and much of the Balkans.

142 *Calicut*: Vasco da Gama's instructions were to make for this city on the Malabar coast in the extreme south-west of India, the main Indian centre for the spice trade. The fleet arrived on 20 May 1498.

Beyond the Indus: this brief survey of India is expanded in canto 10. 91–43. The landscape is described simply: in the Himalayas to the north rise two rivers, the Indus flowing south-west, the Ganges south-east; between them is a vast peninsular, shaped like a pyramid pointing south towards Ceylon. Of the various peoples, Hindu and Moslem, Camões mentions Pathans in what is now Pakistan, Delhis living in the Punjab, and the peoples of the Deccan, Orissa, and Bombay. The two greatest kingdoms are Cambay, that is, the Moslem kingdom of Gujarat to the north-west, and what the Portuguese called Narsinga, that is, the Hindu Empire of Vijayanagar, occupying the whole of southern India. The south-west coast, however, is cut off by a range of mountains called the Western Ghats, behind which Malabar, and other smaller states, preserved their independence.

The people there: perhaps a vegetarian Hindu sect whose followers covered the mouth with a veil to avoid breathing in small insects.

143 *Porus*: a king defeated by Alexander the Great.

A Mohammedan: Vasco da Gama's envoy was 'accosted by two Spanish-speaking Tunisians with the words "What the devil has brought you here?" to which he replied "We have come to seek Christians and spices".' (C. R. Boxer, *The Portuguese Seaborne Empire* (London, 1973), 37).

144 *in ancient Rhodope*: the simile is adapted from Horace, *Odes*, i. 12.

145 *Perimal*: said to have ruled in the ninth century, and to have retired to Mecca but died on the voyage.

Medina: setting of Mohammed's tomb.

146 *Cochin . . .* : these towns are scattered over some three hundred miles of the Malabar coast between Cannanore, north of Calicut, and Quilon to the south.

147 *Pythagoras*: sixth century BC, called by Cicero the founder of philosophy, believed in the transmigration of souls.

148 *One had horns*: Camões's analogies with Roman and Egyptian gods are ingenious and amply convey Portuguese bafflement, but they do not allow us to identify which Hindu deities were displayed.

149 *Hydaspes*: the Jhelum River, a tributary of the Indus. Nysa, home of Bacchus (with the carefree face), was supposedly on its bank. For Semele, see note to p. 17.

149 *Semiramis*: see note to p. 68. She is said to have made her stallion her heir.

third empire: Alexander's empire was counted the third of the ancient world (after the Assyrian and Persian).

154 *first made by Noah*: for Noah's vineyard, see Genesis 9. 20–1.

Cânace's: Aeolus' incestuous daughter. He sent her a sword with which she killed herself after writing to her brother.

155 *shipwreck*: see canto 10. 128.

Hezekiah: Isaiah told him God was adding fifteen years to his life. (Isaiah 38. 5).

Canto Eight

157 *By the first of the paintings*: the shields of Achilles (*Iliad*, xviii) and of Aeneas (*Aeneid*, viii) provide precedents for the use of a series of pictures to illuminate history.

Lusus: see note to p. 10.

Elysium: the Elysian Fields (home of the blessed) were located by the ancients far in the west. Camões's claim that they were in Portugal rests in part on a play on words between Lusus and Elysium.

See another figure . . . : Camões repeats the stories of Ulysses and Lisbon (canto 3. 57), Viriathus (cantos 1. 26 and 3. 22). Sertorius (see canto 1. 26) Henry of Burgundy (see canto 3. 25–7), Afonso I (see canto 3. 38) and Egas Moniz (see canto 3. 35–41). For the Battle of Guimarães, see canto 3. 31.

160 *Postumius*: the Roman Consul Spurius Postumius Albinus, taken by surprise by the Samnites (321 BC) and forced to submit to their symbolic yoke. When the Roman senate rejected these terms, he surrendered again to the enemy.

Dom Fuas Roupinho: (see canto 1. 12) captured the Almoravid governor of Càcares and Valencia de Alcantara who was beseiging him at Porto-de-Mós, near Leira. As admiral under Afonso I, he also won a naval battle against the Arab fleet, off Cape Espichel, opposite Lisbon. He died after being defeated at sea off Ceuta.

this band in foreign armour: for crusaders' help in the capture of Lisbon, see canto 3. 57–8. Heinrich of Bonn, a German crusader, was associated with the miracle Camões records.

Prior Teotónio: prior of Santa Cruz (Coimbra), who lost Leiria to the Almoravids and captured Arronches instead (see canto 3. 55).

161 *Mem Moniz*: the son of Egas Moniz. He fought at Santarém and in Sancho's attack on Seville (cf. canto 3. 75–80).

Gerald the Fearless: see note to p. 60.

161 *this Castilian*: Pedro Fernández de Castro, who quarrelled with Alfonso
VIII of Castile (over a feud with the Count of Lara) and fought along-
side the Almohad amir Ya'qub, who devastated the Tagus valley, cap-
turing Abrantes in 1195. The case scandalized Christendom, leading
Pope Celestine III to excommunicate those involved and to reinstate Spain
as a crusading zone.

this warrior Bishop: the battling Bishop of Lisbon, granted a heavenly vision
at the siege of Alcácer do Sal (1217) was named Dom Sueiro, not Mateus
(cf. canto 3. 90).

162 *Master of the Order of Santiago*: Paio Peres Correia, who helped Afonso
III in the conquest of the Algarve (see canto 3. 95). He had earlier (1242)
attacked Tavira after seven Portuguese hunters had been killed during a
truce.

these three knights: Gonçalo Rodrigues Ribeiro, Vasco Eanes, and Fernão
Martins de Santarém, Portuguese knights of international fame in the
early fourteenth century.

for here is a man: another eulogy of Dom Nuno Álvares Pereira, High
Constable of Portugal and hero of Aljubarrota (cf. canto 4. 14–21 and
34–5). The incident in stanzas 30–1 is said to have occurred at the Battle
of Valverde (see canto 4. 46).

163 *Pompilius*: Numa Pompilius, second king of Rome, in Plutarch's account.

another captain: references follow to Pero Rodrigues (from Landroal, near
Évora), his defeat of the commanders of Calatrava and Alcántara dur-
ing the Spanish invasions of 1384–5 (they are said to have captured 100
ewes and 1,500 she-goats), and his action in freeing his friend, Álvaro
Gonçalves Coitado, whom they had also taken prisoner.

Note Paio Rodrigues . . . : references to the pro-Castilean Paio Rodrigues
Marinho, his act of treachery against the loyal Gil Fernandes, and the
latter's revenge, all in the same campaign. Later, Gil Fernandes, launched
his own raid on Jerez de los Caballeros (Badajoz), while admiral Rui Pereira
kept the Spanish fleet at bay off Lisbon, allowing the Portuguese to cross
the Tagus in safety.

164 *Here you see seventeen Portuguese*: an incident in the same war, when a
group of seventeen Portuguese, lacking water, attempted to descend to
the Tagus at Almada, opposite Lisbon, and were ambushed. The incid-
ents celebrated in these stanzas seem increasingly anecdotal, but they are
connected not only in time but by the coincidence of name and place (i.e.
the two Rodrigues of stanzas 33 and 34, the actions of Gil Fernandes,
the crossing between Lisbon and Almada).

Viriathus: see cantos 1. 26, 3. 22, and 8. 6.

two princes: see canto 4. 50.

Count Pedro: Pedro de Meneses, Count of Viana (d. 1437), first gover-
nor of Ceuta, and his son Duarte who saved the life of Afonso V at Alcácer-
Ceguer (cf. canto 4. 55) in 1464.

169 *What precious gifts?*: see canto 4. 61–5. Vasco da Gama had only the most trumpery presents to offer the Samorin.

Acidalia: this fountain in Boeotia was sacred to Venus.

170 *the sign of Aries*: the tropics.

171 *the southern hemisphere*: see canto 4. 49. Argo, Hydra, Ara (the Altar), and Lepus (the Hare) are all southern constellations.

174 *As the reflected light . . .* : Camões's version of a simile in *Aeneid*, viii. 17–25.

Coelho: Nicolau Coelho, captain of the caravel *Bérrio* (see canto 4. 81–2).

175 *his brother*: Paulo da Gama.

Álvaro and Diogo: Álvaro de Braga, the clerk, and Diogo Dias, the overseer (cf. canto 4. 81–2).

176 *The King of Thrace . . .* : references follow to Polydorus, Priam's son, sent for safekeeping at the start of the Trojan war to the king of Thrace, Polymnestor, and murdered for the treasure he brought; to Danae daughter of Acrisius, imprisoned because of a curse that her son would kill her father, and visited by Jupiter in a shower of gold (she bore Perseus as a consequence, who killed Acrisius by accident); and to Tarpeia, who betrayed Rome to the Sabines for what they wore on their arms (meaning their gold bracelets) and was smothered under the weight of their shields.

Canto Nine

177 *Ptolemy*: King Ptolemy II Philadelphus (285–247 BC) and his sister/wife.

Its annual voyage: this trade route, following the monsoons, was the first threatened by the arrival of the Portuguese.

179 *Reflecting he had laboured in vain*: much that followed historically is anticipated in this stanza. Initially, the Portuguese had hoped to enter the spice trade through peaceful alliances. Unable to provide the goods and bullion from Europe to finance that trade, Portugal devised an entirely new concept of empire—to control the seas and make the system pay for itself by levying duty on all goods carried in the Indian Ocean and China seas. Hence the events described in canto 10. 10–73, as the Portuguese seized the strategic points between East Africa and Macau. The Arab and Indian traders were slow to comprehend what was happening. As the Shah of Gujerat exclaimed when the Malabar coast was first attacked: 'Wars by sea are merchants' affairs, and of no concern to the prestige of kings.' (quoted in Boxer, *The Portuguese Seaborne Empire*, 50).

180 *an interval of joy*: the climax to *The Lusíads* (in all senses of the word) begins here with Venus' preparations for the Island of Love. The intense beauty and carnal pleasures of this island (for Camões was no prude in rewarding his mariners) should not seduce us from his larger purpose —to offer us, in a single episode extending over cantos 9 and 10, a

complete portrait not only of the solar system and of the true dimensions and riches of the planet mankind inhabits (as the context of Portuguese achievements), but of the relationship between the physical and the intellectual, the sensual and the philosophical, the imaginative and the moral, the 'Roman' and the Christian visions of the world, with a due sense of their relative claims. The island is not just a place for love-making; it is the setting for the two visions granted da Gama and his companions, and the cantos should be taken together.

181 *for she owned many*: I have taken this much-debated passage to mean that Venus possessed islands beyond those normally attributed to her in the Mediterranean. For Hercules' pillars, see canto 3. 18.

Such a device: references follow to Dido, her love for Aeneas, and to how she gained land in North Africa by requesting no more than a bullock's hide would cover and then cutting the hide in strips to measure out Carthage.

Peristera: a nymph who beat Venus in a race to pick flowers and was changed by Cupid to a dove.

182 *Actaeon*: see note to p. 32. King Sebastian was obsessed with hunting and disturbingly reluctant to marry.

183 *such as happened . . .*: references follow to Myrrha (see canto 4. 63); to Byblis who fell in love with her brother (Ovid, *Metamorphoses*, ix. 454 ff.); to Amnon, King David's son, who raped his sister Tamar (2 Samuel 13. 1–36); and to Ninyas, possibly the son of Semiramis, with whom he had an affair (cf. cantos 3. 100 and 7. 53), but there are other candidates.

184 *ensnared in Vulcan's net*: the net cast over Venus and Mars when Vulcan caught them together.

Typhoeus: see note to p. 121. The whole speech echoes *Metamorphoses*, v. 365 ff. and *Aeneid*, i. 663–6.

185 *Zephyr and Flora*: the warm west wind and the goddess of flowers.

I wish to populate: the first hint of Venus' larger purpose, to bring about a union between the Portuguese and the sea.

the lovely birds: swans. Cygnus, Phaethon's friend (cf. canto 1. 46), lamented his death and was changed into a swan.

the giant goddess Fame: portrayed as a giantess in *Aeneid*, iv. 178–88 and *Metamorphoses*, xii. 39–63.

187 *Memnon's*: see note to p. 47.

Delos: a floating island until Latona, fleeing Juno's jealousy, hid there to give birth to Apollo and Diana, when it became fixed in its present position.

188 *the various trees*: references follow to Daphne who, pursued by Apollo, became a laurel; and to Cybele's lover Atys, who was changed to a pine for breaking his vow of chastity. The poplar and myrtle were sacred to Hercules and Venus respectively.

188 *Pomona's*: goddess of fruits. There is an untranslatable pun on *amor* (love) and *amora* (mulberry).

189 *Narcissus*: fell in love with his own reflection and became the flower which bears his name.

Adonis: son of Myrrha and Cinyras (see canto 4. 63), was loved by Venus. At his death, the anemone sprang from his wound.

hyacinths: the flower, named after the friend Apollo killed accidentally with a quoit, is supposed to form the letters αι (from the Greek *aiai*, alas) with its leaves.

192 *'Tra la spica e la man . . . messo'*: the line 'Between the corn and the hand, what a wall is placed', (i.e. 'there's many a slip between cup and lip') is quoted from Petrarch, sonnet 56.

195 *the two Thebans*: Bacchus and Hercules.

Canto Ten

197 *adulterous Coronis*: faithless Apollo's unfaithful lover from Larissa.

The smoky wines: Falernian wines were too expensive for Horace (*Odes*, I. xx).

198 *The names of heroes . . .*: here (continuing to st. 73) begins the first of the two visions offered Vasco da Gama and the navigators, as the nymph describes Portuguese conquests in East Africa, Arabia, India, and the China Seas, to establish the seaborne empire first mentioned in canto 1. 1. For Proteus as prophet, see canto 6. 20.

Iopas . . . Demodocus: the bards who sang before Dido and Aeneas (*Aeneid*, i. 740 ff.) and Odysseus and the Phaeacians (*Odyssey*, viii. 62 and xiii. 27) respectively.

Calliope: see canto 3. 1.

199 *King of Cochin*: the Raja of Cochin, south of Calicut, where in 1502 the Portuguese established a station after failing in their negotiations with the Samorin, who attacked Cochin as a consequence.

one who would embark: the 'matchless Pacheco' (canto 1. 4), Duarte Pacheco Pereira, who sailed for India in 1503 to become 'the Portuguese Achilles'. His defence of Cochin, with two ships and less than a hundred Portuguese, is described in stanza 13. Cambalon is an island, opposite the estuary on which Cochin is situated.

Beypore and Tanur: on the coast between Calicut and Cochin. For Narsinga, see canto 7. 21.

201 *Not even Miltiades . . .*: references follow to Miltiades' victory over the Persians at Marathon (490 BC); to Leonidas' stand against Xerxes at Thermopylae (480 BC); to Horatius and his defence of the bridge against the Etruscans (507 BC); and to Quintus Fabius' delaying tactics against Hannibal (from 217 BC).

201 *Belisarius*: the Roman general (AD 505–65), unjustly accused of conspiracy by the Emperor Justinian. Legend has him begging in the streets of Constantinople.

the prize Ajax deserves: Ajax was cheated of the armour of Achilles through the sophistry of Ulysses.

202 *my poet's word*: the theme of the badly rewarded soldier and of royal ingratitude bears directly on Camões's own situation.

Francisco de Almeida: first Portuguese viceroy of India, together with his son, Lourenço, 'the fearsome Almeidas' (canto 1. 14).

Kilwa: (cf. canto 1. 54–5) was attacked in 1505.

Mombasa: (cf. cantos 1. 103 and 2. 1–29) also attacked in 1505.

the powerful Samorin's giant ships: this battle with the Samorin's fleet occurred in 1506.

Chaul: Lourenço died in the first Battle of Chaul against a combined Gujarati–Egyptian fleet in 1508.

203 *Scaeva*: a heroic centurion in Caesar's wars with Pompey.

Mameluke and cruel Cambayan: Egyptian and Gujarati (the Gulf of Cambay is north of Bombay).

204 *sailing into the bay of Diu*: the second battle of Chaul in 1509, against another combined Gujarati–Egyptian fleet, ended in victory for Francisco de Almeida, and secured Portuguese control of the Indian Ocean (see Introduction, p. ix). The battle was fought off Diu at the entrance to the Gulf of Cambay, after the viceroy had first sacked Dabhol, south of Bombay. Melik-el-Hissa was the Muslim governor of Diu, and Emir Hussein (st. 36) the Egyptian admiral.

the dark and mournful outcome: Francisco de Almeida died in 1509 after being shipwrecked at the Cape of Good Hope (cf. canto 5. 45).

But what great light: Tristão da Cunha commanded a fleet sailing for India in 1506. The flagship was blown off course towards Brazil, and da Cunha reached the South Atlantic islands named after him before exploring Madagascar (St Lawrence), and sacking the Swahili cities of Lamu, Oja, and Brava north of Malindi.

205 *That light too*: Afonso de Albuquerque, second viceroy (1509–15), was with the same fleet. Albuquerque 'the fierce' (canto 1. 14) conquered Ormuz (1507), Goa (first 1509, finally 1510), and Malacca (1511), consolidating Portuguese control of the main spice routes.

hissing arrows: the so-called miracle of the reversed arrows when, in the confusion of battle, many of the defenders were shot by their own side (cf. canto 2. 49).

Gerum . . . : Gerum Island, Musquat, Al Quraiyat, and Bahrain Island, in the Persian Gulf, with their pearls and salt mounds.

that morning . . . Catherine: Goa was captured for the second time on St Catherine's Day, 25 November 1510.

206 *the brutal, savage act*: the execution of Rui Dias, an officer from Alenquer, for his relationship with an Indian woman. The details (Was she his mistress? Did he molest her? Was she a prostitute? Was she a slave of Albuquerque himself?) are lost in history, but Camões (unlike some of his editors) plainly feels the punishment was unjust.

Alexander, seeing Apelles . . . : references follow to Alexander the Great, who gave up Campaspe to the painter Apelles; to Cyrus the Elder of Persia (sixth century BC), his captive, Queen Panthea, and her jailor Araspas who became her lover; and to Baldwin I who seized and married Judith, the daughter of Charles the Bald of France (d. 877).

207 *Soares de Albergaria*: (viceroy 1515–18), built the fort at Colombo in Ceylon (cf. Taprobana, canto 1. 1).

Lopes de Sequeira: (viceroy 1518–22) led an expedition to the Red Sea in 1520. Candace and Sheba were queens of ancient Ethiopia. Massawa is capital of Eritrea and Arkiko, a town on the coast.

Duarte de Meneses: (viceroy 1522–4) served formerly in North Africa. He attacked Ormuz in 1523. Vasco da Gama succeeded him but (st. 54) died in his first year of office.

a second Meneses: Henrique de Meneses (viceroy 1524–6). At his death, aged 30, he was rumoured to possess just 13 *reis*; hence Camões's tribute.

208 *brave Mascarenhas*: Pedro de Mascarenhas was elected viceroy in 1526 but was campaigning in Malacca and was denied the post through intrigue and imprisoned in Goa. Bintan (near Singapore) was captured in 1526.

Sampaio: Lopo Vaz de Sampaio (viceroy 1526–9), Mascarenhas's usurping rival. He won naval victories at Bacanore, north of Calicut (1526), and against Kutti Ali (1528), Muslim commander of Tanur (see st. 14). Meanwhile, Heitor da Silveira (the Portuguese Hector of Troy) won a further battle against the Gujarati fleet off Chaul in 1529.

209 *Da Cunha*: Nuno da Cunha (viceroy 1529–38), son of Tristão da Cunha (cf. st. 39), fortified Chale, near Calicut (see canto 7. 35) and captured Bassein, north of Bombay.

After will come Noronha: Garcia de Noronha (viceroy 1538–40) assisted Antonio da Silveira, the governor, in defending Diu from the Turkish siege.

your son: Estêvão da Gama (viceroy 1540–2).

Martim Afonso de Sousa: (viceroy 1542–5), former naval commander in Brazil, captured Damão in 1534, fortified Diu, and in 1537 finally destroyed the Samorin's fleet off Cape Comorin on the southern tip of India, capturing Beadala on the nearby coast. Like Goa, Damão and Diu remained Portuguese possessions until 1961.

210 *João de Castro*: (governor 1545–8, and viceroy for just two weeks before his death) helped defend Diu during the combined siege of 1546–7 led by the Sultan of Cambay. Among the heroes of this siege were João de Mascarenhas, commander of militia at Diu, Fernando de Castro, blown

up by a mine, and Álvaro de Castro, dispatched by his father with rein-
forcements from Goa at the most dangerous time of the year.

211 *He will battle again*: de Castro's victories (1547) over the Sultan of
Cambay, with his squadrons of elephants, and over Hidel Khan, former
ruler of Goa, whose cities of Dabhol (see st. 72) and Ponda he destroyed.

212 *God in supreme wisdom*: the second (continuing to st. 142) of the visions
granted Vasco da Gama is of the workings of the universe and the earth's
true dimensions. The model of the universe is, of course, Ptolemy's, then
current in Europe (Copernicus with his improbable, rival hypothesis being
virtually unknown). According to this theory, the earth lies at the centre
of eleven concentric and transparent spheres. The five known planets
(Saturn, Jupiter, Mars, Venus, and Mercury), together with the sun and
the moon, are each fixed to a sphere of their own whose motion, regular
or otherwise, accounts for their movements against the background of the
eighth sphere which is that of the fixed stars. Beyond the sphere of the
fixed stars lies the crystalline sphere, which accounts for the movements
of the equinoxes. Then comes the Primum Mobile, which drives the whole
system, and beyond, in the eleventh sphere, the empyreal Heaven, or the
abode of the blessed. Tethys guides Vasco da Gama inwards until she
reaches earth at the centre and begins her geographical explanations.

213 *We serve only . . .* : see Introduction, pp. xiv–xvi.

214 *on so tight a rein*: Tethys is describing the crystalline sphere and its barely
perceptible movement compared with that of the moon.

215 *the hostel of humanity*: in her geographical survey (continuing to st. 142),
Tethys begins briefly with Europe, then conducts Vasco da Gama via the
Cape and East Africa to the Middle East and India, and onwards to China
and Japan. With brief glances inland, this journey takes us along the coast,
simulating another immense voyage.

Monomotapa: the Portuguese arrival in Sofala coincided with the decline
and abandonment of the walled city of Great Zimbabwe, and the rise of
the Karanga kingdom, under its first king, Monomotapa, which ruled the
region until the mid-nineteeth century. Modern historians of Zimbabwe
are maddeningly coy about the precise relation between these events.

Gonçalo da Silveira: a Jesuit missionary, killed in 1561 at Monomotapa's
court. Tethys also refers to the region's gold-mines and to the lake (Lake
Victoria) in which both the Nile and the Zambesi were believed to rise.

the fortress at Sofala: built and defended by Spaniard, Pero de Anhaia,
was commissioned by Francisco de Almeida, first viceroy.

216 *Meroé*: the biblical city, which Tethys locates in Nubia on the Upper
Nile.

your unborn child: Cristovão da Gama, brother of Estêvão (see st. 62), died
in Abyssinia, after two outstanding victories, repelling an invasion by the
Sheikh of Zeila. For Malindi, see canto 2. 58. Rapto (Ptolemy's name)
and Quilmance are not identified (unless 'Obi' means the Uebi Shibel
which flows through Somalia into the sea at Mogadishu).

216 *See Mount Sinai*: crossing the Red Sea (like Moses) at the entrance to the Gulf of Suez, and passing above Mt Sinai (for St Catherine, see st. 43), Tethys turns south-east over Tur and Jiddah and the Asir Mountains to Aden (with Arabia to the east), before following the coast of the Yemen north-east past Ras Fartak and making for the Straits of Ormuz.

217 *Notice Dhofar*: a province in southern Oman. Cape Ras el Hadd is the eastern tip of Muscat, at the entrance to the Gulf of Oman. Tethys tours this gulf, noting Cape Ras Musandam, opposite Ormuz (where Pedro de Castello Branco withstood a siege in 1541), together with Bahrein Island and the joint delta of the Tigris and Euphrates rivers.

See mighty Persia: Persia is glimpsed from the coast as Tethys conducts us past New Ormuz (on Gerum Island: old Ormuz was on the mainland) where two governors, Pedro de Meneses and Pedro de Sousa, both probably Camões's friends, won important victories. The almost excessive detail here (st. 105 takes us past Cape Ras Jaskah, east of Ormuz, and past the desert of eastern Persia) suggests close personal knowledge of this region.

218 *the beautiful Indus*: introduces a vast sweep of India's west coast from the delta of the Indus past Sind, the Gulf of Kutch, and Cambay, and the Malabar coast with its 'thousand cities' awaiting the Portuguese, to Cape Comorin opposite Ceylon.

Saint Thomas: the legend of the apostle's martyrdom (cf. canto 5. 12) dates from at least the sixth century, and complements for India the legend of Prester John in Africa. For Narsinga, cf. canto 7. 21.

Mylapore: (or St Thomas), near Madras.

219 *their threads of office*: the Brahmin's insignia of authority.

220 *If, being earth's salt*: see Matthew 5. 13 and John 4. 44.

221 *To return to the coast*: in just six stanzas, Tethys covers some, 3,000 miles on a sweeping tour of the Bay of Bengal from Madras up India's east coast past Narsinga (cf. canto 7. 21), past Orissa, past the vast delta of the Ganges, to Chittagong where the coast turns southwards, past Pegu (of strange tales) and the Arakan mountains of Burma, past the Siamese coastal cities of Tavoy and Tenasserim, past Kedah in northern Malaya and Malacca and the island of Sumatra, to Singapore 'at the land's very tip'.

222 *The coast points east*: touring the Gulf of Siam, Tethys indicates Pahang and Patani on the east coast of the Malaysian peninsula, then the Menam River flowing into the Bight of Bangkok. Camões's knowledge of the interior, however, is shaky. Chieng-Mai is not a lake but a city, and his accounts of the peoples of Laos and Burma are travellers' tales.

the great River Mekong: the last stage is from Cambodia, pausing at the vast delta of the Mekong River where Camões was shipwrecked (see Chronology, p. 25 and cf. canto 7. 80), past Tsian Pa and Cochin China (both now in Vietnam) to the Gulf of Tonkin and Hainan Island, and finally to China with its Great Wall and civilized politics. Japan, where St Francis Xavier founded his mission in 1549, is glimpsed in the distance.

223 *islands beyond number*: the return voyage, with its theme of islands, takes us east of the Philippines through the Molucca Passage. Tidore and Ternate are the tiniest of the islands; then come the countless islands of the Banda Sea with Borneo well to the west; then Timor and, turning sharply west, Java, Sumatra, and back to Ceylon and the Maldive Islands, then Socotra at the entrance to the Red Sea and others off Somalia, and finally Madagascar (see st. 38).

with its burning summit: Camões distinguishes the volcano at Ternate, with its leaping flames, from the one on Sumatra (see st. 135) which merely smoulders.

never alight: the first bird-of-paradise skins sent to Europe had their legs removed, giving rise to the belief that they were unable to perch.

224 *it is fitting you glance westwards*: Tethys concludes with the achievement of another Portuguese Fernão de Magalhães (Magellan: cf. canto 2. 55) who, believing himself snubbed by King Manuel, offered his services to Carlos V of Spain and set out in 1519 to circumnavigate the globe. The Straits of Magellan were discovered in October 1520. Tethys refers to the Spanish conquest of Latin America (st. 139), the Portuguese discovery of Brazil (st. 140), and the tall people of Patagonia (st. 141).

226 *No more, Muse, no more*: Camões concludes with a further address to King Sebastião, again notable for its anxiety over the state of the nation, drawing a sharp contrast between Portuguese serving overseas and Portuguese at home, giving the young king some sound advice, and offering his own services as warrior and as poet.

227 *Phormio*: the philosopher of Ephesus, who lectured Hannibal on warfare (Cicero, *De Oratore*, II. xviii. 75).

228 *Mount Atlas* . . . : cf. cantos 3. 77 and 5. 11. Taroudant remained a city closed to Christians until the nineteenth century. For Sebastião's invasion, see Introduction, p. x.

The Oxford World's Classics Website

www.worldsclassics.co.uk

- Browse the full range of Oxford World's Classics online

- Sign up for our monthly e-alert to receive information on new titles

- Read extracts from the Introductions

- Listen to our editors and translators talk about the world's greatest literature with our Oxford World's Classics audio guides

- Join the conversation, follow us on Twitter at OWC_Oxford

- Teachers and lecturers can order inspection copies quickly and simply via our website

www.worldsclassics.co.uk

American Literature

British and Irish Literature

Children's Literature

Classics and Ancient Literature

Colonial Literature

Eastern Literature

European Literature

Gothic Literature

History

Medieval Literature

Oxford English Drama

Poetry

Philosophy

Politics

Religion

The Oxford Shakespeare

A complete list of Oxford World's Classics, including Authors in Context, Oxford English Drama, and the Oxford Shakespeare, is available in the UK from the Marketing Services Department, Oxford University Press, Great Clarendon Street, Oxford OX2 6DP, or visit the website at www.oup.com/uk/worldsclassics.

In the USA, visit www.oup.com/us/owc for a complete title list.

Oxford World's Classics are available from all good bookshops. In case of difficulty, customers in the UK should contact Oxford University Press Bookshop, 116 High Street, Oxford OX1 4BR.